Instructional Design for Librarians and Information Professionals

LESLEY S. J. FARMER

Neal-Schuman Publishers, Inc.

New York   London

Published by Neal-Schuman Publishers, Inc.
100 William St., Suite 2004
New York, NY 10038
http://www.neal-schuman.com

Printed and bound in the United States of America.

The paper used in this publication meets the minimum requirements of American National Standard for Information Sciences—Permanence of Paper for Printed Library Materials, ANSI Z39.48-1992.

Library of Congress Cataloging-in-Publication Data
Farmer, Lesley S. J.
    Instructional design for librarians and information professionals / Lesley S.J. Farmer.
      p. cm.
    Includes bibliographical references and index.
    ISBN 978-1-55570-736-1 (alk. paper)
    1. Information literacy—Study and teaching.   2. Technological literacy—Study and teaching.
3. Instructional systems—Design.   4. Curriculum planning.   5. Libraries and education.   I. Title.

ZA3075.F365 2011
028.7071—dc23

                                    2011031233

To
Emma Johnson,
my first teacher;

to
my adult education teachers;

and to
Girl Scouts,
my informal education teachers

Contents

||||||||||||||||||||||||||||||||||||||||||||||||||||||||||||||||||||||||||||||||||||||||||||||||||||||

List of
illustrations

Preface

Wanted: Strong vision of a user-focused instructional program and the leadership skills to make it a reality.

Function: Manage the library's instruction program through the development of goals and strategies for program implementation, promotion, and assessment; internally coordinate library instruction including class schedules, instructor assignments, support and faculty training, and statistics; work with faculty to develop collaborative teaching and learning projects; create and maintain print and web-based instructional materials.

Competencies: Instructional librarian qualifications: interpersonal, communication, and technological skills; knowledge of current educational theories and instructional technologies; a creative, flexible, and problem-solving attitude.

These excerpts from current instructional librarian recruitment advertisements attest to the knowledge, skills, and dispositions needed by today's librarians. The 2009 American Library Association *Core Competencies of Librarianship* includes "the principles related to the teaching and learning of concepts, processes and skills used in seeking, evaluating, and using recorded knowledge and information" (p. 4). *Instructional Design for Librarians* aims to help librarians and other information professionals to become competent instructors.

Today, more than ever, people need to not only find information, but find the *right* information and know how to use it. Today, more than ever, you as a librarian need to facilitate users' physical and intellectual access to the surfeit of sometimes overwhelming and complex information. Instruction has become a core function for most librarians, yet academic preparation of librarians does not always include the principles of instruction, especially that of instructional design.

Instructional design is a specific concept: a systematic process to developing education programs. This reflective and iterative process generally involves aligned and congruent analysis, design, development, implementation, and evaluation (Reiser and Dempsey, 2007). As such, it implies that a congruent set of knowledge, skills, and dispositions is being taught, usually to a specified learner population. However, most librarian instruction is just in time, in response to user needs. In that respect, identifying needs, determining content, and figuring out the most effective way to deliver information are all components of instructional design. What librarians need is a systematic process that not only responds to needs but anticipates needs, based on past experience. By thinking about instruction more systematically, you, as a librarian, can plan more strategically, train staff more efficiently, and provide more intentional and scalable instruction for their clientele. Furthermore, because technology has expanded (perhaps exploded) the world of information, you need to instruct people in the effective use of digital information. For that reason, technology issues are woven throughout the text.

This book was originally intended to focus on instructing adults, but the principles of andragogy (the science of teaching adults) applies well to most populations: practicality, blending of intellectual and social activities, building on prior knowledge, and so on. Furthermore, librarians may deal with mixed generations as they instruct, so having a general guide for instructional design that can be applied to many different situations seemed the most logical way to proceed in writing this book. As such, this comprehensive book can be a hands-on guide for day-to-day instructional planning as well as a resource for instructional design courses in library and information science (LIS) programs.

As for my own background, I have worked in all types of libraries over the years, instructing many types of learners. I have also taught in formal educational institutions: K–12 to graduate school. Even my teaching credentials include K–12 library media specialist, secondary school English and math, community college, and adult education. Since I wanted to teach librarianship, and recognized the difference between knowing library/information science and instructing in that field, I earned both an MS in Library Science and an EdD in adult education. Thus, based on the experiences of myself and others, as well as extensive reading,

|||||||||||||||||||||||||||||||||||||||||||||||||||||||||||||||||||||||||||||||||||||||||||||||||||||||||||||

this volume intends to give all types of librarians the tools to design and implement instruction effectively for their library clientele.

Instructional Design for Librarians is arranged with the learner as the starting point, followed by steps in instructional design, its implementation, and its management.

- Chapter 1 provides an overview of the need for instructional design.
- Chapter 2 introduces instructional design. It traces its foundations and theories, and explains its framework.
- Chapter 3 discusses the stakeholders in instructional design: learners, organizations, and instructors. Each entity has associated factors to consider, such as human development and culture, which are explored.
- Significant preplanning is needed to ensure effective instruction. Chapter 4 discusses needs assessment, outcomes and standards, types of learning, and assessment.
- Chapter 5 focuses on design content decisions. It examines curricular issues, resource options, and the importance of formats. The relative advantages of using existing resources or creating them are also detailed.
- Once instruction is planned, it can be delivered. Chapter 6 discusses delivery decisions such as timing, grouping, learning environment, and context.
- Technology plays an increasingly large part in instructional delivery. General principles and instructional strategies are detailed in Chapter 7.
- Instruction exists within a system. Chapter 8 explains how to build curriculum systems and learning communities. It also explores how instructional systems relate to other programs and functions.
- As with resources, instructional design requires effective management. Chapter 9 discusses documentation, support, communication, assessment, and continuous improvement.
- The book concludes with links to a list of instructional design resources and an index.

The book's organization was designed to meld current theories and best practices in order to emphasize how technology can best be integrated into teaching. Throughout the text, instructional examples are provided to show how concepts are implemented for different audiences, different content, and different delivery approaches: from face-to-face to online tutorials and video conferencing. My hope is this approach will prepare readers to compare and contrast instructional design approaches, so that they can make the best choices in a variety of settings and for specific purposes. If so, the book will have achieved its purpose of making every librarian a better teacher.

||||||||||||||||||||||||||||||||||||||||||||||||||||||||||||||||||||||||||||||||||||||||||||||||||||||

References

American Library Association. 2009. *Core Competencies of Librarianship*. Chicago: American
    Library Association. http://www.ala.org/ala/educationcareers/careers/corecomp/
    corecompetences/finalcorecompstat09.pdf.
Reiser, R., and J. Dempsey. 2007. *Trends and Issues in Instructional Design and Technology*. 2nd
    ed. Upper Saddle River, NJ: Pearson.

Introduction

There's a world of information out there, and it keeps on changing and expanding. It's no wonder that people get confused, frustrated, turned off. What information is relevant and accurate? How does one find meaning in this world? How does one fit into it?

Yet in this information society, in order to survive, people must cope with ongoing change, getting prepared for a world they can only imagine and retooling themselves several times during their lives as jobs change. Lifelong learning has become a necessity.

As information experts, librarians and other information professionals (the term "librarian" will be used in this book for both entities)—YOU—facilitate and foster lifelong learning for your clientele. As a knowledgeable member of the community, you try to determine information needs, which can expand to include identifying learning needs. You also work closely with technology, and understand how to match technology tools and information processes. In sum, as a librarian, you are uniquely positioned to provide instruction about twenty-first-century learning skills.

To help provide more systematic instruction, you can use instructional design to translate learning needs and goals into reflective plans for instructional materials, activities, other support, and evaluation.

The information society

To understand the current educational reality and contributing factors, an over-view of the information society and education is needed. At the 2003 World Summit on the Information Society (WSIS), governments and world leaders "made a strong commitment towards building a people-centred, inclusive and development-oriented Information Society for all, where everyone can access, utilise and share information and knowledge" (United Nations, 2006: 6). What constitutes an information society? Fundamentally, an information society is one in which information replaces material goods as the chief driver of socioeconomics. Human intellectual capital has higher currency than material capital, or at least intellect is needed to optimize the use of material resources.

This information society impacts existing institutions and cultures. The speed and globalization of information leads to constant change, which can be difficult to digest and manage. The majority of jobs now involve technology and other related new skills, so that the idea of a "terminal" degree or a static skill set is becoming an outdated paradigm. Rather, people often need to "retool" themselves throughout their work lives. Particularly for adults who are largely digital immigrants, this new world of information, especially in electronic form, can be puzzling and overwhelming. Do they have enough background information to understand and use the *new* information?

Impact of technology

Since information and material have always been needed, what particularizes the recent notion of an information (or knowledge) society? New information and technology have vastly increased the speed, access, and interconnectedness of information worldwide. Simultaneously, information and communication have converged, such as telecommunications and broadcasting, giving rise to informational industries. The cost of technology has dropped precipitously so that the majority of people can access it, thereby reinforcing mass media and other information entities. As a result, new forms of organization and social interaction have emerged (Webster, 2002).

By 2008 the majority of the world's population had mobile phones and more than a billion fixed lines connected people to information and communication technologies (ICT) (International Telecommunication Union and United Nations, 2007). On the other hand, 90 percent of Internet traffic consists of spam, including increasing malicious viruses and phishing efforts. The digital divide now focuses more on quality (such as speed) rather than quantity. In the United States, almost two-thirds of adults use e-mail or the Internet at work, and 96 percent are making some use of new telecommunications tools (Madden and Jones, 2008). While these employees state that their work has improved because of technology, they also assert that technology has also increased their stress and brought new demands into their lives.

The 2009 *Digital Economy Fact Book* (Eskelsen and Ferree, 2009) and the Center for State and Local Government Excellence (2010) provide several indicators of ICT's impact on the United States (U.S.) economy:

- Almost 70 percent of government employees (which constitute about 17 percent of the total employee population) are knowledge workers.
- Telecommunications and media constitute one-sixth of the U.S. economy.
- In 2008 online retail sales reached $204 billion.
- More than 90 percent of U.S. adults regularly or occasionally go online before making a purchase.

In the 2010 *Economist*'s Intelligence Unit analysis of economies worldwide, the researchers emphasized the centrality of ICT in the digital economy; indeed they concluded, "The Internet is now fundamental to commercial success and social prosperity" (p. 17). The report asserted that ICT impacts the economy only to the degree and quality of its usage. Furthermore, they stated, such usage is determined by the society's value of ICT, which depends on education, including digital literacy.

Learning skills and lifelong learning

In order to process and deal with the surfeit of information and ever-changing technology, people need lifelong learning skills. As early as the 1991 Secretary's Commission on Achieving Necessary Skills (SCANS) report, governmental agencies have noted the need for employees who can: locate, interpret and organize information; communicate information; create documents; solve problems; work with a variety of technology; and know how to acquire new knowledge. In a landmark study of CEOs from 28 countries, Rosen and colleagues (2000) documented four global literacies needed in today's business world: personal literacy (self-knowledge and self-esteem), social literacy, business literacy, and cultural literacy. As businesses increasingly realize the importance of intellectual capital, knowledge management has become a key ingredient for success. In 1995, G-7 leadership agreed that a global information society needed to be built, providing infrastructure and applications as they impact societies and cultures. Particularly since one of the main reasons for education is to prepare its students to contribute to society's economic well-being, it makes sense to incorporate information literacy into the curriculum.

International stakeholders at the World Summit on the Information Society stated their shared values of information literacy:

Information Literacy lies at the core of lifelong learning. It empowers people in all walks of life to seek, evaluate, use and create information effectively to achieve their personal, social, occupational and educational goals. It is a basic human right in a digital world and promotes social inclusion of all nations. (Garner, 2005: 3)

The concept of lifelong learning seems self-evident. As long as one is alive, one is likely to encounter new situations that need to be resolved; each of these encounters is a potential learning moment. Nevertheless, because today's information society drives change in so many aspects of life, lifelong learning takes on new and explicit meaning. People consciously have to pay attention to the world around them and decide if they want to change—and what they need to do to accommodate that change. In this respect, the information society has sometimes been called the learning society to emphasize the dynamic nature of social change throughout people's lives (Field, 2006).

Instructional design

As information and technology increase, the need for help in accessing, evaluating, and using information efficiently rises. As a librarian, you are uniquely trained and experienced in this arena, so your instructional role has the potential to serve as a central function. Therefore, as you assume the role of teacher or instructor, you need to be intentional about instructional planning and implementation. Informal coaching and one-shot presentations no longer suffice.

The term *instructional design* refers to a systematic process to developing education programs. It is systematic in that it is "an integrated set of elements that interact with each other" (Gustafson and Branch, 2007: 11). The system monitors itself and its environment, and makes adjustments as needed. It is a process in that there are defined phases of analysis, design, development, implementation, and evaluation (ADDIE) (Dick and Carey, 1985), although these phases need not be lockstep; rather, they are iterative and self-correcting.

This instructional design approach has several characteristics that can help you facilitate intellectual access to information (Reiser and Dempsey, 2007).

- **Learner centered**: Librarian instructors begin by assessing learner needs and wants. Similarly, library services respond to community needs.
- **Goal oriented**: Goals are articulated so that instructors and learners clearly know the intent of the instruction, and can determine when the goal is met.
- **Performance focused**: Can learners perform the intended skill; can they apply their newly learned knowledge? Being able to demonstrate competence authentically is usually how instructional and learning effectiveness is measured. This philosophy melds well with librarians' approach to information

services: for example, can users find the information source? Can they read a map so that they can plan a trip?

- **Data driven**: Data are collected throughout the process. Steps are documented. Observations are made. Sample work is collected. Both the instructor and the learners generate data (e.g., learning aids, student notes) that can be used to make informed instructional decisions.
- **Self-correcting**: Each step in the instructional design process is analyzed and evaluated, based on the collected data. For instance, did the needs assessment ask the right questions about the user population? Did the instruction lead to meeting the intended goal? The instructional designer makes adjustments throughout the design process to ensure optimum learning. Librarians intuitively do the same thing; if the user is not successful with his or her research, for instance, the librarian usually tries a different tactic to help that user be satisfied.

Librarian's instructional role

Libraries, be they physical or virtual, have collections of informational resources, which are developed and maintained by staff, hopefully including at least one librarian/information professional. These library staff members help users gain physical and intellectual access to information, and this function constitutes their instructional role. The users typically define the library setting since the raison d'être of the library is to fulfill the users' informational needs.

The public library serves the widest spectrum of users—the entire community—, and the most broad-based mission—to inform, inspire, and entertain its public. Therefore, public librarians theoretically could have the broadest instructional role. Because public librarians have such a broad constituency to serve, with a high turnover rate for those patrons, they tend to focus on locational instruction because such questions are common and predictable over time; reference or informational services offer individualized just-in-time instruction that is usually very specific. Because of the scale of operations, public librarians tend to systemize their instructional aids: signage, FAQs, bibliographies and pathfinders, and reference sheets (such as "how to print"). Formal instruction tends to focus on literacy, such as helping parents provide positive reading experiences with their children (that is, family literacy) or facilitating English-language learning in collaboration with other literacy agencies. Formal instruction is sometimes woven into library programs, such as looking for a job or managing money. With the advent of technology, public library formal instruction is most likely to focus on computer use, a task that is frequently delegated to library volunteers or other agencies.

In contrast, special libraries serve a very specific, stable population: employees or agency members (such as museum donors). As such, librarians need to keep up with advances in the employer's field as well as generic or library-specific information tools. In terms of instruction, most of it consists of individualized just-in-time training, usually in terms of using emerging research tools.

Academic and school libraries have as part of their central mission the education of their clientele, particularly students. School librarians provide developmentally appropriate information literacy instruction that supports the school's curriculum. Ideally, school librarians collaborate with classroom teachers to provide course-specific context for learning skills; for example, students learn how to read different kinds of maps so they can see how geography impacts civilization. Academic librarians focus more instructional attention on scholarly research tools and resources for both students and faculty. University libraries tend to offer standardized workshops for basic research skills, and work with specific academic departments to offer more specialized or domain-specific training upon need. School librarians are the most likely librarians to create a planned sequence of instruction, although academic librarians are increasingly developing "stepped" instruction: freshman overview, basic domain-specific instruction, and graduate-student thesis research strategies. Both types of librarians offer individualized instruction for students and teaching faculty. It should also be noted that public academic and school libraries serve their local community; parents may use school libraries, and local residents may use postsecondary libraries.

As a whole, librarians also serve as mediators between their institutions and the community at large. As such, they may provide instruction to and about outside entities, particularly through educational program venues. For instance, public libraries might serve as polling stations, and sponsor programs that help people get informed about political issues. School libraries routinely invite authors to explain the publishing process. With their connections to other libraries and community entities, librarians might provide instruction to their clientele on how to access these community resources. Usually, librarians have to pro-actively seek such community connections, although they might well have that outside agency provide the relevant instruction since that agency is the best informed about its own sources.

Regardless of the setting, technology has not only entered the library picture but has sometimes taken center stage. Even archivists handling incunabula (books printed before 1501) usually use an integrated library management system. Digital resources constitute a growing percentage of the library collection, which librarians need to maintain and help their constituents use. In addition, librarians incorporate technology into their instruction, both in terms of learning aids and delivery mechanisms: print and digital documents, presentation applications, audiovisual (AV) tools, instant messaging and other online real-time services, and social media. These technologies have several benefits: ability to combine media, recordability, flexibility for repurposing, scalability for large audiences and duplicative efforts, ability to overcome space and time constraints. On the other hand, each tool requires some time to learn and apply appropriately. In addition, each application needs equipment to access and use on the part of both the instructor and learner. Nevertheless, as library users become more diverse and technology facilitates resource sharing, technology will continue to play an increasingly important role in library instruction.

The need for instructional design becomes apparent in the face of societal needs. It also becomes apparent that instructional issues can be complex. For this reason, this book guides librarians in considering and dealing with the various aspects of instructional design, always keeping in mind the learner, and his or her needs and interests. Starting with the learner, you can find out ways to assess those needs and identify the kind of knowledge to be gained. You can develop the appropriate curriculum, identify the resources and activities to convey the curriculum, implement that curriculum, and assess the design and the learner throughout the process in order to optimize the experiences. As a result, both you and the people you help become more knowledgeable.

References

Center for State and Local Government Excellence. 2010. *Survey Findings: The Great Recession and the State and Local Government Workforce.* Washington, DC: Center for State and Local Government Excellence.

Dick, W., and L. Carey. 1985. *The Systematic Design of Instruction.* New York: Harper Collins.

Economist Intelligence Unit. 2010. *Digital Economy Rankings 2010.* London: Economist. http://graphics.eiu.com/upload/EIU_Digital_economy_rankings_2010_FINAL_WEB.pdf.

Eskelsen, G., A. Marcus, and W. Ferree. 2009. *Digital Economy Fact Book.* 10th ed. Washington, DC: Progress & Freedom Foundation.

Field, J. 2006. *Lifelong Learning and the New Educational Order.* Sterling, VA: Trentham Books.

G-7 Ministerial Conference on the Information Society: Cooperation on Applications and Testbeds. 1995, January 12. Brussels. International Federation of Library Associations. http://www.ifla.org/documents/infopol/intl/g7/g7-113qa.txt.

Garner, S. 2005. *High-Level Colloquium on Information Literacy and Lifelong Learning.* Alexandria, Egypt: International Federation of Library Associations.

Gustafson, K., and R. Branch. 2007. "What Is Instructional Design?" In *Trends and Issues in Instructional Design and Technology,* 2nd ed., edited by R. Reiser and J. Dempsey, 10–16. Upper Saddle River, NJ: Pearson.

International Telecommunication Union and United Nations. 2007. *World Information Society Report.* Geneva: International Telecommunication Union and United Nations. http://www.itu.int/wisr.

Madden, M., and S. Jones. 2008. *Networked Workers.* Washington, DC: Pew Internet & American Life Project.

Reiser, R., and J. Dempsey, eds. 2007. *Trends and Issues in Instructional Design and Technology.* 2nd ed. Upper Saddle River, NJ: Pearson.

Rosen, R., et al. 2000. *Global Literacies.* New York: Simon and Schuster.
United Nations. 2006. *World Information Society Report.* Paris: United Nations.
United States Department of Labor. 1991. *Secretary's Commission on Achieving Necessary Skills (SCANS).* Washington, DC: Government Printing Office.
Webster, F. 2002. *Theories of the Information Society.* 2nd ed. London: Routledge.

2

Instructional design overview

As information and technology increase, the need for help in accessing, evaluating, and using information efficiently rises. Librarians are uniquely trained and experienced in this arena, so your instructional role has the potential to serve as a central function. In this capacity, you must be intentional about instructional planning and implementation. Informal coaching and one-shot presentations no longer suffice. This chapter gives an overview of instructional design and explains several instructional design models.

Defining instructional design

Instructional design may be defined as a systematic process used to develop educational programs in a consistent, reliable manner. This reflective and iterative process generally involves aligned and congruent analysis, design, development, implementation, and evaluation (Reiser and Dempsey, 2007). More broadly, instructional design includes "a collection of activities to plan, implement, valuate, and manage events and environments that are intended to facilitate learning and performance" (Spector and Ohrazda, 2004: 687). You can see that not all instruction reflects instructional design.

Instructional design emerged from general systems theory, the intent of which was to apply the concept of interdependent system elements to efficient training for aerospace and the military. The model is now the basis for most adult education and much of higher education, and its principles apply to all ages. Using a systematic instructional design has several benefits for libraries: it focuses on the learner, it supports effective instruction, it provides a systematic way to address learning problems, it fosters coordination among all the instructional components and stakeholders, and it facilitates diffusion and adaptation (Smith and Ragan, 2005). Thus, you can collaborate more effectively with library partners as well as optimize the library's efficiency in instruction. For these reasons, this book focuses on instructional design.

Instructional design builds on the assumptions that the learner's past experiences reflect a complex network of concepts, and that the learner actively processes information, which impacts that existing network. Furthermore, instruction, evaluation, and time on task impact the learner's cognitive activities (Di Vesta and Rieber, 1988). You can see how this assumption fits well with the idea of information literacy.

While several models of instructional design exist, they all share some common properties (Reigeluth, 1999):

- Focus on design (the means) rather than results (the end).
- Identify instructional methods, which are situationally contextualized.
- Parse instructional methods into contributing components (such as clear information).
- Increase the chances of achieving a goal but not guaranteeing it (non-deterministic).

Instructional design emerged about the same time that educational technology became a significant element in training. The term "instructional media" is sometimes used to describe physical means to present instruction (Reiser and Gagne, 1983), with an emphasis on audio-visuals and other technology. While visual education via slides and film existed in the early twentieth century, and radio captured the attention of educators in the 1930s, instructional media did not take off until World War II when large-scale training was needed. In the 1950s, the advent of television and computers spurred educational technology. Language labs also emerged at this time. However, installation and maintenance costs of these technologies minimized their impact. Only when the availability of affordable computers with user-friendly interfaces and relevant content became widespread did educational technology significantly impact instructional design. At this point, the fields of instructional design and technology have merged to become instructional technology (Reiser and Dempsey, 2007).

Likewise, only in the twenty-first century can libraries be said to have ubiquitous technology: from integrated library management systems (ILMS) to digital resources, from a variety of equipment for users to online reference services. Most libraries now have web portals, which include guidance to information use such as LibGuide wikis and web tutorials. The next step is for you as a librarian to design instruction systematically in collaboration with your stakeholders.

A word about educational philosophy

Educational philosophy establishes the purpose and shapes the role of education: curriculum and instruction practices, student behavior norms (which might differ from the institution's expectations), and learner-specific experiences.

Wiles and Bondi (2010) identified ten areas that can be observed in schools which reflect educational philosophies. These factors can also be applied to library settings, as noted in italicized questions.

1. **School buildings and grounds**: Restricted facilities may indicate controlled structure in contrast to flexible walls and use of outside space. *Is the library program limited to one location on site? Where is the library located: centrally or remotely from the public?*
2. **Classrooms**: Furniture arrangements impact learning in that rigid rows are more conducive for lecture while moveable furniture and circular tables facilitate collaborative peer learning. *How much flexibility exists in the library's use of space? Is space arranged for different purposes, and then repurposed upon need?*
3. **Learning materials**: Exclusive use of textbooks suggests a liberalist or perennialist philosophy while extensive use of library materials suggests a constructivist approach. *To what degree does the library collection reflect a variety of formats and perspectives? Are digital resources accessible from classrooms and remotely?*
4. **Teaching strategies**: Didactic questioning and lectures indicate a teacher-centric approach in contrast to I-Search projects, which are student-centric. *Does the librarian use a wide repertoire of teaching strategies?*
5. **Organization of knowledge**: Sequential skills mastery may be pragmatic in contrast to group-determined exploration, which might indicate a radical or postmodernist philosophy. *To what degree are learning activities structured; to what degree are they open-ended or customized according to user needs?*
6. **Staffing patterns**: The presence or absence of interdisciplinary teams or co-teaching reflects differing philosophies such as behaviorist or postmodernist. *Does the librarian teach in parallel to other educators? Does instruction interact or build upon other instruction, or is it co-planned and co-taught?*
7. **Administrative conditions**: Traditional philosophies would play out in centralized authoritative leadership in contrast to inclusive, distributive leadership, which might be radical or postmodernist. *What role does the librarian play in decision making?*

8. **Climate**: A focus on efficiency, which might be pragmatic, differs significantly from relaxed, informal working relationships facilitating humanism.
   *What is the library's climate or atmosphere; does it foster quiet independent
   work or chatty group work?*
9. **Participant roles**: Uniform roles reflect high structure while flexible and
   dynamic roles can lead to change. *Is library staffing hierarchical or team based;
   what is the training and decision-making process?*
10. **Community involvement**: Predetermined, perennial school missions often
    limit community interaction while radical and constructivist philosophies
    are more apt to solicit community input and involvement. *Does the library
    have a steering or advisory committee, or foster a friends group? How much
    input do library stakeholders have? How and to what degree are volunteers
    used?*

Educational philosophies exist at all levels, from personal to societal, from one
learning activity to an entire program or institution, although as a whole they
are socially constructed and culturally defined. Educational philosophies are also
reflected in governmental policy such as the No Child Left Behind Act (2001),
and may have religious roots such as exhibited in traditional Arab education.

When educational stakeholders hold different educational philosophies, conflict at least at the intellectual level is likely to occur. For example, if you are
a school librarian who embraces constructivist inquiry, and the school pushes
"back to basics" lectures, you might not get many class visits. International students who come from a different educational structure and philosophy are likely
to experience confusion when entering a progressive U.S. library. Such disequilibrium can foster insightful dialogue and learning as people come to understand
and negotiate different perspectives. It is helpful if all parties are open-minded
and respectful of differing educational philosophies, although as long as the
expectations and norms implicit in an educational philosophy are explained,
learners usually adapt to that environment. Unfortunately, educational philosophy is sometimes so deeply embedded that it might not even be considered at
the conscious level. Thus, when you encounter the manifestations of a different
educational philosophy (such as a fixed schedule for class activities) you might
not realize why you feel uncomfortable in the learning situation. Therefore, educational philosophy should be explicitly expressed and addressed so that expectations can be clarified.

Most librarians tend to support a humanist/constructivist philosophy since
their approach to service is to satisfy their clientele's needs and interests. That is,
the clientele sets the parameters for the interaction, which reflects a learner-centered philosophy. To some extent, librarians also possess a pragmatist/progres-
sive philosophy as they help their clientele negotiate the library's organizational

structure. Clientele often frequent the library in order to solve a problem, and the librarian helps facilitate that process.

Because educational philosophy impacts instructional design choices, you should reflect upon your own educational philosophy. Being self-aware can help you identify your instructional comfort zones, and help you determine where you might want to broaden your instructional design assumptions and skills. In any case, you must be aware of your own educational philosophy as well as others' when you design instruction autonomously and with others and teach within your institution, be it a college or corporation. The following set of questions provides a starting place for you to self-reflect on your personal educational philosophy.

- What are your beliefs about knowledge?
- What are your beliefs about what is worth knowing and worth teaching?
- What are your beliefs about teaching and learning?
- Who do you consider to be a learner?
- What are your beliefs about learners?
- What do you think should be the librarian's role in teaching and learning?

Next, examine your institutional mission and charge in light of the above educational philosophies—and your own philosophy.

- What drives the institution: the bottom line, high graduation rates, learner self-fulfillment, social change?
- What role does the library have within this philosophy?
- How do *you* fit within that philosophy?

Instructional design theory

In its conceptualization, instructional design grew out of cognitive psychology and a behaviorist philosophy. Developed by industry human resource personnel with an eye on technology-enhanced training, instructional design is a structured way of looking at learner needs and creating learning activities that will help them meet desired outcomes. By standardizing the process, the designer can focus on the specific task. As a theory, instructional design not only provides a predictable process but also includes criteria for assessing its effectiveness and impact on learning. Over the years, instructional design theory has taken on a more pragmatist and humanist philosophical bent as learners have become more involved in the design process.

Reigeluth described instructional theory as "explicit guidance on how to better help people learn and develop" (1999: 5), identifying methods of instructional conditions and the situations in which to use those methods. The former involves what is being learned, learner characteristics, learning environment character- istics, and instructional constraints. The latter focuses on how well instruction works as indicated by how well the student attained the learning goal, how effi- cient the instruction is, and how satisfied learners are with the instruction.

Perkins (1992) stated that the instruction should provide clear information about expected goals and performance, opportunities for students to practice and reflect on their learning, informative feedback, and strong motivation. Unlike some other theories, instructional design theory is design oriented, focusing on process rather than describing a product or results; emphasis is placed on the instructional outcome rather than on the specific learning goals.

Andrews and Goodson (1995) posited four purposes of instructional design models:

1. To improve teaching and learning through a systematic approach of problem solving and feedback
2. To improve instructional design management through monitoring and con- trolling the system
3. To improve assessment through attention to each component and sequence of events within the instructional design
4. To test instructional design theory through theory-based design

Other theories contribute to instructional design theory. Learning theory and instructional theory are discussed in Chapters 3 and 4. Communications theory traces ideas from internal development to externalized messages, which are trans- mitted as a signal via a communications channel to be received at the destina- tion, which may or may not communicate back to the originator. This theory emphasizes the elements that impact informational dialogue that occurs between teacher and learner (Shannon and Weaver, 1949).

System theory deals with the dynamic interrelated qualities of systems, where a system may be considered as a "set of interrelated and interacting parts that work together toward some common goal" (Smith and Ragan, 2005). Each part has a function, and depends on other parts, such that change of one part causes a change in other parts. In instructional design, the nature of the learner and learn- ing environment needs to be assessed in order to determine the strategy, and each component of the design needs to be monitored to assess the process's effective- ness. For example, in a special library, the learners are the employees (who have several different functions—such as accountants, technicians, managers, etc.), and the learning environment might be the library, a training room, the com- pany's intranet, or the employee's work desk. The job's function, the employee's work status (entry level versus senior, for instance), as well as personal learning differences all impact the content and instructional strategy needed. Furthermore, different strategies fit for online learning in contrast to face-to-face delivery, and most instruction would need to be developed in collaboration with management or human resource personnel. The impact of the instructional design might also be hard to gauge, and again is likely to be done in consort with other entities of the corporation.

Instructional design models

At its most basic level, instructional design has three components: analysis, instructional strategy, and evaluation. Several models concretize the principles of instructional design. Sometimes the term instructional systems design (ISD), a concept that has been around since the 1950s, is used interchangeably with instructional design. In some circles, ISD is a broader concept, with the idea that instructional design focuses mainly on analysis and design. However, other researchers have an opposing view. In this book, the term instructional design will be used almost exclusively.

Andrews and Goodson (1995) compared 40 instructional design models developed since the 1960s. In their synthesis, the researchers created a schema to capture the models' processes. The elements included the following:

1. **Origin**: theoretical or empirical experience/research
2. **Theoretical underpinnings**: learning or instructional theory, systems theory monitoring, analysis function
3. **Purpose and uses**: instructional design teaching, production of processes or products, nonformal education, formal education, small-scale lesson/course development, large-scale curriculum/system development, cost reduction of education
4. **Documentation**: documenting, applying, or validating data relative to part or all of the model

In the next decade, Jerrold Kemp's (1971) model was found to be very useful. It has as its center learning needs and goals, taking into consideration priorities and constraints. He then posits nine steps in the design process.

1. Identify instruction problems, and specify goals.
2. Analyze learner characteristics that need attention.
3. Determine contact and task components.
4. State learner objectives.
5. Sequence content.
6. Design instruction strategies.

7. Plan the instructional message and delivery.
8. Identify and develop assessment instruments.
9. Select resources to support instruction and learning activities.

These steps exist within the larger context of formative and summative evaluation, which inform revision.

ADDIE: analysis, design, development, implementation, evaluation

The most popular instructional design model, ADDIE, was created at Florida State University for the U.S. Armed Forces (Branson and Rayner, 1975). It posits five design steps:

1. **Analysis**: What do students need, and what are their present skills? What is the nature of the learning environment and its constraints?
2. **Design**: What strategy will help students meet identified outcomes? How should content be organized? How should ideas be presented to learners? What delivery format should be used? What types of activities and exercises will best help learners? How should the course measure learners' accomplishments?
3. **Development**: How should the strategy be "packaged"? What resources are needed? Does content need to be created? How will the strategy be pilot-tested?
4. **Implementation**: How will the activity be implemented? Where and when will it occur, and who is responsible for each aspect?
5. **Evaluation**: What learning occurred? How effective was the instructional design planning and product?

Watson (1981) elaborated on each step, as follows.

- **Analysis**: Analyze the system, select task functions, construct performance measures, analyze existing curriculum, select learning setting, estimate costs.
- **Design**: Develop objectives, develop assessments, describe entry behavior/ identify pre-requisite skills, identify learning steps, determine structure and sequence.
- **Development**: Specify learning activities, specify instructional management plan and delivery system, select and create materials, develop and validate instruction.
- **Implementation**: Implement instructional management plan, conduct instruction.

- **Evaluation and control**: Conduct internal and external evaluation, revise system.

Over the years, ADDIE has evolved. Management has been added as another aspect. Other components have been added as needed, such as prototyping and action mapping. ADDIE is also being used alongside other models, such as performance models.

The BLAAM model adjusts ADDIE to the needs of academic librarians, who often do not have the capacity for full-scale instructional design development. The acronym stands for Blended Librarians Adapted ADDIE Model, and its phases follow (Bell and Shank, 2007).

1. Assess the users' needs and develop a problem statement.
2. Develop clear, measurable objectives.
3. Design prototypes, implement plans, and create materials needed to instruct.
4. Deliver instruction.
5. Measure how well the instruction met the identified objectives.

The ASSURE model was developed to support classroom teachers who incorporate technology into their lessons, and may be useful for school librarians (Smaldino, Lowther, and Russell, 2008). This model incorporates Ellen Gagne's 1985 conditions of learning (detailed in Chapter 3) to ensure effective use of media. Its acronym serves as a mnemonic for the model's six stages (p. 86).

1. Analyze learners. What are the learners' general characteristics? What specific competencies do they start with? What are their learning styles?
2. State objectives in terms of the target learner. State the behavior to be demonstrated, and conditions under which the behavior is to be demonstrated, and the degree to which the skill or knowledge must be mastered.
3. Select materials, technology, and strategies based on the learners' existing status and the desired outcome identified by the objectives.
4. Utilize materials and technology to help learners meet the objectives. Specifically, preview the materials and technology, prepare the materials and technology, prepare the learning environment, prepare the learners, provide the learning experience.
5. Require learner participation. Learners should be mentally engaged. Learning activities should allow learners to practice new knowledge and skills, and receive feedback on their efforts.
6. Evaluate the lesson in terms of its impact on student learning, critiquing the instructional process and the resources used. Revise the lesson to address issues of concern.

The ARCS instructional design model focuses on motivational factors within the ADDIE construct (Keller, 1973). The acronym stands for four components of the instructional design framework.

1. Attention refers to the learner's interest level.
2. Relevance of the instruction is determined from the learner's perspective.
3. Confidence refers to the learner's sense of self-success.
4. Learner satisfaction is based on intrinsic motivation and response to extrinsic motivation.

As instructors analyze learner perceptions, they can identify motivational objectives and strategies, such as using positive praise and formative informational feedback to maintain satisfaction and improve performance.

The ADDIE model is also the basis for Wiggins and McTighe's (2006) backwards thinking model. The underlying concept is that by starting with the intended results, instructional designers can identify the indicators for success and thus be able to design learning experiences that lead to that success.

An even more integrated approach was refined by van Merriënboer (1997) in his 4C-ID model. The cognitive and instructional design dimensions are integrated with four components: learning tasks, supportive information, procedural just-in-time information, and part-task practice. As learners practice their new skill, they need less support, and they integrate the parts of the learning task until it becomes automatic.

How might the ADDIE model or its variations be played out in library settings? Here is a real-life case study (Farmer, 2000, 2001).

- **Analysis:**
    - The school librarian wanted to foster information literacy. She noticed that students were not using the full range of relevant library resources, and were often off task. Teachers complained that the students were plagiarizing, and that they did not know how to find magazine articles.
    - The librarian formed a research study group to analyze the problem and recommend action. First, the librarian shared the 1998 American Association of School Librarians (AASL) information literacy standards with the study group. Together the librarian and the study group developed a list of research skills that all students needed to have by the time they graduated.
    - Next, the entire school faculty assessed their students' present skills based on the research skills list, and identified the extent to which students are taught these skills and have opportunities to practice and demonstrate those skills.

- One of the identified skills was to avoid plagiarism, and a need was recognized to teach students ways to take notes, organize, and synthesize findings that preclude plagiarism. In addition, teachers needed information about websites that fostered plagiarism so that they could counteract the use of such websites.

- **Design**:
  - The study group decided to focus on teacher learning. They concluded that teachers need to become aware of websites that provided ready-made reports that students could easily plagiarize and use. Teachers also needed to share methods that students used to plagiarize (some teachers already figured out those methods, based on reading student reports). Furthermore, teachers needed to design learning activities that would minimize the possibility of plagiarism.
  - The study group decided that the instructional content should consist of the following: (1) representative websites that provide ready-made reports; (2) methods of plagiarizing; (3) representative assignments that could be easily plagiarized; (4) methods of designing assignments that would minimize the possibility of plagiarism.
  - The study group decided that a simulation activity would be an effective way to present content. Teachers would use sample websites to create a plagiarized report. Teachers would then brainstorm ways to develop plagiarism-proof lessons.
  - Outcomes would be measured by assessing the reports, teacher discussion, and suggested lesson plans. Longer-term outcomes would be measured by analyzing future lesson plan handouts and sample student work.
  - The study group built on the school's strong professional development structure that provided monthly faculty in-services.

- **Development**:
  - Two study group classroom teachers packaged the professional development in-service activity as a scenario simulation and faculty brainstorming session. They created a one-hour in-service that was advertised as a professional development session for addressing student plagiarism.
  - Resources needed included a list of websites that provide ready-made reports, a worksheet that detailed the research project simulation, a computer lab with Internet connectivity, newsprint and markers for brainstorming, tape and walls for posting the newsprint, and awards for the best plagiarized reports.
  - The two study group classroom teachers created the worksheet, with help from the librarian who researched the list of websites.

- The worksheet was tested by the rest of the study group, who gave feedback to the two classroom teachers so they could refine the in-service activity accordingly.

- **Implementation**:
  - The activity occurred on a scheduled faculty in-service afternoon in the school's computer lab.
  - One of the activity developers introduced the simulation scenario, and asked the teachers to pretend they were high school juniors who had to create a computer word-processed research report in 30 minutes using the websites provided. Participants were given the worksheet guidelines, and told that they could work alone or in pairs. Participants were also told that awards would be given for the most credible plagiarized report.
  - Participants printed out their reports, and gave them to the two activity developers and the librarian, who critiqued the reports to determine who won. The librarian gave out awards for the most credible report, the most plagiarized report, the fastest report, and the longest report. The librarian also led a five-minute group, sharing the methods teachers used to plagiarize the reports (e.g., evaluating which websites had the most relevant papers and using word-processing "tricks" such as global replacement terms to hide plagiarism).
  - The second activity developer then led a ten-minute group brainstorming session on ways to modify assignments so that opportunities for plagiarism would be reduced (e.g., breaking down assignments into discrete steps so students would show work at each point, reformatting the report into a video or debate, modifying the report so that students have to compare two concepts or events). Ideas were recorded on newsprint by the two other activity leaders, to be published by the librarian and disseminated to the participants afterward.

- **Evaluation**:
  - The first activity developer conducted a quick "whip" to ask teacher participants what they learned (recorded by the second activity developer).
  - The research study group debriefed the in-service and analyzed the brainstorming ideas to determine the effectiveness of the instructional design planning and product.
  - A month later the research study group sampled assignment handouts and student work to determine the wording and nature of the assignments, and to determine the extent of student plagiarism.

Systems approach

Dick and Carey (1985) developed their own Systems Approach instructional design model, which emphasizes systems thinking. As such, it examines the inter-relationship among context, content, learning, and teaching. Their components include the following:

- Identifying the instructional goal
- Conducting an instructional analysis
- Analyzing learners and contexts
- Writing performance objectives
- Developing assessment instruments
- Developing instructional strategies
- Selecting and developing instructional materials
- Designing and implementing formative assessment of teaching
- Revising instruction
- Designing and implementing summative assessment

Along the way, assessment analysis may result in modification of earlier compo-nents, such as instruction revision may necessitate changing objectives.

Another model that takes a systems approach is Roger Kaufman's Organizational Elements model (1992). It consists of five elements; inputs, pro-cesses, products, outputs, and outcomes. The instructional designer sets up the means (inputs and processes) with the intent of having the learner accomplish certain ends (products) and the system accomplish outputs. The ultimate out-come is societal impact. Typically, this model is used to identify and address gaps between the current situation and the desired one.

In the ADDIE school site example above, the overarching student graduation outcome of information literacy is a good candidate for a systems approach to instructional design. All teachers need to be involved in the design and imple-mentation of instruction, and curriculum across disciplines needs to be addressed and modified to some extent. This process fosters cross-curricular collaboration and interdependence, and also requires schoolwide agreement and administra-tive support. The librarian plays a pivotal role in this effort, yet the ownership for information literacy needs to be broad-based.

Iterative approach

Several models use an iterative approach in that the design is incrementally developed and refined based on feedback. In other words, each step in the design informs and potentially changes the prior steps. The DID (Dynamic Instructional Design) model explicitly integrates technology into its iterative process (Lever-Duffy and McDonald, 2011). The six steps, each of which incorporates formative and summative feedback, follow.

1. Know the learners through formal and informal assessment. What are the developmental stages and skill levels of the learners? Did the design meet the needs of the learners?
2. State performance objectives. Are the objectives measurable, valid, and reliable? Did the objectives capture the content that students needed to learn?
3. Establish the learning environment. Does the environment allow for learner choice and interaction? Did the environment promote learning?
4. Identify teaching and learning strategies. Do the strategies meet the diverse needs of the learners? Were the strategies sufficient and effective for the objectives?
5. Select technologies. Is the technology appropriate to the teaching and content? Did the technology support the intended teaching and learning?
6. Perform summative evaluation. Does the assessment instrument accurately measure the achievement of objectives? Did the assessment provide the data needed to determine the effectiveness of the design?

Throughout the process, the instructor is both designing and revising, based on the feedback.

Probably the most popular iterative model is called Rapid Prototyping, which originated with software development (Fisher, 2003). The steps follow.

1. Plan the project, getting buy-in from the main stakeholders.
2. Analyze the potential instructional design, taking into consideration the learner, the content, and the objective.
3. Design and develop a prototype with the essential features of the ultimate learning tool, and test it with expert target learners.
4. Modify and refine the product, based on learner response and key stakeholder evaluation.
5. If further refinement is needed, analyze the cost-effectiveness of those making those changes (known as "return on investment). For instance, if another field in a learning database is requested, how much time would it take to redo the database records? If the feature is not essential, the added cost and delay might not be worth the effort.
6. Stabilize the design, and complete the product.
7. Disseminate the product, and evaluate its use.

This model is more appropriate when designing online tutorials that the learner uses independently. It enables target learners to shape the learning to meet their needs, and provides built-in support when it is time to implement the learning tool. For example, an academic librarian might create a web tutorial on evaluating websites. She would work with discipline faculty about the kinds of resources that might be consulted when doing reports in a course, and test possible websites and criteria for judging those websites with sample students in the course. The librarian would also need to upload and test the web tutorial to make sure students can physically access the tutorial and follow it.

Agile design

The philosophy reflected in rapid prototyping has led to the recent concept of agile design, which values response to change more than following a plan, and leverages interaction rather than processes. Sidky and Arthur (2008) developed five principles for agile design:

1. Focus on people.
2. Collaborate.
3. Embrace change to deliver clientele value; be adaptive.
4. Frequently plan and implement integrated learning processes; be evolutionary.
5. Strive for technical excellence.

Generally, agile instructional design begins by envisioning future curriculum and its overall modules. Learner roles and context are identified so that needs connect with the curriculum. A team of instructional designers determine learning modules based on the emerging themes and learners. Planning involves identifying strategies, timing, and resources. Typically, module building and testing is done by designing pairs who meld expertise in content matter, design, and technology. Learners pilot-test these modules-in-progress. Once modules are completed and reviewed for quality assurance, they can be integrated into learning management systems and stabilized. When these modules are ready for release, they can be deployed (Douglas, 2007).

Agile design blends cognitive flexibility theory (Spiro and Jehng, 1990) and constructivist learning theory, involving learners in design instruction, at least in terms of curriculum development. Agile instructional design is particularly useful for cross teams, such as librarians and teachers, who incorporate technology. Wikis lend themselves well to the model, for instance, because they demonstrate how stakeholders can be cocreators.

Implications for you

Instructional design should resonate well with librarians since the basic service model in librarianship is user based. As you try to determine the user's intent or goal within the constraints of the situation (such as a report due the next day), you need to determine the strategy to meet the need, and assess the user's prior knowledge and skills. With that information, you can then determine which resources are appropriate and how to help the user physically and intellectually access the information. You then evaluate the process: Did the user meet his or her goal or seem satisfied? How effective was your process? All along the way, you might change your course of action, depending on the results of each step. For example, if you are showing someone how to use keywords in combination to locate journal articles, and realize that the user does not know how to use a database aggregator, then explicit training in that skill is needed—or an alternative resource that is more familiar to the user might be used instead, such as a search engine.

What instructional design provides is a systematic way to deal with instruction in a scalable and efficient way. Because instructional design supports many different curricula and instructional strategies, it can be applied across academic and workplace domains with a variety of learners. You and your librarian colleagues can choose a model that supports your institution's mission and educational philosophy, and then structure all of the library's instructional efforts accordingly in order to provide a cohesive, aligned service. Moreover, by using one design model, the entire instructional library staff can facilitate evaluation and analysis in order to improve their efforts more efficiently. In this book, an enhanced ADDIE model is used as the design framework. It is learner centered and flexible, both characteristics of librarian instruction.

You can use ADDIE or other models independently or as a starting point in collaborating with teachers and trainers, addressing information literacy needs in the process. For example, because you constantly observe users' information behaviors, you can provide valuable input about current competencies. You can leverage your expertise about resources in developing relevant learning activities. You can also share strategies that were effective in teaching users how to locate and evaluate information purposefully. You should also strive to be included in evaluating resultant user work so that you can help your colleagues improve their own instruction and related information services.

References

American Association of School Librarians. 1998. *Information Power*. Chicago: American Library Association.

Andrews, D., and L. Goodson. 1995. "A Comparative Analysis of Models of Instructional Design." In *Instructional Technology*, edited by G. Anglin, 161–182. Englewood, CO: Libraries Unlimited.

Bell, S., and J. Shank. 2007. *Academic Librarianship to Design: A Blended Librarian's Guide to the Tools and Techniques*. Chicago: American Library Association.

Branson, R., and G. Rayner. 1975. *Interservice Procedures for Instructional Systems Development: Executive Summary and Model.* Tallahassee, FL: Center for Educational Technology, Florida State University.

Di Vesta, F., and L. Rieber. 1988. *Characteristics of Cognitive Instructional Design: The Next Generation.* Syracuse, NY: ERIC (ED295636).

Dick, W., and L. Cary. 1985. *The Systematic Design of Instruction.* Glenview, IL: Scott, Foresman.

Douglas, I. 2007. "Issues in Software Engineering of Relevance to Instructional Design." *TechTrends* 50, no. 5: 28–35.

Farmer, L. 2000. "Copy Me: Cyber-Plagiarism Faculty Workshop." In *Student Cheating and Plagiarism in the Internet Era: A Wake-Up Call,* edited by A. Lathrop and K. Foss, 159–160. Englewood, CO: Libraries Unlimited.

Farmer, L. 2001. "Building Information Literacy through a Whole School Reform Approach." *Knowledge Quest* 29, no. 3: 20–24.

Fisher, N. 2003. "Rapid Prototyping." Paper presented at the TechEd conference, Ontario, CA, March 24–26.

Gagne, E. 1985. *The Cognitive Psychology of School Learning.* Boston: Little, Brown.

Kaufman, R. 1992. *Strategic Planning Plus.* Newbury Park, CA: Sage.

Keller, H. 1973. "The Processes of Causal Attribution." *American Psychologist* 28: 107–128.

Kemp, J. 1971. *Instructional Design.* Belmont, CA: Fearon.

Lever-Duffy, J., and J. McDonald. 2011. *Teaching and Learning with Technology.* 4th ed. Boston: Pearson.

Perkins, D. 1992. *Smart Schools.* New York: Free Press.

Reigeluth, C., ed. 1999. *Instructional-Design Theories and Models, Volume II.* Mahwah, NJ: Lawrence Erlbaum.

Reiser, R., and J. Dempsey. 2007. *Trends and Issues in Instructional Design and Technology.* 2nd ed. Upper Saddle River, NJ: Pearson.

Reiser, R., and C. Gagne. 1983. *Selecting Media for Instruction.* Englewood Cliffs, NJ: Educational Technology Publications.

Shannon, C., and W. Weaver. 1949. *The Mathematical Theory of Communication.* Urbana, IL: University of Illinois Press.

Sidky, A., and J. Arthur. 2008. "Value Driven Agile Adoption: Improving an Organization's Software Development Approach." In *New Trends in Software Methodologies, Tools and Techniques: Proceedings of the Seventh SoMeT_08,* edited by H. Fujita and I. Zualkernan, 149–164. The Netherlands: IOS Press.

Smaldino, S., D. Lowther, and J. Russell. 2008. *Instructional Technology and Media for Learning.* 9th ed. Upper Saddle River, NJ: Pearson.

Smith, P., and T. Ragan. 2005. *Instructional Design.* 3rd ed. New York: John Wiley & Sons.

Spector, J., and C. Ohrazda. 2004. "Automating Instructional Design: Approaches and Limitations." In *Handbook for Research for Educational Communications and Technology,* 2nd ed., edited by D. Jonassen, 685–699. Mahwah, NJ: Lawrence Erlbaum Associates.

Spiro, R., and Jehng, J. 1990. "Cognitive Flexibility and Hypertext: Theory and Technology for the Nonlinear and Multidimensional Traversal of Complex Subject Matter." In *Cognition, Education and Multimedia: Exploring Ideas in High Technology,* edited by D. Nix and R. Spiro, 163–205. Hillsdale, NJ: Lawrence Erlbaum.

van Merriënboer, J. 1997. *Training Complex Cognitive Skills: A Four-Component Instructional Design Model for Technical Training.* Englewood Cliffs, NJ: Educational Technology Publications.

Watson, R. 1981. "Instructional System Development." Paper presented to the International Congress for Individualized Instruction, Tucson, AZ, October 29.

Wiggins, G., and J. McTighe. 2006. *Understanding by Design.* 2nd ed. Upper Saddle River, NJ: Prentice Hall.

Wiles, J., and J. Bondi. 2010. *Curriculum Development.* 8th ed. New York: Macmillan.

3

Learners in instructional design

Because instructional design is learner centered, the place to start designing is the learner. To that end, learning theory and its principles are discussed in this chapter. Learning behaviors change as people grow up, so developmentally appropriate pedagogical and andragogical (adult learning) concepts are detailed.

The other party in learning is the teacher: you. Learning may be defined as change in behavior; to that extent, librarians can be considered change agents. Since librarians tend to help clientele at the point of need, the instructor as facilitator and coach is a natural fit for you. Nevertheless, expertise in information science constitutes just part of your knowledge base relative to instructional design. You also must understand how teaching and learning work, and you need effective interpersonal skills.

Both learner and teacher operate within social contexts, so instructional design needs to address these issues. Cultural values and experiences, not only by ethnicity but also gender and other social groupings, shape learning, so these factors are also discussed in this chapter.

Principles of learning

At its most basic philosophical level, learning involves change: of personal behaviors or dispositions. If incoming information repeats existing information, it may *reinforce* or *affirm* learning, but that does not constitute *new* learning. Nor does a student *have* to learn; teachers can only teach—students must take responsibility for their own learning. Rather like a gift, if the student does not accept the information, then she or he does not learn. Thus, learning truly is a self-monitoring activity, which changes in nature over time.

At the cranial level, learning involves connecting neurons. On the physical level, individuals connect with their environment through their senses; how they perceive that environment—be it natural or human—influences the possible related learning. Internally, learners connect the known and the unknown. As learners perceive patterns in information—be they intellectual or psychological—those patterns can become organized into mental models (Popper, 1990). Interestingly, as children become more self-aware, they also become more "other" aware, noting how their own limited knowledge gives rise to others making the connection for them (Helwig and Kim, 1999).

Indeed, learning is ultimately a social activity, connecting people in potentially meaningful relationships. Even if a person reads a book and tells no one, the ideas originate with another person so a meeting of the minds still occurs, although the acquired knowledge would be considered *tacit* knowledge. On the other hand, when readers explicitly share their experience and knowledge, they make their knowledge external; they also usually increase their involvement and understanding through immediate feedback that results in negotiated learning (Nonaka, 2008). Collaborative learning offers the opportunity to learn something that could not be accomplished alone: a situation where the whole is greater than its parts. Film-making is a good example. A community of learners offers a socially acceptable way to initiate people into group-generated knowledge and value sets as well as shape one another's internalized learning. Thus, an oppressive environment that tries to stifle learning or has few learning assets also impact's one's learning, in a deleterious manner (Todd, 2000).

Still, as one matures and becomes more information literate, one's self-identity is based on autonomous comparisons more than social comparisons (Ruble and Flett, 1988). The learner finds a niche *within* society, and contributes to it, for ultimately, learning is more than receiving or consuming information. The flip side of learning is doing. As one thing *impacts* another, then they are related. Thus, learning can be connected with action as one relates to the environment, typically as a way to influence surroundings. For instance, once a person learns CPR, that person might well save another person's life.

Note that schooling has hardly been mentioned so far. Learning is a natural process that can potentially occur anytime anywhere for the conscious individual. Formal education tries to determine the content and conditions for learning that will optimize purposeful learning that will be useful within society. Information literacy constitutes a distilled set of processes that help people engage with information and act upon it, wherever the situation calls for such need.

Learning styles

Another way to think about learning is to consider "the typical ways in which a person takes in and processes information, makes decisions, and forms values" (Hand, D'Archangelo, and Robbins, 1992: 1). Individuals get information through their senses, which may differ because of biology, environment, or personal preference. Internal processing is again a factor of biology and circumstance, such as emotional upheaval. Sternberg (1985) posited three approaches to internal processing—analytical, creative, and contextual—each of which then impacts how learning occurs.

How people interact with their environment impacts their learning style. The most famous theory that addresses this issue is Gardner's 1983 theory of multiple intelligences that reflect nine approaches: linguist, spatial, kinesthetic, mathematical/scientific, social sense, intrapersonal, musical, naturalist, and existential. Several other models exist:

- Personality model: how personality impacts interaction (e.g., Myers-Briggs Type Indicator)
- Kolb's (1984) learning style dimensions: concrete to abstract, and observation to experimentation
- Cognitive styles: field dependent versus field independent; timing (reflective versus impulsive)
- Social interaction model: interaction in learning situations
- Environmental preferences: learning space characteristics (e.g., time of day, amount of light, quality of sound, visual qualities)

The bottom line is that individuals are likely to learn more effectively with self-knowledge so that they can leverage their learning preferences and gain expertise in areas that are less developed. Likewise, as a librarian, when you understand the impact of learning styles, you can design instruction that addresses these processing preferences. Particularly as you provide learners with choices of resources, you can optimize the conditions for learner interaction with information.

Developmental issues and learning

To a large extent, learning is developmental in nature, both in terms of changing mind-sets as new ideas meet head-on with prior experience and impressions as well as in being shaped by personal human development (e.g., brain growth and refinement). Thus, babies tend not to be cognitively aware that they are learning, although they are certainly modifying their behavior in response to their surroundings. Similarly, teens may be able to manipulate audio files, but they may lack the moral imperative to realize the ethical implications of pirating such files.

In addition, because different aspects of humans develop at diverse points in life (e.g., emotional maturity lagging behind physical growth spurts), no simple path to learning exists. Nevertheless, learning is usually considered as a cumulative activity as one builds a repertoire of learning tools and information.

Developmental psychologist Erik Erikson (1980) ascertained a unique set of issues that a person needs to address at each point in life.

- Infants deal with basic trust.
- Toddlers deal with will: autonomy versus shame and doubt.
- Kindergartners deal with purpose: initiative versus guilt.
- Elementary children deal with competence: industry versus inferiority.
- Teenagers deal with fidelity: identity versus role confusion.
- Young adults deal with love: intimacy versus isolation.
- Adults deal with caring: generativity versus stagnation.
- Seniors deal with wisdom: ego integrity versus despair.

Within this context, learning takes on different characteristics.

Child development

Learning changes with physical development, even at the prenatal stage as billions of neurons are formed and connected (Sousa, 2005). That interconnectivity activity continues unabated until puberty when the brain determines which connections should be permanent. Other windows of learning opportunity also occur in childhood. For instance, children's ability to learn motor skills peaks at age six. The window for developing emotional control is the first two and a half years. The window for language acquisition closes largely by age eleven.

Jean Piaget (1952) is known for his research on developmental patterns of intellectual growth. Even at the pre-language stage, babies learn concepts of space, time, and causality. Until age seven, children learn concretely at the pre-operational stage. They learn distinctions through categorization, breaking down differences into subclasses, although they sometimes cannot distinguish between main concepts and distracting details. Moreover, young children have a difficult time when faced with conflicting information such as maps with different keys or terms with different meanings (Moore, 1995; Leong and Jerred, 2001). Intellectually, children cannot distinguish between valid and invalid inferences or distinguish between explicit and inferred information until fourth grade, although by third grade children can differentiate between inductive and deductive inferences (Beal, 1990; Pillow, 2002). Part of the problem is that children have a hard time seeing other points of view because they are egocentric. Nevertheless, Glaubman and Glaubman (1997) found that even kindergartners could understand and use metacognitive methods to generate high-level questions; explicit training in questioning also improved reading comprehension and retention. The underlying message is that children need to have active learning activities where they can explore concrete items. It should be noted that in many cases, the more realistic and active the learning experience, the more likely it is to be effective for any age group (Dale, 1946).

Vygotsky (1978) asserted that language development, which is a social phenomenon, was critical to learning. Unlike Piaget, Vygotsky thought that preoperational children began speech by talking to themselves internally. His theory, called the zone of proximal development, stated that children could accomplish tasks with assistance if given external help prior to doing them independently; this scaffolding helped children integrate their learning. Vygotsky's theories can apply to any age, in that with external help, individuals can go just beyond their comfort zone to acquire new knowledge, skills, and attitudes.

In terms of moral development, the most noted psychologist was Lawrence Kohlberg. He posited three levels of moral reasoning, each with two stages. At the preconventional level, individuals focus on obedience and punishment, and then on self-interest compliance. Teens are most likely to operate at the conventional level, either conforming to social norms or maintaining a social-order mentality of law and order. The postconventional level is usually exhibited by only self-realized adults. As librarians address responsible and ethical information behavior, they need to work with children at the level that they can respond to. For instance, younger children would respond to personal consequences while older children would understand fairness.

Adolescent development

This generation of adolescents is probably the most diverse in terms of ethnicities, backgrounds, and experiences. Each teenager is unique, yet all teens share certain developmental tasks to ensure successful transition into adulthood as well as positive experiences in adolescence. On the most basic level, teens need to move toward independence, deal with the future, address sexuality issues, and develop personal values and direction. These developmental tasks and needs represent most teenagers' realities, behaviors that are usually successfully fulfilled over time. However, the approaches that teens use to address these tasks differ significantly in early, middle, and late adolescence, as noted by the American Academy of Child and Adolescent Psychiatry (2003). See the following list for examples. Information literacy instruction examples are italicized.

- In **middle school years**, ages 12 to 14, early teenagers are somewhat self-conscious, struggling with their own sense of identity and "normalcy" while trying to fit in as they transition to middle school. They fluctuate between a need to rely on parents and on friends, and see parents for their flaws. They often act out of emotion, so they may be moody. They are growing rapidly and unevenly, so they may be physically awkward, restless, and tired. In general, they are eager to explore the world around them. Living mainly in the concrete "now," these early teenagers test adult rules, and may start experimenting with risky behaviors. Girls usually are more mature than boys at this age. *At this age, students can learn evaluation skills by identifying points of view expressed in articles about social issues such as global warming.*

- **Beginning high schoolers**, ages 14 to17, alternate between poor self-esteem and high self-expectations as they experience rites of passage. They may seem overly critical of their own appearance and of their parents. They search actively for peer acceptance and group identity, and yet feel sad about their loss of closeness with their parents. They are starting to develop career goals, and are exploring their sexuality. *At this age, students can learn critical thinking skills by analyzing advertisements in terms of the body images that they use.*
- **Older teenagers**, ages 17 to 19, have a more realistic self-concept and more stable personality. They are able to think independently and abstractly. They take pride in their own work, and are able to delay gratification and make reasonable compromises. They feel stress, and look for skills to help them survive day to day as well as to prepare for an uncertain future. They are making serious postsecondary educational and career decisions, and are considering serious sexual relationships. They also accept social institutions and cultural traditions. *At this age, students can learn digital citizenship skills by developing positive digital reputations.*

Obviously, attitudes and behaviors vary among individual teenagers, but the progression of steps cross most cultures. Moreover, most teenagers manage to grow up without too much difficulty. As long as teens learn how to be productive, are able to navigate through difficulty, stay healthy, have healthy relationships, and get involved in communities, they will succeed (Gambone, Klem, and Connell, 2002). Nevertheless, personal and societal problems can disrupt adolescent growth. When these issues are difficult to avoid, such as rural isolation or endemic poverty, then persistent problems can impact adult success if teens do not know how to cope. Symptoms of stress and difficulties include personality changes, low self-esteem, social problems, disconnectedness, academic problems, withdrawal, and avoidance (Williams-Boyd, 2003).

If you are a youth-serving librarian, you should pay attention to the social and emotional skills of adolescents. To this end, you can design instruction that provides teens opportunities to take intellectual risks in safe learning environments. More specifically, you can help younger teens think about how their behaviors impact their academic performance by using metacognitive exercises that concretely show the relationship between social-emotional behavior and research processes. This reality check can help students become more objective and accurate in their self-assessments. Peer review of these self-reflections can offer a socially acceptable and developmentally appropriate way to examine research efforts.

Millennials

The millennial generation, born since 1980, exhibits a unique set of characteristics, largely the result of societal and cultural changes. Globalization has led to fewer cultural distinctions, greater interaction, and a greater common language (often based on music and television) (Ousley, 2006). While this generation seems to have a sense of entitlement and appears egocentric, they are very social and more tolerant than past generations. While they can be surface oriented, they seek active involvement. Likewise, while their attention span may seem short at times, they can also spend hours on some activity of their own choosing. Nevertheless, they highly value authenticity and directness, and want to make a difference in society. Although they can be very conventional in their thinking and need a sense of security, they also tend to be greater risk takers and more creatively expressive (McLester, 2007).

Millennial learners tend to learn by doing, making choices, and customizing their learning (Carlson, 2005). In terms of information seeking, millennials are not intent on looking for the right answer; in fact, they tend to value all information as being equal. Likewise, the format of information makes little difference to them in terms of credibility. They expect instant information, and feel comfortable doing several tasks simultaneously, yet experience information overload (McLester, 2007). They are high communicators, although their formal knowledge of grammar and speaking may not be well developed. In fact, for most millennials, their overall scholastic goal is "good enough" learning and intellectual "skimming," partly because they feel overstressed and partly because schools themselves do not always teach deep learning engagement (Carlson, 2005).

If you work with millennials, it is important to instill in them a sense of personal pride that can be gained through a desire for excellence and optimum learning experiences. With their natural tendency to question authority, you can encourage millennials to analyze available resources critically. You can also parlay their technological expertise in showing them how to work smarter, not harder, to gain information fluency.

How adults learn

Development does not stop at adulthood; people develop cognitively and psychologically throughout their lives. The immediate issues of a 30-year-old, for instance, usually differ from the issues of a 60-year-old. This factor becomes critical in professional development where an entire faculty or professional group is participating. In instruction, illustrative examples need to cross generational experiences, such as drawing upon natural disasters in teaching locational skills.

Psychologist Daniel Levinson (1978) studied men's interactions between their inner life and external events, and identified their development as "seasons in a man's life." Building on Erikson's stages, Levinson detailed three eras. Each stage includes seasons of upheaval and change as well as seasons of stability and synthesis. Implications for instructional design follow in italics.

- **Early adult**: 22–28 years old entering the adult world, 28–33 transitioning between old life structures and new life challenges, 33–40 settling down. *Librarians should emphasize the benefits of skill building to optimize career options.*
- **Middle adult**: 40–45 midlife transition, 45–50 entering middle adulthood, 50–55 transitioning as in early adulthood, 55–60 culmination and peaking of middle adulthood. *Librarians can show adults how their information literacy, for instance, can provide them with balance in their lives, both by being more productive as well as using skills for personal growth.*
- **Late adult**: 60–65 late-adult transition, 65 and onward old age. *Older adults can mentor younger learners. Their cognitive processes may be slower, so self-paced learning may be more comfortable than strict class-time learning, especially if it incorporates socializing.*

Generational issues

When you consider the age of an individual within the context of an era, such as reaching adulthood in the 1950s as opposed to reaching it in the 1990s, then the picture becomes even more complex. Each generation exhibits trends of behaviors and expectations. While individual differences trump any generalization, some patterns do emerge (Hicks and Hicks, 1999; Howe and Strauss, 2003). Instructional design implications for librarians are indicated by italics.

- **Gen Xers** (1966–1980) are individualistic career nomads. Self-starting and resourceful, they seek autonomy and purpose. *Web tutorials are a welcome way to learn for them.*
- **Baby Boomers** (1946–1965) are the counterculture turned mainstream, hardworking citizens who still carry a torch for ideals. Continuing to be competitive (because of their numbers), they seek public recognition before it is too late. *This population may need digital retooling to keep competitive.*
- **Traditionalists** (born 1945 and before) are retiring after loyal service to a single employer, if possible. They tend to be patriotic (partially because of World War II experience) and conforming in behavior. *This population has*

time to volunteer in the library, and will need relevant training to match skills to library duties. They are a good target for computer training to keep in contact with family and get health information.

These developmental issues do not take into consideration cultural differences. Each culture has its own rites of passages and adult roles, which may be determined by age, gender, and life situation. Ethnicities are often set in different cultures, such as a 60-year-old Chinese woman in a rural village in Western China as opposed to a 60-year-old Chinese woman in a Los Angeles corporate office. Most basic of all, personality can vary wildly among any group of individuals.

Andragogy

Interestingly, earlier centuries considered children as miniature adults, and taught them through example; children mimicked adults. The idea of *pedagogy* marked a consciousness about the unique aspects of children and the way they learn. Ironically, *andragogy*, the science of adult education, is a late-twentieth-century concept. In fact, many universities still refer to the act of instruction in higher education as pedagogy, which does not recognize the special attributes of adult learners.

Building on growing research about lifelong human development, andragogy pioneers Malcolm Knowles, Swanson, and Holton (2011) leveraged the idea of adult self-concept and responsibility to explain the needs of adult learners. These factors need to be considered when designing instruction for this population, and library-specific recommendations are italicized.

- **Self-direction**: Adults want to be treated as responsible, self-directed learners. They want to be in control of their learning. *Therefore, librarians should develop a learning environment that provides adults choices in what they learn, how they learn, and how they demonstrate their learning.*
- **Experience**: Adults have extensive and diverse experiences, which help them to construct meaning from learning activities. *Librarians should help adult learners identify what they already know, and then build on that knowledge in a community of learners, each contributing to the group's body of knowledge.* In addition, experienced adults build up high expectations, so instructors should be responsive to those demands and set clear and reasonable norms. *Librarians should also realize that adult learners may have experienced negative learning situations, so they have to overcome those negative connotations.* This issue becomes more glaring in light of technology ignorance or past technology failure.
- **Motivation**: Adults are motivated internally: by job needs, personal desire, and self-esteem. Whenever possible, instruction should be developed in

response to adult interests and needs, and should be offered on a volunteer basis to ensure that the participants are willing, committed learners, thus offering a positive atmosphere. *Since libraries are usually frequented on a volunteer basis, librarians can leverage their users' internal motivation.*

- **Readiness**: Adults learn when they see a need to learn in order to cope with their lives or improve them. As with motivation, readiness should dictate the creation of learning opportunities. In addition, learning activities should be contextualized so adults see how it they fit into their daily experience. *Librarians can survey their clientele, or consult their reference statistics to identify high-interest topics for instruction.*
- **Need to know**: Adults need to know what they are going to learn and why they are learning it before they commit to the learning. *Librarians should explicitly state the learning outcomes and benefits of each learning activity.*
- **Timing**: Adults have many demands on their time, so they need to fit learning within the framework of the rest of their lives. *Librarians need to provide reasonable deadlines and provide a structure that allows for self-pacing.*
- **Practical**: Adults appreciate immediate and close transfer of learning and practical instruction. Hands-on, concrete learning activities that are domain specific work well with adults. *Therefore, librarians should include opportunities for learners to reality-check content by testing it in real-world situations.*
- **Social**: Adults want their social needs to be met as well as their academic, intellectual needs. Moreover, adults learn through shared knowledge construction. *Librarians should provide interactive structures and opportunities for adult learners to share their thoughts, be it face-to-face or online.* By offering these outlets, instructors find that learners are more satisfied and learn more.

As the need for continuous education becomes more evident and life spans increase, it is possible that four generations of adults may be learning together. Therefore, as a librarian instructor, you need to balance the universal with the particular. To address a diverse group of adult learners, establish a common goal and some common values. Provide choices for the learners to personalize their experiences, and elicit from them appropriate examples as well as offer universal illustrations that can resonate for everyone. Incorporate social opportunities to help younger adults feel that they belong, to help adults mentor their younger peers, and to enable older learners to share their knowledge. In addition, acknowledge differences in processing time as people age. Older learners may need repeated instruction or slower pacing, so online instruction may actually be more effective for them than strict face-to-face sessions.

Gender issues in learning

Gender differences in learning start with early biological differences. Males' right brains, where abstract thinking and sequencing dominate, are thicker than girls', although girls tend to have thicker left brains, which impact image and holistic thinking. Girls' brain hemispheres are more connected than boys' so their brains are more coordinated (Sousa, 2005). Because of these differences, boys respond better to things, and girls respond better to people. When crises occur, the lower part of boys' brains dominate: fight or flight; in contrast, girls' upper thinking brain dominates in such cases, which may explain why girls tend to take fewer risks (Moir and Jessel, 1991).

In infancy, boys are less bothered by loud noises than girls, who prefer soft tones and singing; on the other hand, girls have better hearing and are able to distinguish emotional nuances. Boys are more active and more easily angered; girls are more easily saddened. As toddlers, boys have greater muscle and roam more. Girls develop better vocabulary and have better visual memory; they also multitask better than boys (Gurian and Stevens, 2010). In terms of emotional development, even as early as the primary grades, boys are better able than girls to separate emotion from reason. On the other hand, by sixth grade, boys are more likely to take aggressive action to solve problems. While some differences even out over time, having initial advantages in specific modalities of perception and processing can impact later learning.

Puberty accentuates other gender-linked learning issues. For instance, boys achieve academically after puberty while girls start to drop out of some advanced science courses. Girls' IQ scores drop off during middle school, although they rise again in high school. Boys tend to pursue power while girls pursue a comfortable environment. Boys' social hierarchies tend to be stable while girls' are fluid (Park, 2004). Because learning is largely a social process, the emotional lives of adolescents need to be acknowledged and leveraged to bring out the best in each gender—and build up their less-utilized traits.

Not surprisingly, education is a different experience for boys and girls (Black, 1995). For example, because beginning reading requires both sides of the brain, girls are, again, at an advantage. On the other hand, by third grade, reasoning math skills showcase boys' natural lead (Gurian and Stevens, 2010). In terms of learning overall, girls tend to be concrete experiential learners while boys favor abstract conceptualization, the latter being the main instructional approach in formal education. Because of their more split brain hemispheres, boys can be more field-independent, competitive learners, which is favored in schools. In contrast, girls tend to think more about the relative quality of ideas and their interrelationships. Boys focus more on the product while girls focus on the process. Because girls develop earlier than boys overall, it takes more time for boys to learn; moreover, boys' attention span is shorter, and they need more attention than girls. While primary-age boys are more rule-bound than their female peers, by their teenage age years, boys rebel against those rules (Gurian and Henley, 2001). Girls generally enjoy school more, and work harder than boys. As a result, girls tend to get higher grades in school (Black, 1995; Philbin et al., 1995). Even females' worldview often differs from males': time is considered fluid, measured in terms of relationships rather than in objective units; power is limitless rather than zero-sum; leadership is based on facilitation rather than power; and the world is to be lived with, not exploited (Miller, 1976).

As touched upon above, societal expectations carry as much weight as nature. Social development has continued to start with the family, grow to include neighbors and relatives, and then include community and larger entities. Within the last half-century, societal expectations about females and males have been tested repeatedly; today's youth grow up in a different social climate than their parents or grandparents did, by and large. Many businesses reflect "flatter" bureaucratic hierarchies, and deal with organizational well-being as much as the bottom line. The glass ceiling has become more permeable, and career options have increased for both males and females. Both sexes can self-realize their full potential to a greater extent. On the other hand, stereotypical images and expectations are communicated daily in the mass media and in daily life. Particularly when learners are stressed or uncertain about themselves, they are more likely to regress to stereotypical behavior.

As a librarian, you are uniquely positioned to address gender issues in designing instruction. First of all, you have specialized training and technological expertise, which models positive achievement. In addition, the library is usually considered a safe, neutral place to take intellectual risks. Information literacy requires a variety of skills and processes that draw equally from male and female learning preferences, so both sexes can build on their strengths while gaining fluency in their less strong learning modes. Furthermore, by becoming information literate, both sexes become empowered. When designing instruction, you should make sure that examples are suitable for both sexes (such as health or politics), that learners have choices in source material, and are offered alternative ways to practice and demonstrate competency.

Who are instructors?

Education is usually considered in terms of teaching and learning. The teacher is assumed to have more knowledge about the content matter, and is able to share that knowledge with learners. In that respect, parents, clergy, and siblings can serve as teachers. Although some people consider themselves auto-didacts, even they are learning from another person via recorded information.

More formally, though, teaching is a profession in that its members have specialized knowledge gained from advanced formal preparation, which they apply to solve educational problems. The National Education Association's 1975 *Code of Ethics* describes the teacher's responsibility as follows: "The educator strives to help each student realize his or her potential as a worthy and effective member of society. The educator therefore works to stimulate the spirit of inquiry, the acquisition of knowledge and understanding, and the thoughtful formulation of worthy goals" (p. 1).

Librarian instructional competencies

Increasingly, librarians are considered teachers, at least informally, as they help users gain physical and intellectual access to information. In terms of professional expertise, the American Library Association's (ALA) 2009 list of core competencies of librarianship include the following teaching elements:

- The methods used to interact successfully with individuals of all ages and groups to provide consultation, mediation, and guidance in their use of recorded knowledge and information
- Information literacy/information competence techniques and methods, numerical literacy, and statistical literacy
- Principles of assessment and response to diversity in user needs, user communities, and user preferences
- Principles and methods used to assess the impact of current and emerging situations or circumstances on the design and implementation of appropriate services or resource development
- The role of the library in the lifelong learning of patrons, including an understanding of lifelong learning in providing quality service and leveraging lifelong learning in promoting library services
- Learning theories, instructional methods, and achievement measures; and their application in libraries and other information agencies
- Principles related to the teaching and learning of concepts, processes, and skills used in seeking, evaluating, and using recorded knowledge and information

The American Library Association also recognizes that the library/information profession includes several specialties, which have more specific teaching competencies. The most obvious specialty is school librarianship. The 2011 National Council for Accreditation of Teacher Education standards for initial preparation of school librarians requires content knowledge about learning and content pedagogy as well as competency in providing effective learning environments.

Similarly, the National Board for Professional Teaching Standards (2001) stated that school librarians need to be knowledgeable about learners, teaching and learning, and information studies as they integrate instruction. In support of this instructional role, most school librarians have post-baccalaureate preparation in both library/information science and education. Pre-service school librarians are also usually required to have extended field experience to hone their instructional skills.

Youth-serving librarians in public library settings are also expected to have teaching competencies. For instance, the Association of Library Service to Children (ALSC) (2009) stated that their librarians need to understand youth learning and development, and instruct children in the use of library resources and tools, including research skills. Similarly, the Young Adult Library Services Association (YALSA) (2010) expects their librarians to be familiar with adolescent development, to instruct them in basic research and other information literacy skills, and to create an environment that supports informational needs.

Librarians in higher education serve mainly adults. In their role, they are expected to provide instruction in a variety of services: course-related activities, hands-on learning activities, orientations, tutorials, and point-of-use instruction. Academic librarians also need to collaborate with classroom faculty in curriculum planning, instruction, and assessment. The Association of College and Research Librarians (ACRL) 2008 standards define 41 core proficiencies for instruction librarians and 28 additional proficiencies for instructional coordinators. These standards address curriculum knowledge and ten categories of skills: administration, assessment, communication, information literacy integration, instructional design, leadership, planning, presenting, promotion, and teaching.

Special Libraries Association's (SLA) 2003 competencies for information professionals considers information services to include researching client groups' information behaviors and problems in order to identify solutions and provide customized information services so clients have the capabilities to integrate and apply information in their work or learning processes. More narrowly defined special librarians, such as law librarians, are also expected to teach research strategies and methods (American Association of Law Librarians, 1988).

It should be noted that librarians are expected to be resource and technology experts, particularly in terms of management. These skills are vital, especially in the digital world that makes up much of current instructional design.

Current instructional roles

While there is always room for formal presentations and on-the-fly assistance, neither of these efforts portray the spirit of the teacher, especially in light of instructional design. Core library service actually holds the key to good teaching in that librarians try to help people become effective users of information and ideas, to which end they need to know about users, information, and information use.

Instructional design favors a more analytical coordinator role, a process-centric effort in which the instructor carefully establishes and monitors an environment that fosters learning, based on assessing learner needs. Indeed, a current term for an instructional designer is a knowledge engineer. These design processes cross content and delivery systems, making them applicable and scalable for many settings.

Structuring the interaction among learners, content within a context makes the librarian instructional designer a facilitator. Such a role builds on effective communication and the ability to delegate power and responsibility.

On a one-to-one basis, the instructional designer serves as coach and mentor. Like a coach, you work with the learner to create a personal development plan, analyzing the learner's current performance and giving advice on how to improve such action. As a mentor, you enter a working relationship with the learner, and ease the learner's way to knowledge.

Perhaps the most impactful instructional design role for librarians, though, is as a change agent. A change agent is a person or group with technical expertise and human relations skill who can facilitate change through a helping relationship (Houle, 1996). Not only do change agents design instruction to optimize learning, they also try to help learners contextualize their learning and incorporate it into their daily lives. In effect, change agents try to provide the conditions for effective and sustainable change on the part of their clientele. They can help clientele identify social support, help them identify and overcome obstacles, and encourage small steps for immediate success. Change agents also help individuals' sense of self-efficacy by providing clear instructions, modeling the behavior, providing opportunities for practice, and reinforcing changed behavior.

Havelock's 1973 theory of change posited four ways that a person can act as a change agent:

1. As a catalyst or troublemaker whose efforts stir up change
2. As a solution giver
3. As a resource linker, be it financial, material, human, or knowledge based
4. As a process helper who can recognize and define needs, diagnose problems, set objectives, acquire needed resources, help implement solutions, and evaluate solution success

Havelock emphasized the need for change agents to gather relevant information by inquiring and listening to clientele, observing and measuring systems outputs, and then reflecting on that data in order to diagnose the existing situation and determine how best to facilitate change. These processes are practiced by librarians daily at the reference desk!

|||||||||||||||||||||||||||||||||||||||||||||||||||||||||||||||||||||||||||||||||||||||||||||||||||||||||||||||

The social side of teaching

It has been said that teachers teach students—teachers don't teach subjects. The underlying message is that without students, no learning occurs. Regardless of a librarian's expertise, if positive interactions do not occur, then the instructional design will not be effective. Thus, for students to learn, you need to provide opportunities for learners to be actively engaged, participate in groups, interact frequently with their instructors, get timely and specific feedback, and see connections with real-world contexts. In short, socialization is a vital part of education.

Therefore, librarians need to examine their own social style. Introverts may interact with students differently from extroverts; intuitive thinkers may behave differently from individuals who prefer reacting to concrete external realities. Even the comfort zone of physical space between two individuals differs by culture and personality. Some people prefer interacting with others of the same sex while others enjoy working with the opposite sex. Some librarians like whole-class discussion while others prefer coaching individuals. Whatever the social style, self-awareness can help explain the reasons for initial instructor-student interaction. Although the two parties may have different ways of reacting to each other, it is the librarian instructor's responsibility to identify the possible disconnect and to figure out ways to overcome those first miscommunications, particularly if teaching youth. In the latter situation, that adult can help youth learn different ways to interact socially as well. What is your own social style? Through self-reflection, you can better negotiate instruction approaches with learners, even if your style preference does not match your learners.

Types of learning situations

The concept of lifelong learning seems self-evident. As long as one is alive, one is likely to encounter new situations that need to be resolved; each of those encounters is a potential learning moment. Nevertheless, because today's information society drives change in so many aspects of life, lifelong learning takes on new and explicit meaning. People consciously have to pay attention to the world around them, and decide if they want to change—and what they need to do to accommodate those changes. In this respect, today's society has sometimes been called "the learning society" to emphasize the dynamic nature of social change throughout people's lives (Field, 2006).

Within the context of lifelong learning, the types of learning may be divided as follows (Marsick and Watkins, 2001):

- **Formal learning**: institutionally sponsored structural learning with an identified curriculum and delivery system, sometimes known as academic preparation

- **Informal learning**: semi-structured instruction that usually happens through daily interaction at home or work or other social settings; language acquisition and social norms are usually taught this way
- **Incidental learning**: usually unintentional learning, such as accidentally touching a hot burner and learning to avoid direct touch

As a librarian, you are potentially involved in all types of learning.

Types of youth learning and libraries

Informal learning begins at birth, as a child learns to make accommodations in order to be fed. That informal learning continues nonstop in the family, and expands to the neighborhood and community in which one lives. Religious, health, and recreation institutions are early sites for informal learning as children learn doctrine, hygiene, and rules of play. The public library constitutes one of those early informal learning settings, depending on the parents' or other care-givers' initiative to bringing children to the facility. Nowadays, that first exposure to the public library might well be online.

Complementing early informal learning is PK–12 formal education. Schools are social institutions that are structured with the intent of preparing youth to enter successfully into society and become contributing citizens. Schools empha-size academic success, but also have to attend to students' physical and mental well-being. Schools are expected to transfer societal norms and expectations, while helping youth prepare to be responsive to—and to initiate—change as they will encounter it in society. School libraries are considered the main type of library setting for school-age children for several reasons: the facility is physi-cally convenient, the collection is age-appropriate and supports the school cur-riculum, and the school librarian has the expertise and opportunity to design instruction that aligns with the school's mission and fosters learning literacies.

Postsecondary formal education bridges youth and adulthood. Community colleges, in particular, may include students as young as 16 (or even younger for the gifted) and as old as nonagenarians. In the United States, higher education tends to focus on degree- and certificate-bearing programs, which are largely populated by young adults. However, reentry students comprise a growing per-centage of the student body population.

Informal education continues throughout childhood and adolescence: in clubs and other social groups, in social environments such as recreational centers and libraries, and via mass media such as television and video games. Each of these venues has social norms and philosophies, which they may share explicitly. In most cases, the emphasis is on the social entity such that the learning is usually focused on ways for the individual to be accepted and successful within the social environment.

In studying youth, Besharov (1999) found that as teens grow up, about one-third of them feel disconnected from institutions (e.g., school) or people (e.g., peers, families, community) for at least six months, with at least 50 percent of Latino and African-American males exhibiting these signs, although ethnicity in itself has no significant effect on how teens respond to these factors. However, youth who feel disconnected for three or more years suffer long-term social and financial problems. For them, both formal and informal learning may be limited, which further impacts their later success. Public libraries have a unique opportunity to provide a safe learning environment for these at-risk youth.

Types of adult learning and libraries

Although some adults do not think of themselves as lifelong learners, informal learning characterizes most people's daily lives. Librarians acknowledge the validity of such learning approaches, and can leverage informal learning opportunities. Nevertheless, the implications of a learning society lead to a more systematic approach to adult learning rather than trial and error on a personal basis (Selwyn, Gorard, and Furlong, 2006).

Workplace learning constitutes the most common venue for both formal and informal learning. While hallway conversations and e-mail advice are ongoing informal learning situations, formal learning is also increasingly part of the workplace. Career and technical training may consist of a lengthy set of courses, such as a university degree program, or specific, just-in-time technical information. Education options largely depend on the person's career status (Mullowney, 1980):

- Pre-career preparation: foundational principles and practices
- Beginning entry-level position: company-specific processes and minor technical gaps
- Mid-level position shift: advanced study or new aspects of the industry (e.g., management issues)
- Midlife career change: condensed information in order to switch careers quickly and efficiently, perhaps with suggestions on transferring knowledge from one domain to another
- Senior years: refreshed/new information in the field

Corporations may well have libraries, which can serve as centers for self-initiated learning. In addition, special librarians may work with other divisions, such as human resources, to create formal training sessions.

Current society is marked by ongoing change rather than event-specific change, so it might be posited that widespread adult education would result. Evidence supports that assumption; about 46 percent of the U.S. population participated in adult education activities in 1999 (Westat and Creighton, 2000). Nevertheless, a forced government-based adult education initiative, such as proposed in Great Britain (Istance, Schuetze, and Schuller, 2002), would be likely to fail if for no other reason than adult learners need to feel in control of their own learning experience, choosing if and how to participate. Rather, the conditions for adult formal learning, which reflect instructional design, need to be provided widely and systemically so that adults have opportunities for meaningful learning. Libraries can serve in that capacity. As is, they tend to provide resources that support all kinds of lifelong learning, although the collections are rarely developed in tandem with lifelong learning providers. Such an approach is a great opportunity for libraries to become even more essential in the community.

Groups of learners

As you know, learning is largely a social process. People may gather in several ways, either as a self-defined process or by some outside entity. The grouping may be ad hoc or permanent, project based or functional based. Learners tend to be grouped officially through formal education, such as schools, and at the workplace. However, spontaneous groups may form as a result of mutual interest, and are most likely to endure because of added social value. Group learning has several benefits: increased motivation because of member interdependence, a greater social presence as a whole group, greater communication, improved collaboration, and more efficient gaining of knowledge. Your expertise in optimizing learning experiences can come in handy for such groups; you can become an excellent member of these groups and can act as a valuable consultant.

Learning communities and communities of practice

In this light, a learning community consists of a group of people who want to learn something in common, and act on their learning to achieve a common goal. The learning community may learn from one another, or seek expertise from outside their circle. Another socio-educational trend is "communities of practice": making tacit information explicit, bringing the newcomers into the center of learning, and sharing best practices in order to improve the entire organization. In this latter type of community, expertise exists *within* the group. Wenger, McDermott, and Snyder (2002) asserted that the structure of a community of practice consisted of three dimensions: the domain of knowledge, which provides a common ground of understanding; a sense of community, which fosters social interaction and sharing; and the specific practice focus. Wenger (1998) also noted three stages of community of practice: mutual engagement, during which time norms and relationships are established to bind the group together; joint enterprise, which establishes the intellectual domain of the group; and shared repertoire, in which the members produce and share communal resources.

Communities of practice tend to begin informally, based on mutual need. In some organizations, such communities are instituted formally; however, if an authentic need is not recognized, and the social interaction is not positive, then the community will die. In that respect, informal communities are more likely to be sustained because the members have buy-in and can operate autonomously. On the other hand, an organization that is open to, and supports, communities of practice will likely benefit those communities, and the communities of practice themselves will contribute significantly to the organization's overall productivity and impact.

Levels of engagement

Wenger, McDermott, and Snyder (2002) defended the notion of a range of involvement. They asserted that most learning communities consist of 10 to 15 percent core members who often assume leadership roles, 15 to 20 percent active members, a majority of peripheral members on the sidelines, and nonmembers who are interested in the learning community and may "lurk" there occasionally. The researchers contended that each set of individuals contributes to the learning community, and derives benefits that may, in turn, contribute to the members' other learning communities as well as to themselves. While most learning communities want high-level interactivity among all members, this idea of different levels of participation recognizes individuals' learning preferences. Furthermore, learners may well be applying their newfound knowledge to the professional settings to which they belong outside of their learning community, which can improve their profession as a whole. As a librarian, you can serve as a valuable member of the learning community, and can offer both content and organizational information.

The learning organization

With the advent of the information society has come the concept of the learning society and more specifically the learning organization. In the information age, organizations realize the importance of their intellectual capital or assets, and they are couching enterprises within a framework of a learning organization. The enterprise has a vision, identifies the gaps between reality and that vision, and sets about ways to bridge those gaps (Laiken, 2001). Senge (1990) defined learning organizations as "organizations where people continually expand their capacity to create the results they truly desire, where new and expansive patterns of thinking are nurtured, where collective aspiration is set free, and where people are continually learning to see the whole together" (p. 3).

Increasingly, the workplace is adopting the concept of learning communities as a way to cope with internal and external change. Theoretically, educational and professional associations have embraced this philosophy for a long time, but supporting learning communities is more important now than ever. Entities have to keep nimble and flexible in response to changing external environmental factors such as changing clientele demographics, technological advances, economic turns, and political priorities of the moment. Change comes from within the organization as much as from without; for example, the concept of company loyalty is less valued among young workers. Therefore, enterprises need to manage knowledge efficiently so exiting employees can transfer their knowledge to their successors and new employees can get up to speed quickly in order for the enterprise as a whole to keep operating smoothly between human resource transitions. Both individual and organizational learning is needed to keep a competitive edge. Special libraries tend to maintain collections to support the workplace; increasingly, they are embracing the concept of knowledge management, creating in-house repositories of corporate documents as a sort of brain trust.

Within the working environment, which may also consist of an educational institution, learning communities have several benefits.

- New employees are trained more efficiently because they can get help from mentors and other experts.
- Institutional knowledge is shared so that operations can function successfully if employees are absent or leave.
- Employees can keep current in their fields by sharing their learning experiences, such as conferences and professional reading.
- Individual learning and group learning inform each other.
- Camaraderie and interdependence are facilitated through joint, meaningful actions.
- Employees can analyze and reflect on their practice with the aim of improving individual and organizational efforts.

As Laiken (2001) noted in her study of organizational learning models, "a focus on information organizational learning contributes to employees' collective ability to move beyond simply coping with stress to engaging in creative action, for the benefit of both the individual members and the organization as a whole" (p. 4).

Technology impacts learning communities in several ways:

- Communication and actions can be recorded more easily through e-mails, online chat, and videoconferencing.
- Documents can be digitized for easier access, storage, and retrieval.
- People can communicate anytime, anywhere.

The explicit focus on a learning organization transcends these informal and arbitrary practices to provide a predictable and sustainable system of knowledge sharing. Senge (1990) identified five principles within this framework: personal mastery, mental models, shared vision, team learning, and systems thinking. Instructional design can play a key role at each stage. Librarian implications are noted in italics.

1. **Personal mastery** connotes an ongoing process of self-assessment and self-improvement. While individuals can choose to learn or not learn, their attitude and actions impact the overall organization as a whole, particularly if they share their new knowledge. Instructional designers can provide the conditions for learning by announcing learning opportunities, linking learners to resources and experts, and facilitating the public recognition of gained knowledge. *Librarians are well positioned to provide these communication links.*
2. **Mental models**, such as educational philosophies, impact individual and group learning in that they codify the organization's assumptions and expectations. If, for instance, the mental model of *statis* permeates the organization, then learning that leads to innovation will probably not be supported or encouraged. If, on the other hand, a mental model of mutual support and encouragement exists, then shared learning is more likely to blossom. Generally, an organizational attitude of open dialogue and positive problem solving tends to support the principles of a learning organization. *Instructional designers, including librarians, need to recognize the organization's mental models in order to frame their own work and support. Even in a static organization, librarian instructional designers can support individual learning if for no other reason than to enable new employees to gain the knowledge needed to maintain the status quo.*
3. **Shared vision** offers a touchstone to anchor the learning organization. Individuals can determine whether their learning efforts contribute and manifest the vision—or detract from it. Usually, shared vision also demonstrates a commitment to long-range planning and innovation that mark a learning organization. *As a librarian, you usually serve the entire organization, so you can design instruction that supports and applies that vision across entities.*
4. **Team learning** acknowledges the social aspect of learning. Individuals want to check their understanding to confirm their learning or make needed changes. More importantly, team learning appreciates the unique skill sets of each person, and builds on those individualities to produce a significant product that no one person could do independently. *Instructional designers, including librarians, can help individuals gain expertise in collaboration:*

building mutual respect and trust, communicating and negotiating effectively, understanding group interaction and dynamics, sharing control, assessing efforts and progress, and making adjustments to optimize results (Greenberg, 2010). Indeed, a basic premise of information literacy is collaboration, which undergirds and promotes team learning.

5. **Systems thinking** frames learning within the organization in order to allocate and manage the necessary resources to support such learning. Especially since organizations are comprised of interdependent functions, those relationships need to be examined as a whole in order to optimize results. For instance, if accounting learns how to track workflow more efficiently using technology, they may find that certain departments are not using their time efficiently and may call them to task—and suggest that they learn more effective ways to conduct business. Instructional designers, in this case, probably human resource developers (HRD), need to be informed of this development, and help impacted departments understand the consequences and gain the knowledge needed in order to improve their practice. *As an informational mediator between divisions or functions, the library often observes those interrelationships and overlaps, and can provide valuable input into system analysis. The library collection, including repositories, also serves a cost-effective central information hub. Likewise, information literacy training can link several functions.*

Culturally sensitive learning contexts

All too often, cultural sensitivity is overlooked when designing instruction, even though each society's culture reflects educational philosophies and impacts learning organizations. Biggs, Kember, and Leung (2001) emphasize the importance of identifying which factors are universal and which are culturally defined. Most significant are those practices that are imposed as if universal (e.g., outlining a report) that actually reflect specific cultural norms (e.g., North American); learners outside that teacher-centric culture may feel discounted or underprepared. Not only should you as a librarian be aware of the impact of culture in designing instruction, but you should leverage those cultural differences to provide a richer educational experience.

McMahon and Bruce's (2002) examination of learners led to several contributing cultural factors that can impact instructional design effectiveness:

- **Language (idioms)**: native/primary language skills of reading and writing; the quality and quantity of second-language experience and skill; formal versus informal language usage; vocabulary and idiomatic knowledge
- **Educational philosophy and experiences**: role of education; curriculum and instruction practices; student behavior norms (which might differ from the institution's expectations); learner-specific experiences

- **Gender issues**: sex-linked educational, career, and workplace expectations/ norms that are culturally defined
- **Age-linked cultural norms**: generation-specific roles and expectations; familial roles and norms; roles and expectations impacted by global/social realities (e.g., digital natives)
- **Knowledge of career**: transmission of information patterns (e.g., family, academic counseling, libraries); cultural expectations and norms relative to specific careers; community needs and practices (e.g., local agricultural economy versus globalized knowledge economy)

If the learning is linked to careers in general or to a specific workplace, librarian instructors need to know this. Particularly if the career ethos contradicts familial values, learners might artificially separate those two worlds, try to integrate the two, or reject one set of values. As a librarian instructor, you should take care to respect each student's cultural stance while noting the importance of learning about the social climate to be experienced as an employee. Furthermore, it is helpful to contextualize content in terms of students' local reality or at least build on those realities as students need to assimilate new cultural understandings (McMahon and Bruce, 2002).

Kalyanpur and Harry (1999) further assert that the following elements should be established at every level of a system to facilitate cultural sensitivity and eventual competency as it is manifested in instructional design:

- A belief in the value of diversity
- The capacity for cultural self-assessment
- Awareness of the dynamics of cultural interaction
- Institutionalization of cultural knowledge
- Service adaptation and accommodations that respect diversity within and between cultures

Fortunately, librarians have a strong belief in inclusivity and diversity, along with a commitment to individual needs, so you can serve as a positive model for sensitive, culturally aware instructional design. Therefore, as you design library instruction with learners from different cultures, you should strive for cultural proficiency: open to learning about other cultures and sharing one's own culture, able to change personal perspectives, and able to communicate effectively across cultures (Liaw, 2006).

Online environments and learning

Online teaching differs from face-to-face instruction in terms of physicality. Teachers and students are not in the same space at the same time. For that reason, the senses play a lesser role in digesting information; a disconnect occurs. For instance, gestures are not as easily interpreted, even in videoconferencing venues. Theoretically, when instruction exists without any images or sounds of teachers or students, context is minimized; people are less likely to impose their preconceived notions of generations in the educational setting. With that assumption made, some instructors may think that online courses can be standardized for a global audience.

However, such an assumption is false. People bring their backgrounds and experiences to their online learning situation, and interpret the course in light of their existing mental schema. In comparison to face-to-face interactions, it may be more difficult for instructors and students to ascertain the basis for individuals' contributions and responses in the online environment. With less information about the individual available, misinterpretations may actually increase in number. For example, if an e-learner asserts that birth control is bad, it helps to understand that person's statement if it is known that the learner is a 20-year-old black male rather than a 60-year-old Latino.

Age and gender impact online instructional design and delivery in two ways: developmental/biological and social/cultural. As the brain develops, it processes and communicates information in different ways. Furthermore, the time period in which individuals live shapes their online experience; for instance, millennials, as opposed to most baby boomers, have grown up with digital technology. As noted previously, learning preferences may also be sex linked, and certainly experiences have gendered implications. Therefore, as the online community reflects lifelong learning, it behooves you to factor in age and gender when developing and delivering online instruction.

Implications for you

Instructional design may be viewed as a series of embedded circles that represent stakeholders. At the center is the learner, with his or her learning needs and goals. The immediate learning environment is designed by the librarian instructor—you—bringing your own experiences and expectations. These two parties, learner and instructor, are surrounded by organizations: groups of people with their own beliefs and agendas. These groups are contextualized by societies, each with their own cultural values and norms.

Librarians can be found in each of these circles, both being influenced by those values and behaviors as well as having some influence within each circle. Certainly, you need to be aware of each stakeholder and his or her role in instructional design as it supports instructional design. Beyond that understanding, you need to collaborate with these stakeholders so that the resultant learning will be relevant and effective for all those entities.

|||||||||||||||||||||||||||||||||||||||||||||||||||||||||||||||||||||||||||||||||||||||||||||||||||

Sample instructional design about culture and learning

The following online lesson is geared toward postsecondary underclass students, who are likely taking a social studies or wellness course. The instructional design builds on students' self-perceptions, and uses interactive media to leverage social learning. The online quiz enables students to be self-revealing without having to disclose possible prejudices publicly, and gives them instant feedback.

|||||||||||||||||||||||||||||||||||||||||||||||||||||||||||||||||||||||||||||||||||||||||||||||||||

Lesson

Title: Cultural Competence: The First Step

Lesson overview: As learners deal with multicultural resources and people of different cultures, they need to be culturally competent. The first step in cultural competence is self-awareness of one's own culture and culture-based perspectives.

Time frame: 2 hours

Learning objectives: Learners will:
- Describe aspects of culture.
- Self-assess their own cultural competency.
- Develop cultural competency goals for their course work.
- Incorporate selected information into one's knowledge base.
- Use information effectively to accomplish a specific purpose.
- Understand the economic, legal, and social issues surrounding the use of information.

Curriculum standards
- Foster respect for human diversity in the USA.
- Promote the understanding of diversity to encourage tolerance and acceptance of others.
- Recognize the significant influence of diverse populations and cultures within the USA.

Resources
- Technology: Internet-accessible computer; class blog (optional)

Planning for diverse learners
- Students may work in pairs.
- Text can be translated using an online translator, or read aloud using a computer reader.

Instructional strategies and study activities

Instructor posts the following content online.

Cultural Competence

As we deal with people of different cultures, we need to be culturally competent. Health issues can be particularly culturally sensitive.

Culture may be defined as "the customary beliefs, social forms, and material traits of a racial, religious, or social group" and "the set of shared attitudes, values, goals, and practices that characterizes an institution or organization" (*Webster's Dictionary*). In health professions, cultural issues apply to the clientele, the health worker, the setting, and the profession in general (e.g., resources and services).

READ the Cultural Competency webpage: http://diversity.vc.ons .org/page/132853/;jsessionid=g7r7hsqlt5s

This issue has been emphasized in the health professions, and can apply well to other social services.

Think about your own culture. A useful construct is this set of cultural factors categorized as RUTSMAP: Religion / Unions / Traditions / Space-time / Medicine AND Money / Academics / Pastimes. An example is provided at the end of the tutorial.

Cultural Bias

All of us are prejudiced in some way, be it against fast foods or for flossing ;-)

In order to deal with the myriad of constant stimuli, we make pre-judgments in order to find some order in the chaos. However, those pre-judgments can sometimes be inaccurate, misleading, or even harmful. We certainly know that 9/11 has sparked prejudice, and as students, we try to learn how to deal with such prejudice. In terms of attitude, it's probably best to "own up" to one's own prejudice (I have an aversion to phone salespersons), and then try to get beyond the bias to the actual person and content.

READ this webpage on bias: http://www.tolerance.org/activity/ test-yourself-hidden-bias (I didn't find the test to be very helpful.)

TAKE the multicultural awareness quiz: http://www.mhhe.com/ socscience/education/multi_new/activities/awarenessquiz.html

Task

Create your own RUTSMAP, and answer 1 part of question 5 of the multicultural awareness quiz guide. Based on these and cultural competency reading, where do you see yourself in terms of cultural competency—and what do you hope to achieve in this arena during the course?

Your reflection will probably be about two pages single-spaced.

POST your reflection in your class blog. You are encouraged to compare your RUTSMAP with a peer's.

Sample RUTSMAP

I was raised in a Danish-American family (both parents had grand-parents from Denmark). I was an only child.

Religion / nominally Lutheran. Doing good was more important than being religious or spiritual. My mother became more active in the (conservative) Protestant church once I converted to Roman Catholicism (based on my international experience).

Unions / The key union was the nuclear family, and marriage was more important than children. The extended family was passively important. Professional associations were very important too. Friends were also important: few but loyal. I have the same values.

Traditions / Birthdays and holidays (especially Christmas) were important. My mother went all out for Christmas with decorations, gifts, and Danish cookie baking. I have the same values. Other traditions were usually food-related: pancakes after church, Saturday night waffles, coffee breaks. (I don't keep these traditions.) However, I keep the tradition of the family dinnertime and its sacredness.

Space-time / Personal space was (and is) very important. Timeliness was/is important, although we tended to be last-minute for events. I'm the same.

Medicine / We avoided medicine, and believed in liquids/rest remedies in general. We believed in seeing the dentist and doctor (who were supposed to be trusted, although we should not have always) for checkups, and in doing a little exercise. We were pretty ignorant of advanced health issues, except upon need (i.e., Dad's cancer, my knee surgery).

M can also be Money / FRUGAL. My mother loved a good sale. Lots of leftovers and recycling. Mom handled the money; she saved and also invested (unsuccessfully). I'm the same.

Academics / VERY important. My parents were the only ones in their families to attend—and graduate—from college. Both earned advanced degrees. They pursued professional careers (professor and architect). They didn't think they were any better than repair-men or waitresses (Mom was one for a while), but they said: "If you had a good mind, you should use it and contribute to society." I'm the same.

Pastimes / reading, card and board games, sewing, camping, travel, art, music, TV. Pastimes were usually done alone or with family/friends. Dad was very creative, and Mom was a great appreciator of culture. We didn't go to events often, mainly because of cost. I'm a combo of my parents.

Variations

- Deliver instruction face-to-face.
- Learners can be paired for the activity.
- Learners can interview something according to the RUTSMAP.
- Learners can create a class grid or database of RUTSMAP information.
- Learners can produce a RUTSMAP for someone else rather than themselves.

Student assessment

Learners are assessed in terms of their self-assessment and their application of cultural competency to their course (Table 3.1, p. 56).

Additional resources

Alpi, Kristine M. 2001. "Multicultural Health Information Seeking: Achieving Cultural Competency in the Library." *Journal of Hospital Librarianship* 1, no. 2: 51–59.

Table 3.1　Cultural rubric

Objectives	Low performance	At or below average	At or above average	Exemplary performance
Learner describes aspects of culture.	Few aspects of culture are described. Cultural aspects are inaccurate and prejudicial.	Some aspects of culture are described. Cultural aspects are inaccurate or prejudicial.	All RUTSMAP aspects of culture are described. Cultural aspects are accurate.	All RUTSMAP aspects of culture are described, with specific examples. Cultural aspects are accurate and insightful.
Learner self-assesses cultural competency.	Self-assessment is off-target. Self-assessment is vague; elements are missing. Little or no insight is evident.	Self-assessment is realistic. Some insight is evident.	Self-assessment is realistic and justified. Some insight is evident.	Self-assessment is realistic and well-justified. Assessment is very insightful.
Learner develops cultural competency goals for his or her course work.	Goal is weak or vague. Goal does not link to cultural competency. Goal does not link to course.	One goal is provided, which links to course.	One achievable, specific goal is provided, which links to course.	Two achievable, specific goals are provided and well-justified. The goals take advantage of the course's content and approach.

References

American Academy of Child and Adolescent Psychiatry. 2003. *Facts for Families*. Washington, DC: American Academy of Child and Adolescent Psychiatry. http://www.aacap.org.

American Association of Law Librarians. 1988. *AALL Guidelines for Graduate Programs in Law Librarianship*. Chicago: American Association of Law Librarians.

American Library Association. 2009. *Core Competences of Librarianship*. Chicago: American Library Association. http://www.ala.org/ala/educationcareers/careers/corecomp/corecompetences/finalcorecompstat09.pdf.

Association of College and Research Librarians. 2008. *Standards for Proficiencies for Instruction Librarians and Coordinators: A Practical Guide*. Chicago: American Library Association.

Association of Library Service to Children. 2009. *Competencies for Librarians Serving Children in Public Libraries*. Chicago: American Library Association.

Beal, C. 1990. "Development of Knowledge about the Role of Inference in Text Comprehension." *Child Development* 61: 1011–1023.

Besharov, D., ed. 1999. *America's Disconnected Youth*. Washington, DC: CWLA Press.

Biggs, J., D. Kember, and D. Leung. 2001. "The Revised 2-Factor Study Process Questionnaire R-SP2-2F." *British Journal of Educational Research* 71: 133–149.

Black, G. 1995. *CSMpact for Education: Do Boys and Girls Experience Education Differently?* Rochester, NY: Harris Interactive.

Carlson, S. 2005. "The Next Generation Goes to College." *The Chronicle of Higher Education* 52, no. 7: A34–A37.

Dale, E. 1946. *Audio-Visual Methods in Teaching*. New York: Dryden.

Erikson, E. 1980. *Identity and the Life Cycle*. New York: Norton.

Farmer, L. 1995. *Informing Young Women: Gender Equity through Literacy Skills*. Jefferson, NC: McFarland.

Farmer, L. 2007. "Developmental Social-Emotional Behavior and Information Literacy." In *Information and Emotion: The Emergent Affective Paradigm in Information Behavior Research and Theory*, edited by D. Nahl and D. Bilal, 99–120. Medford, NJ: Information Today.

Field, J. 2006. *Lifelong Learning and the New Educational Order*. Sterling, VA: Trentham Books.

Gambone, M., A. Klem, and J. Connell. 2002. *Finding Out What Matters for Youth*. Philadelphia, PA: Youth Development Strategies.

Gardner, H. 1985. *Frames of Mind: The Theory of Multiple Intelligence*. New York: Basic Books.

Glaubman, R., and H. Glaubman. 1997. "Effects of Self-Directed Learning, Story Comprehension, and Self-Questioning in Kindergarten." *Journal of Educational Research* 90, no. 6: 361–374.

Greenberg, J. 2010. *Behavior in Organizations*. 10th ed. Englewood Cliffs, NJ: Prentice Hall.

Gurian, M., and P. Henley. 2001. *Boys and Girls Learn Differently! A Guide for Teachers and Parents*. San Francisco: Jossey-Bass.

Gurian, M., and K. Stevens. 2010. *Boys and Girls Learn Differently! A Guide for Teachers and Parents*. Rev. ed. San Francisco: Jossey-Bass.

Hand, K., M. D'Archangelo, and J. Robbins. 1992. *Teaching to Learning Styles; Leader's Guide*. Alexandria, VA: Association for Supervision and Curriculum Development.

Havelock, R. 1973. *The Change Agent's Guide to Innovation in Education*. Englewood Cliffs, NJ: Educational Technology Publications.

Helwig, C., and S. Kim. 1999. "Children's Evaluations of Decision-Making Procedures in Peer, Family, and School Contexts." *Child Development* 70, no. 2 (March): 502–512.

Hicks, R., and K. Hicks. 1999. *Boomers, Xers and Other Strangers.* Wheaton, IL: Tyndale House.

Houle, C. 1996. *The Design of Education.* 2nd ed. San Francisco: Jossey-Bass.

Howe, N., and W. Strauss. 2003. *Millennials Go to College.* Washington, DC: The American Association of Collegiate Registrars and Admissions Officers.

Istance, D., H. Schuetze, and T. Schuller, eds. 2002. *International Perspectives on Lifelong Learning: From Recurrent Education to the Knowledge Society.* Berkshire, UK: Open University Press.

Kalyanpur, M., and B. Harry. 1999. *Culture in Special Education.* Baltimore: Paul Brookes.

Knowles, M., R. Swanson, and E. Holton. 2011. *The Adult Learner.* 7th ed. Burlington, MA: Butterworth-Heinemann.

Kolb, D. 1984. *Experiential Learning: Experiences as the Source of Learning and Development.* Englewood Cliffs, NJ: Prentice-Hall.

Laiken, M. 2001. *Models of Organizational Learning: Paradoxes and Best Practices in the Post Industrial Workplace.* Toronto: University of Toronto.

Leong, C., and W. Jerred. 2001. "Effects of Consistency and Adequacy of Language on Understanding Elementary Mathematics Word Problems." *Annals of Dyslexia* 51: 277–298.

Levinson, D. 1978. *The Seasons of a Man's Life.* New York: Knopf.

Liaw, S. 2006. "E-learning and the Development of Intercultural Competence." *Language Learning and Technology* 10, no. 3: 49–64.

Marsick, V., and K. Watkins. 2001. "Informal and Incidental Learning." *New Directions for Adult and Continuing Education* 89, Spring: 25–34.

McLester, S. 2007. "Technology Literacy and the MySpace Generation." *Technology & Learning* 27, no. 8: 17–22.

McMahon, C., and C. Bruce. 2002. "Information Literacy Needs of Local Staff in Cross-Cultural Development Projects." *Journal of International Development* 14, no. 1: 113–137.

Miller, J. 1976. *Toward a New Psychology of Women.* Boston: Beacon Press.

Moir, A., and D. Jessel. 1991. *Brain Sex.* New York: Dell.

Moore, P. 1995. "Information Problem-Solving: A Wider View of Library Skills." *Journal of Contemporary Educational Psychology* 20: 1–31.

Mullowney, T. 1980. *Policy Paper for the Evaluation of Programs for Indian Tribes and Organizations.* Washington, DC: Department of Education.

National Board for Professional Teaching Standards. 2001. *Library Media Standards.* Arlington, VA: National Board for Professional Teaching Standards.

National Council for Accreditation of Teacher Education. 2011. *ALA/AASL Standards for Initial Preparation of School Librarians.* Washington, DC: National Council for Accreditation of Teacher Education.

National Education Association. 1975. *Code of Ethics.* Washington, DC: National Education Association.

Nonaka, I. 2008. *The Knowledge-Creating Company.* Cambridge, MA: Harvard Business School Press.

Ousley, M. 2006. "Hope for a More Equitable Society." *Journal of College & Character* 7, no. 4: 1–10.

Park, A. 2004. "What Makes Teens Tick?" *Time* 163, no. 19: 56–65.

Philbin, M., E. Meier, S. Huffman, and P. Boverie. 1995. "A Survey of Gender and Learning Styles," *Sex Roles* 32, no. 7/8: 485–494.

Piaget, J. 1952. *The Origins of Intelligence in Children.* New York: International University Press.

Pillow, B. 2002. "Children's and Adults' Evaluation of the Certainty of Deductive Inferences, Inductive Inferences, and Guesses." *Child Development* 73, no. 3 (May): 779–792.

Popper, K. 1990. *World of Propensities.* Bristol, England: Thoemmes.

Ruble, D., and G. Flett.1988. "Conflicting Goals in Self-Evaluative Information Seeking: Developmental and Ability Level Analyses." *Child Development* 59: 97–106.

Selwyn, N., S. Gorard, and J. Furlong. 2006. *Adult Learning in the Digital Age: Information Technology and the Learning Society.* New York: Routledge.

Senge, P. 1990. *The Fifth Discipline: The Art and Practice of the Learning Organization.* Rev. ed. New York: Doubleday.

Sousa, D. 2005. *How the Brain Learns.* 3rd ed. Thousand Oaks, CA: Corwin Press.

Special Libraries Association (SLA). 2003. *Competencies for Information Professionals.* Alexandria, VA: Special Libraries Association.

Sternberg, R. 1985. *Beyond IQ: A Triarchic Theory of Human Intelligence.* Cambridge, MA: Harvard University Press.

Todd, R. 2000. *Information Literacy in Electronic Environments: Fantasies, Facts, and Futures.* Paper delivered at the Virtual Libraries: Virtual Communities IATUL Conference, Queensland University of Technology, Australia, July 3–7.

Vygotsky, L. 1978. *Mind in Society.* Cambridge, MA: Harvard University Press.

Wenger, E. 1998. *Communities of Practice.* Cambridge, England: Cambridge University Press.

Wenger, E., R. McDermott, and W. Snyder. 2002. *Cultivating Communities of Practice.* Cambridge, MA: Harvard Business Press.

Westat, K., and S. Creighton. 2000. *Participation in Adult Education in the United States: 1998–1999.* Washington, DC: U.S. Department of Education.

Williams-Boyd, P., ed. 2003. *Middle Grades Education.* Santa Barbara, CA: ABC-CLIO.

Young Adult Library Services Association. 2010. *Young Adults Deserve the Best.* Chicago: American Library Association.

4

Preplanning

One essential feature of instructional design is needs assessment; instruction is not arbitrary or "boilerplate," but rather builds on explicitly identified needs. Oftentimes, the community perspective drives instructional design as ways to address a local issue arise (e.g., massive layoffs and a need to retool skills). Assessment can focus on knowledge needs, such as academic preparation for college. Perhaps individuals need to know how to use a specific set of resource tools (e.g., reference sources), so that the assessment focuses on their skill sets. Alternatively, a needs assessment can start with the individual's own specific cluster of learning needs.

This chapter provides a number of assessment tools to help librarians diagnose needs. Administrative factors of dissemination and data collection are detailed. Strategies for analyzing the responses are also suggested.

Based on the diagnostic assessment, you are ready to start the design process. General goals and more specific objectives are determined, often in collaboration with the target learner. Outcomes stipulate what learners should know and do, and indicators operationalize these outcomes. Standards specify how well learners should perform, and assessments enable one to measure if those standards have been met.

Categories of educational situations

While instructional design starts at the point of need, the origin of the needs assessment typically rests outside the ultimate learner. Typically, an individual does not apply a formal instructional design process to independent learning, although one can certainly plan learning experiences for oneself. Instead, instructional design, being a systematic approach, usually starts outside the learner, be it one teacher or a consortium of organizations.

Houle (1996) identified several categories of educational situations, which establish the configuration in which instructional design occurs. Librarians fit well into each of these situations, as noted in italics.

- **Tutorial teaching** ideally represents the most learner-based, interactive, responsive instructional design. The tutor assesses the need and the learner, usually performing a discrepancy analysis to determine the gap between the learner's current status and the desired goal, in order to design an individualized instructional plan. *The reference interview and thesis consultation best capture the spirit of tutoring.*
- A **learning group** consists of a group of people with a common purpose, who interact with one another to reach that purpose. *A research group that involves librarians fits this situation.*
- **Teacher-directed group instruction** is the most common learning situation because of its ease in planning and delivery; instructional design fits well in this situation. *Librarians find themselves in this situation as guest lecturers, co-teachers, or stand-alone instructors for a variety of learning activities (such as orientations, one-shot workshops, a series of lectures, or a course).*
- **Committee-guided group learning** is found in professional development venues such as conferences. Planning checklists facilitate the process, and lend themselves well to instructional design. *Librarians who are involved in professional organizations often find themselves in this situation.*
- **Collaborative group education** reflects consensus building and negotiation, and fosters authentic instructional design. *Librarians may be part of a coalition or system of libraries, which would offer learning activities.*
- **Creating an educational institution** involves using an existing structural or content model to start a separate entity, such as a parallel group in another state. Establishing and sustaining a new institution requires much motivation and flexibility, and instructional design takes on an organizational tenor. *Librarians are likely to create such an institution as part of a major new initiative, such as information literacy or new cataloging standards.*
- **Designing a new institutional format** focuses on a new pattern of service or delivery system. Such a development has to consider not only its own value but also its fit with existing formats and services. Pilot-testing new formats is facilitated by instructional design. *Librarians are experiencing this situation as they incorporate Web 2.0 into professional development, particularly in professional organizations.*

- **Designing new activities in established formats** helps keep an institution viable and responsive to needs. Instructional design is likely to occur at two or more levels: the institutional level (which would examine issues of scheduling and allocation of resources) and the instructional level (which would focus on sequencing, assessment, and so forth). *Librarian educators are most likely to operate in this situation, although library programs in general should be involved in such strategic planning.*
- **Collaborative institutional planning** occurs when two or more organizations interrelate their activities. Each organization has to determine what resources it contributes to the effort and what role it plays. Obviously, another layer of administration is needed in order for this situation to succeed. Instructional design can become quite complex in this situation. *The above noted issues-based councils exemplify librarian experiences in this situation.*
- **Mass education** tends to be defined by time, place, or method: i.e., a live broadcast, a museum or fair, a film or podcast. Instructional design reflects a more abstract approach in this situation because it is unlikely to be responsive to individual learners, but the individual learner can decide whether to participate or not. *One could make a case that the library entity itself reflects mass education in that it provides a variety of services that can be experienced by its users.*

This book focuses on the teacher level of instructional design, but the organizational level of instructional design should also be kept in mind since libraries tend to exist within larger institutions. As an active librarian, you should participate regularly in professional organizations that offer learning activities.

Needs assessment

Basically, a needs assessment, per se, is a process to determine gaps between a current and a desired condition, and to address them—in this book, through instruction, which is designed. The basis for a learning activity can arise from a variety of sources and for a variety of reasons. You might need to learn how to design a webpage. A soon-to-retire employee might want to learn about estate planning. A school librarian might observe students ignoring the subscription databases as they conduct research, and think that students need instruction in their use. An organization might start a digitization project, which requires staff training. A university might require information literacy competency of its students. Either a person becomes aware through internal reflection or in response to some external event. Such awareness might result in deciding to do nothing (the need is not that important or the resources are not available), or further action might ensue: looking for resources or learning opportunities.

In any case, you need to conduct some kind of needs assessment as part of instructional preplanning. Technically, a needs assessment could be done throughout instructional planning and delivery as gaps are uncovered, such as a student's lack of technological skill or a missing link in a sequence of learning activities. In fact, a loosely designed workshop can include a quick needs assessment at the beginning of the session to help refine content matter to be covered. However, the term is usually reserved for the onset evaluation (Popham, 2010).

Needs, interests, and values

Before conducting a needs assessment, some definitions are in order, which Ingalls (1972) provided. Needs may be considered as basic wants and tendencies. The most well-known hierarchy of needs is Abraham Maslow's: survival, safety, love, ego/esteem, and self-actualization. Maslow (1954) contended that an individual is not motivated at a higher level if needs at a lower level are not satisfied, so, for example, librarians would not be successful talking about Internet safety if the audience is concerned about daily survival. It should be noted that one person's needs may differ from their wants, especially in the eyes of an expert. For example, a student may want a tool that will automatically create a citation, but the librarian may think that the student *needs* to learn how to produce an accurate citation by hand.

In contrast, interests are more peripheral: examples are personal preferences in terms of attraction or stimulation. They arise from life experiences, and may vary with social differences. It's a good idea for you to find out people's interests before you develop the instructional design because it helps if the learner can connect the intended content with personal preferences. Values reflect commitment to patterns of choice. Raths, Harmin, and Simon (1966) developed seven criteria to measure one's values:

1. Is the value the result of free choice?
2. Is the value chosen from among alternatives?
3. Is the value chosen after careful consideration of the consequences of each alternative?
4. Is the value prized and cherished?
5. Does one publicly affirm it?
6. Does one act upon the value?
7. Does one repeat that value; is it a pattern in one's life?

Values are important in that individuals seldom commit to learning something if they do not value it. Particularly in today's world of so much choice in education, the effort to design instruction must be predicated on the potential learners' valuing of the subject matter.

Identifying the bases of needs, interests, and values

You can do a needs assessment as part of an ongoing effort to improve performance or service in general, or it may arise when conscious consideration about learning exists. The need may arise from identifying a goal and then assessing what should be done in order to achieve the goal, or the assessment might be in response to a perceived problem or lack. A needs assessment may be an internal process, such as self-reflection or an organization self-study, or it may be externally driven, such as part of accreditation.

At the learner-based level, a needs assessment is often a self-awareness exercise or a reaction to a problem. For instance, a person may feel stressed, and realize that time is a factor, and further determine that she needs to manage her time better. Thus, the person might look for ways to learn that skill. On the other hand, another person, such as a supervisor, might assess the potential learner as part of a periodic evaluation process or in response to perceived behavior that requires attention.

At the organization level, a needs assessment is often tied to the group's overall mission. If the organization is not meeting its charge, or it wants to improve its quality, then a needs assessment can identify areas to address. An organization might even take a marketing approach to their needs assessment as a way to educate their potential market about available resources and services. The needs assessment can vary its scope, from a general overview to a focus on one function or one group of people. Specificity can facilitate assessment, but you should remember that functions are usually interdependent, so that changes to one area will probably impact another area.

A needs assessment can focus on the effectiveness of a resource. This approach is a typical endeavor for librarians as they manage collections. However, in terms of instruction, a needs assessment can focus on physical *and* intellectual access to resources. A resource approach can also be used to ascertain the effectiveness of instructional resources.

Assessment can also focus on a specific knowledge base, comparing what is known to what *should* be known. Such an approach may apply to both individuals and organizations. Furthermore, knowledge may be assessed in terms of what is available as well as what is used or applied.

Assessing the learning context

Not only should you assess the learner, but you should assess the learning environment as well. Such an environment includes not only the physical attributes but also the temporal and social environment. At the very least, the conditions in which the learner performs must be considered. Moreover, a need might change over time as personnel and resources change.

When you assess an educational environment, for instance, a number of factors emerge that should be considered when designing instruction:

- Courses, curriculum, and programs
- Student performance and graduation
- Teacher performance and collaboration
- Resources: facilities and infrastructure, instructional materials, student information, finances, time allocation
- Support: specialists, staff development, governance structures
- Involvement of parents and the community

If, for instance, students are dropping out, the cause may be financial, academic, or personal. Perhaps students expect faculty to incorporate more technology, in which case faculty development in the use of technology would be called for. If, on the other hand, students are dropping out because their courses require the use of course management systems, and students do not have easy access to technology, then resource allocation of computers, including laptop circulation, and student training in course management systems might be called for. You can see the value of participating in institutional assessments.

Assessing needs, interests, and values

Here are several ways that you and other librarians can assess the needs, interests, and values of potential learners, as suggested by Ingalls (1972).

- **Conduct a competency model.** Have an expert list the competencies for a specific job or literacy, such as conducting research or digital literacy. Then have the expert state the degree of competency that is acceptable. For instance, how technologically adept does one need to be in order to conduct research? The resultant model can be used as an assessment tool to diagnose a potential learner's competency level and need for training. This tool (Table 4.1) can be used as a self-assessment exercise or as a way for you to discuss competency with a learner to design an action plan for professional development.
- **Observe behavior.** Particularly if the goal is performance based, the instructional designer or content expert can watch how the target population is acting. A competency model, performance checklist, or rubric can be used as a way to measure performance.
- **Conduct a discrepancy analysis.** If a goal or desired behavior has been identified, then you can assess the current situation to determine the gap between the status quo and the wanted end. You should perform further analysis to identify the factors that impact the success or failure of the performance so that you can design appropriate instruction.

- **Consult experts.** Experienced reference librarians can be good sources of information about user needs and interests. Supervisors can tell what knowledge or skills are critical, or which are not used well.
- **Conduct an interview.** Both experts and neophytes can provide useful information, and reveal aspects of valuing. Ideally, you should interview every stakeholder entity in order to get a clear picture of the situation. For instance, each stakeholder (teenager, parent, classroom teacher, librarian, administrator, technology specialist, board member) may have a unique attitude about digital literacy.
- **Conduct a focus-group discussion.** Group members can share their perceptions and clarify their needs in order to achieve group understanding and consensus about needed instruction.
- **Administer a survey or questionnaire.** This assessment tool tends to measure perceptions, which may or may not be accurate, particularly of incompetent people. These tools can be helpful for people by making them aware of current situations or possible options, such as uses of the library.
- **Conduct a content analysis.** Student work, meeting minutes, lesson plans, organizational reports, and research studies all provide information about a potential learning need. For instance, several types of documents may reveal that students do not know how to critically evaluate information.
- **Use a problem-solving approach.** Identify a problem in the organization that might benefit from instruction. Determine possible factors that cause the problem, and brainstorm ways that instruction might address the underlying cause.
- **Conduct a systems analysis.** Identify a goal, and then list contributing factors: inputs, processes, outputs, outcomes. Identify the relevant impact (positive, negative, none) of each factor. The areas for improvement lead to needed instruction. For instance, if students are not successful using subscription databases, is it because they don't know about them (because the library has not publicized them) or because they don't practice their skills (because the library provides limited access to the databases)? Two different solutions arise from two different causes.
- **Conduct an environmental scan, sometimes known as a SWOT analysis.** This activity draws upon marketing research, and can be applied to libraries as they seek to plan targeted instruction to segmented populations. The internal environment is analyzed in terms of its strengths and weaknesses; the organization's mission, resources, services, and relationships are examined. Analyze the external environment in terms of threats/obstacles/challenges and opportunities. You can look at a number of trends: demographic, economic, technological, political-legal, social-cultural, and competitive (Wood, 2008).

Table 4.1 Competency model								
	Analyze task	Strategize research	Locate resources	Evaluate info	Extract info	Manipulate info	Organize info	Generate info	Communicate info
Excellence			X		X				
Competence				X			X		X
Adequacy	X	X				X		X	
Marginal Failure									
Incompetence									

- **Review the professional literature.** What needs and interests have been identified by researchers and practitioners? How have those needs been addressed successfully?

Knowledge dimensions

As you analyze the needs assessments, you and stakeholders can identify the kind of learning that would best address the need. Learning goals and knowledge are multidimensional, and may be categorized in different ways.

Gagne (1985) identified six types of learning outcomes, plus a combination of the other types:

1. **Declarative knowledge**: recall and summarize knowledge (such as memorizing the basic multiplication table); knowing "what"
2. **Intellectual skills**: apply knowledge to new situations (for example, discriminate, categorize, predict, solve problems); knowing "how"
3. **Cognitive strategies**: self-manage learning; metacognition
4. **Attitudes**: be predisposed to choose to behave in a certain way (for example, read as a leisure-time activity)
5. **Psychomotor skills**: coordinate muscular movement
6. **Learning enterprises**: purposeful activity that combines different types of learning

Gagne further stipulated that different types of learning required different internal or external conditions. For instance, one needs to manipulate materials to learn motor skills, while learning attitudes requires credible role models or compelling reasons. The kind of learning and associated tasks thus lay the groundwork for making instructional decisions, to be covered in Chapter 6.

Anderson and colleagues (2001) categorized cognitive knowledge into four domains:

1. **Factual**: basic elements needed to comprehend a discipline or solve problems in that discipline
2. **Conceptual**: interrelationship of elements within a larger structure that enable them to function
3. **Procedural**: how to do a task; using skills, techniques, or methods
4. **Metacognitive**: knowledge about cognition; awareness of one's own cognitive processes

Using McREL's knowledge taxonomy, Hubbell (2010) posited four types of knowledge:

1. **Declarative knowledge** addresses what learners need to know. This kind of knowledge tends to be factual and more objective.
2. **Procedural knowledge** explains how to use knowledge or perform a skill. In some cases, processes are content neutral, such as the process of word processing. Other procedures may have content connotations, such as interviewing techniques.
3. **Contextual knowledge** helps learners know when to use knowledge or a skill. For example, a spreadsheet would be useful when making predictions based on numerical manipulations such as budgets. Contextual knowledge is more apt to be subjective when "soft skills" are involved, such as determining at what point to ask about domestic child-discipline practices, which might be considered a private matter or a possible "face" threatening situation.
4. **Experiential knowledge** identifies the reason that specific knowledge is important. For instance, testing a patient's blood is important because it provides important clues as to the person's health and possible disease symptoms. Knowing how a discipline is practiced can impact what information literacy curriculum will be included.

Ng and Bereiter (1991) posited three levels of learning goals, which map well onto information literacy:

1. **Completion**: Learners "do" the answers (unmotivated).
2. **Instructional**: Learners do what the teacher wants them to do (other-motivated).
3. **Knowledge-building**: Learners have a personal stake in the activity (self-motivated). In this construct, Ng and Bereiter also note the correlation between (1) the time horizon and goal level, with knowledge-building having the longest time frame, and (2) the degree of abstraction and goal level, with knowledge-building leading to the most abstract.

Limberg (1998) examined information-seeking behavior, and noted students' psychological responses to information. Her research resembles Ng's and Bereiter's.

- **Find facts**: Toss out whatever does not fit or is inconvenient to find.
- **Find the right answer**: Find a balance between pros and cons; resolve subjective information.
- **Scrutinize and analyze**: Get at underlying values.

Although instructors may value different kinds of knowledge more than others, such as privileging creating over recalling, a complex learning task may involve several different kinds of abilities. Instead, helping the learner to develop a broad repertoire of knowledge, skills, and attitudes and the metacognitive ability to determine which approach to use in a particular situation is probably the most effective overarching instructional attitude. When you as the instructional designer control the type of knowledge, it is likely that learners will meet that level but will rarely surpass that level. On the other hand, when learners "own" the task or have choices when interacting with information, they are more likely to engage in deeper learning. Such a shift in control usually requires an inquiry-based or constructivist approach to teaching and learning (Griffith and Ecological Society of America, 2007).

Developing objectives

Once you conduct and analyze the needs assessment, you and other decision makers must determine if some action is required. If you decide that education can help close the gap and aid in meeting the organizational goal, then you can work with the stakeholders to identify the relevant outcomes of the learning.

The goal of business is to make profit while providing a valued product or service. Education has as among its goals to prepare students to become effective life-long learners and responsible contributors to society. School libraries have as their goal facilitating the school community to be effective users of information and ideas (AASL, 1998).

Consider goals as the beginning point for planning an educational program. They are broad statements about general purposes. Outcomes represent the impact that the program has on its participants. Impact may take the form of change in behavior, attitudes, and knowledge. Educational standards help define what learners should be able to know and do independently of the instructor: the degree to which they meet an outcome. Indicators operationalize these standards into concrete and measurable behaviors and dispositions. Objectives are specific, measurable, short-term learner behaviors that occur within defined conditions. You then decide what kinds of learning activities and what conditions for learning will provide the most effective impact on self-knowledge and performance.

Here is an example of these concepts, as excerpted from the 2010 *California Model School Library Standards.*

Goal: Information literacy

Outcome: Students will be able to locate, evaluate, use, manage, and communicate information effectively and responsibly.

Standard: "The student will evaluate and analyze information to determine appropriateness in addressing the scope of inquiry" (p. 5).

Indicator: The student will "access the comprehensiveness, currency, credibility, authority, and accuracy of resources" (p. 5).

Objective: The student will "evaluate information from visual media as a primary and secondary source, and distinguish the differences" (p. 33).

Translating needs assessment results into instructional objectives requires careful analysis. Malcolm Knowles (Knowles, Swanson, and Holton, 2011) developed an algorithm for this process.

1. Prioritize needs, categorizing them into educational and operational (that is, facilities, resource allocation) objectives.
2. Filter needs in terms of institutional needs and educational philosophy, feasibility, and learner interests.
3. Translate ultimate needs into program objectives and learning objectives.

When crafting the wording of objectives that describe desired behaviors, include the following elements: the learner(s), the targeted behavior, the conditions under which the behavior is performed, and the criteria for determining acceptance level of performance (Alberto and Troutman, 2008). The behavior should be external and measurable, and may be part of a larger objective. For instance, an overall objective might be effective researching, and subsets of that objective might focus on locating or evaluating resources.

The specific wording of such objectives reflects the type of learning to be attained: cognitive, affective, or kinesthetic. Bloom, Mesia, and Krathwohl's 1964 taxonomies in these domains have provided guidance in stipulating the kind of action to be assessed; Anderson and colleagues (2001) have updated these taxonomies to take into account technology and other educational advances. Ohio State University's website on learning objectives provides a good overview of the cognitive taxonomy (http://www.celt.iastate.edu/teaching/RevisedBlooms1.html), and shows examples of learning objectives for different knowledge dimensions.

Smith and Ragan (2005) discussed how to word objectives based on the desired learning outcome:

- **Declarative knowledge**: Learners can define information literacy in their own words.
- **Concepts**: Learners can give examples of scholarly journals.
- **Principles**: Learners can evaluate websites based on identified criteria.
- **Procedures**: Learners can locate a peer-reviewed article on a predetermined topic using a subscription database aggregator.
- **Problem solving**: Learners can use a presentation tool (e.g., PowerPoint) to develop a set of talking points during an oral debate.
- **Cognitive strategies**: Learners can develop a research strategy.
- **Attitudes**: Learners choose to cite resources used when writing a research paper.
- **Psychomotor skills**: Learners can type 50 words per minute.

Assessment at the preplanning stage

Assessment and support mechanisms take time and effort, from deciding what to assess through choosing an appropriate instrument, gathering the data, and analyzing the results. Any slip along the way can lessen its effect and benefits, so you need to plan and implement the processes carefully.

As a vital part of aligned instructional design, assessment should be addressed at the same time that the objectives are determined. Although you might think that choosing the assessment instrument before designing the learning activity itself feels like teaching to the test, a more accurate reading would be that pre-knowledge about the desired outcome and a valid way to measure competency helps ensure that instruction and practice will have an optimum result. Ideally, each assessment should include the following components (Smith and Ragan, 2005):

- objective,
- description of the assessment instrument,
- mastery criteria,
- number of item and sample,
- question characteristics (including difficulty), and
- response characteristics (including common errors).

You can assess learning effectiveness on several levels. On an individual level, student learning can be assessed in pre- and posttests or other evidences of knowledge (e.g., concept mapping, journaling, short-answer test). You can measure the differences in knowledge and skill based on instructional goals, new concepts learned outside of the intended content, retention of knowledge from pre- to posttest, and mental models or schema changes. You can measure the same differences on a group level through group-generated concept maps, vocabulary lists, and know already and want to learn (KWL) lists, to name a few.

You can conduct assessments at several points in the instruction and learning process:

- As a diagnostic tool before learning in order to identify appropriate instructional strategies
- As a formative tool during learning in order to identify appropriate interventions
- As a summative tool after learning in order to make decisions about the learner and the instructional design

You should assess conditions and supports for learning at several levels: the individual learning activity, the series of instruction such as a course, the overall program, the organization, and possibly a consortium of groups. What is the system's capacity? How are material, space, time, and staff allocated and monitored?

Determining the assessment instrument

Locating or developing a valid and reliable assessment instrument (or set of tools) requires answering a number of questions:

- What is being assessed?
- Who is being assessed?
- Who is doing the assessing?
- When and how frequently will the assessment be done?
- How will the assessment be done?
- How will the data be analyzed?
- Who will analyze the data?
- How will the findings be acted upon?
- Who will act upon the findings?
- What accountability is present?

It's best to make these decisions and act upon them in collaboration with the relevant stakeholders.

To this end, the American Association of Higher Education (AAHE) Assessment Forum (2003) identified nine principles to guide assessment of learning.

1. Use educational values as the assessment touchstone. Measure what is valued.
2. Assess learning as a complex set of skills, knowledge, and dispositions gained over time. Therefore, use a variety of assessment methods from different points of view and time.
3. Have clear, specific educational goals. Assessment should lead to improvement, so all stakeholders should agree on precisely what needs to be examined—and why.

4. Consider both processes and products. How a learner approaches a task may be distinct from the end results.
5. Assess on an ongoing basis. Assess baselines, benchmarks, and culminating experiences so that timely interventions can be incorporated to optimize learning.
6. Foster broad involvement. Each stakeholder brings a unique perspective that can impact others' efforts; together, stakeholder participation facilitates systematic coordination.
7. Focus on the use of assessment, especially to take justified action on issues that people truly care about.
8. Consider assessment as an integral part of the larger picture to improve the learning community and organization.
9. Consider assessment as an accountability issue. Assessment keeps education "honest" in the eyes of the public.

Typically, the level of assessment aligns with the level of learning. For instance, a multiple-choice test can measure use of a driver's manual. A concept map can measure knowledge of terms and their interrelationships. A questionnaire can measure simple perceptions about health care. Authentic assessment can work for a range of competencies, from locating a local auto supply store to conducting a sophisticated research project to addressing a local social issue problem.

The assessment not only measures learners' performance but it can be used to validate the objective variable itself. For example, if learners know how to outline, does that lead to better reports? If not, then the true contributing variable must be found. As with learning activities, determining and designing assessments should be an institutional or at least programmatic effort in order to leverage measurements so that learners do not need to be tested constantly and so that you can impact learning in several courses simultaneously.

Some typical assessment instruments follow. Their strengths and weaknesses are noted.

- **Individual interview**: Provides open-ended, interactive, in-depth data. Labor-intensive and time-consuming, the data are only as accurate as the questions being asked and the individual being interviewed, so this approach requires training; language and technical barriers may exist as well.
- **Focus group**: Provides open-ended, interactive, in-depth data and group dynamics. Data may be skewed or missing because of group norming; this approach requires training, and communication barriers may exist.
- **Content analysis**: Provides unobtrusive data that can be repurposed. Confidentiality may limit access or application; data may need to be contextualized.

- **Portfolio**: Provides longitudinal and self-reflective evidence of competency. A portfolio consists of a collection of student work that documents a learner's efforts and achievement over time. Usually the learner chooses work that demonstrates that he or she has met (or is progressing to meeting) standards of competence. Ideally, the learner explains the selection process, and provides a self-reflection of his or her learning. Portfolios are typically assessed according to a rubric. Portfolios might not be valid in that they may measure a learner's organizational and communication skills more than his or her actual curricular knowledge and ability.
- **Authentic assessment**: Asks for the behavior that the learner is expected to exhibit if the intended learning outcome is met. Usually a realistic task is called for that closely approximates the real-world application of the identified competency. Because the simulation task is complex and often "fuzzy" (ill-defined), to measure complex behavior, authentic assessment requires careful delineation of critical criteria, close observation, and holistic grading. An example of an authentic assessment is critiquing learner-produced anti-smoking advertisements. Authentic assessment may assume a different form in an online environment; for instance, simulations can record each decision point if so programmed.
- **Performance-based assessment**: Direct observation of learner behavior that usually involves creating products. Learners' actions thus reflect their knowledge and skills within a real-world or simulated context. Usually descriptive rubrics are used to assess the relative quality of the learner's performance. Videotaping a performance is one way to capture some of the nuances of a performance, although camera angle limits the assessor's perspective. Learners can also demonstrate competence, particularly conceptual knowledge, through true-false, multiple-choice, and/or short-answer tests (which tend to measure recall knowledge) and essays (which tend to measure organizational and communication skill).

The most common commercial assessment tools are standardized tests. High-quality ones have been validated with many populations, and provide longitudinal reliability. Government licensure and accreditation processes frequently rely on these tests because they provide cross-site comparisons. They may be norm-referenced (i.e., test results are compared, such as "grading on the curve") or criterion-referenced (i.e., results are compared to the correct answer), the latter usually being preferred. In those areas where experts can agree on measurable criteria, representative prompts, and correct answers, these tests offer a way to assess many learners efficiently. However, for high-level career-specific competencies, such agreements are difficult to achieve. Standardized tests are most appropriate for assessing declarative knowledge such as the use of basic tools or the application of straightforward processes. Most of these tests are stand-alone products that are not explicitly aligned with curriculum; nor do librarians have access to the tests themselves or the results. On the other hand, textbook publishers are increasingly creating online quizzes and tests that instructors can embed into the online learning environment.

Here are factors to consider when determining which assessment instrument to use, regardless of its format:

- **Validity**: whether or not the assessment measures what is to be learned; for instance, writing about how a mathematical problem is solved might measure writing skills more than mathematical skills
- **Reliability**: whether reusing the same instrument will result in the same kind of response
- **Cost**: for the instrument itself, recording forms, labor involved in development, administration, data entry, and analysis
- **Time**: for development, administration, coding, analysis
- **Availability**: of instrument, of associated technology, human resources for development, administration, and analysis
- **Feasibility or practicality**: in terms of administrative and analysis ease (for example, analyzing a semester's worth of videotaped sessions of information-seeking behaviors would be very labor-intensive)
- **Skills**: for development, administration, data collection training, data entry and coding, analysis
- **Legalities**: of confidentiality and privacy, use of instrument, parental permission
- **Culture**: attitudes toward the instrument, language issues, fear of high stakes or repercussions

Developing assessment tools

Developing assessment tools "from scratch" can be time-consuming and unproductive. Since the main considerations are validity (measuring the intended competence) and reliability (obtaining consistent results), evaluating the assessment instrument itself is key. If a credible entity has already designed and validated an assessment tool that measures a desired outcome with the same kind of population, then seriously consider using it if it is feasible to so do (that is, affordable and doable).

Nevertheless, sometimes an assessment instrument needs to be developed "from whole cloth" because the objectives are site specific or the target audience has unique needs. Fortunately, technology has facilitated this task; you can easily repurpose documents as assessment instruments and disseminate them efficiently.

One obvious way to find out if someone is competent is to ask him or her to create a product that reflects the specific competency. Traditionally, written critiques have been used to demonstrate that a student has understood the source, and research papers have been used to demonstrate that a student can conduct research independently. Ideally, the products should demonstrate conceptual and procedural knowledge applied to real-world contexts. With the advent of digital technology, the repertoire of products has grown exponentially. Here are representative products that reflect competency:

- **Text**: report, white paper, essay, bibliography, biography, article, brochure, press release, résumé, instructions, poem, dramatization
- **Visuals**: illustration, storyboard, timeline, cartoon, photojournal, concept map
- **Video**: commercial, documentary, interview, drama
- **Audio**: podcast, soundscape documentary
- **Multimedia**: webpage, multimedia presentation, computer-aided design, spreadsheet, database, simulation, e-story

In assessing these products, you should consider both the end results and the supporting processes. Rubrics serve as a customizable tool for assessing the different elements either holistically to get a general picture or analytically to examine each factor—during the production as a means to make adjustments as well as at the end. In each case, assessment lists of grids provide qualitative and quantitative descriptors for each identified key criterion. Typically, rubrics are built based on sample work, identifying the key features that distinguish high-quality products from mediocre ones. The rubric is then constructed by specifying the assessment indicators, each criterion measuring one unique aspect. The rubric should be pilot-tested with additional work samples and refined. As much as possible, learners can learn how to use rubrics to guide their efforts by calibrating their assessments using exemplar samples. Rubistar (http://rubistar.4teachers .org/) and Web Tools for Educators: Rubrics and Rubric Makers (http://www .teach-nology.com/web_tools/rubrics/) offer good starting points.

As you choose assessment instruments, remember to maintain learner confidentiality, and be sensitive to learner self-disclosure. Learners should be able to "pass" on discussing personal matters, exploring relevant existing public accounts instead. In that respect, "drop boxes" and direct e-mail are two ways for learners to submit work for instructor eyes only.

Preplanning implications for you

At this point, it should be obvious that instructional design requires careful and systematic forethought and planning. In most cases, such planning needs to involve a number of stakeholders: potential learners, other personnel who are connected with the learners, and the organization as a whole, especially decision makers.

As a librarian, you continuously observe information using behaviors, and are likely to identify instructional needs. Triangulate those informal assessments with systematic needs assessments that involve potential learners and other stakeholders in the process, such as academic faculty or employers. Furthermore, remember that you are viewing users from the perspective of their interaction with library resources, which might be just a small part of the total task to be done or job function. Thus, collaborating with the entire affected enterprise is more likely to result in an accurate picture of the contributing factors for reaching a learner or organizational goal, which can be translated into viable objectives.

As a librarian, you realize the importance of the environment in which people learn and interact with resources. Leverage that knowledge as you identify those tools that measure the conditions for learning. In the process, you can improve the library program itself as it supports learning.

Sample workshop using needs assessment

The following face-to-face workshop can be an effective way to teach K–12 parents about their role in digital citizenship, particularly because it customizes content based on "on-the-fly" assessment. It also sets up conditions for parents to work with each other and the school following the session. The presenter needs to know the content material well, and should collaborate ahead of time with school administrators and parent leaders to make sure that the content and approach is appropriate.

Workshop

Title: Digital Citizenship: What's a Parent to Do?

Subject: Digital Citizenship

Lesson overview: Today's society, including most youth, uses technology daily. Such technology use has consequences, both good and bad. As children's first teachers, parents are uniquely positioned to help their children become good digital citizens. This session explains digital citizenship, and parents' roles in promoting it.

Time frame: 60–90 minutes

Learning objectives: Learners will:
- Describe impact of technology use.
- Identify examples and counter-examples of digital citizenship.

- Give recommendations on ways that parents can promote digital citizenship.

Curriculum standards

- Model digital-age work and learning.
- Promote and model digital citizenship and responsibility.

Resources

- *Net Cetera* booklets (http://www.onguardonline.gov/topics/net-cetera-introduction.aspx) (optional)
- Digital citizenship bookmarks (optional)
- Index cards or equivalent (enough for three per person)
- Technology: Demonstration computer with projector/screen

Planning for diverse learners

- Translators can be present.
- Presentation can be disseminated for participants to comprehend later.
- Presentation is both oral and visual.

Instructional strategies and study activities

0. Before the lesson, librarian makes sure that the room is set up in theater arrangement, and that the technology is set up and operational. Librarian locates and transfers PowerPoint presentation (found under "For Parents" at http://k12digitalcitizenship.wikispaces.com/) onto the demonstration computer.
   Librarian has index cards on hand, which may be placed on each person's chair, or disseminated before the PowerPoint presentation. Librarian may identify volunteers ahead of time to help with dissemination.
   Librarian obtains print copies of *Net Cetera*, or produces bookmarks with that website to disseminate (Figure 4.1).
1. Librarian welcomes the group and introduces himself or herself. Librarian gathers demographic information (grade level of children, technology at home, parent level of comfort using technology) about the participants using "hands-up." This icebreaker activity helps parents see commonalities among themselves, and helps librarian to customize the presentation (for instance, if most parents have elementary children, then recommendations will focus more on selecting sites and family activities).
2. Librarian briefly defines digital citizenship: the ability to use technology safely, responsibly, critically, and proactively to contribute to society. Librarian explains the learning objectives, and provides the rationale for the session (see overview).

3. Librarian has a couple of volunteers disseminate index cards on which to write questions, which will be picked up at the end of the PowerPoint presentation. Alternatively, the index cards can be placed on each person's seat ahead of time.

4. Librarian presents PowerPoint presentation. Librarian tells group where to find the PowerPoint after the session. Librarian also tells group that they will be given the relevant website addresses at the end.

5. Librarian asks volunteers to pick up any questions written on the index cards (giving participants a last chance to jot down questions. Cards are given to the librarian.

6. Librarian has a few participants report on their learning.

7. If there is time, librarian can answer a couple of the questions. There should be a venue for answering more of the questions, such as a parent newsletter. The questions also serve as a needs assessment for follow-up workshops.

8. Librarian thanks the group, and encourages participants to take a bookmark or booklet as they leave. Librarian makes sure that the volunteers have the products to hand out, and are stationed at the room's exit doors.

9. After the session, librarian debriefs with the host (parent organization chair and site administrator) to suggest follow-up activities.

Variations

- Session may be conducted online.
- PowerPoint may be voiced-over, and linked to the agency's website.
- The topic can be narrowed to cyberbullying, family activities using the Internet, how to modify technology settings, etc.
- Part of the session can be hands-on, with participants exploring relevant websites.
- Session can be conducted as a family event, with children accompanying the parents.

DIGITAL

http://www.onguardonline.gov/topics/net-cetera.aspx

http://k12digitalcitizenship.wikispaces.com

Name of Group

CITIZEN

Figure 4.1   Digital citizenship bookmark

Student assessment

Learners are assessed in terms of their presentation and their index card questions.

Table 4.2   Digital citizenship rubric

Objective	Low performance	Basic performance	Competent performance	Exemplary performance
Learner participates in session.	Learner is not attentive.	Learner responds to prompts.	Learner responds to all prompts and comments appropriately.	Learner regularly contributes insightfully to discussion.

Additional resources

http://k12digitalcitizenship.wikispaces.com/

References

Alberto, P., and A. Troutman. 2008. *Applied Behavior Analysis for Teachers.* 8th ed. Columbus, OH: Merrill.

American Association of Higher Education. Assessment Forum. 2003. *9 Principles of Good Practice for Assessing Student Learning.* Brevard, NC: Policy Center on the First Year of College.

American Association of School Librarians. 1998. *Information Power.* Chicago: American Library Association.

Anderson, L., D. Krathwohl, P. Airasian, K. Cruikshank, R. Mayer, P. Pintrich, J. Raths, and M. Wittrock, eds. 2001. *A Taxonomy for Learning, Teaching, and Assessing.* Upper Saddle River, NJ: Addison Wesley Longman.

Bloom, B., B. Mesia, and D. Krathwohl. 1964. *Taxonomy of Educational Objectives.* New York: David McKay.

California State Department of Education. 2010. *Model School Library Standards for California Public Schools, Kindergarten through Grade Twelve.* Sacramento: California State Department of Education.

Gagne, E. 1985. *The Cognitive Psychology of School Learning.* Boston: Little, Brown.

Griffith, A., and Ecological Society of America. 2007. Semester-Long Engagement in Society Inquiry Improves Students' Understanding of Experimental Design. *Teaching Issues and Experiments in Ecology* 5. http://www.esa.org/tiee/vol/v5/research/griffith/article.html.

Houle, C. 1996. *The Design of Education.* 2nd ed. San Francisco: Jossey-Bass.

Hubbell, E. 2010. "Using McREL's Knowledge Taxonomy for Ed Tech Professional Development." *Learning & Leading with Technology* 37, no. 8 (June-July): 20–23.

Ingalls, J. 1972. *A Trainer's Guide to Andragogy.* Rev. ed. Waltham, MA: Data Education.

Knowles, M., R. Swanson, and E. Holton. 2011. *The Adult Learner.* 7th ed. Burlington, MA: Butterworth-Heinemann.

Limberg, L. 1998. "Information Seeking and Learning Outcomes." *Scandinavian Public Library Quarterly* 31, no. 3: 28–31.

Maslow, A. 1954. *Motivation and Personality*. New York: Harper.

Ng, E., and C. Bereiter. 1991. "Three Levels of Goal Orientation in Learning." *Journal of the Learning Sciences* 1, no. 3: 243–271.

Popham, W. 2010. *Everything School Leaders Need to Know about Assessment*. Thousand Oaks, CA: Corwin Press.

Raths, L., M. Harmin, and S. Simon. 1966. *Values and Teaching*. Columbus, OH: Merrill.

Smith, P., and T. Ragan. 2005. *Instructional Design*. 3rd ed. New York: John Wiley and Sons.

Wood, M. 2008. *The Marketing Plan Handbook*. 3rd ed. Upper Saddle River, NJ: Prentice Hall.

5

Design content decisions

The curriculum includes the content to be covered. Several types of knowledge and literacies that drive curricular decisions may be involved. Curriculum must also fit into the larger mission of the organization so it can be contextualized meaningfully.

Aligned resources are needed to convey the curriculum content. These may consist of texts, videos, and other learning objects. As an expert in resources and their uses, you should be able to leverage their skills in these aspects of instructional design.

Curriculum bases

Curriculum provides the content that learners must be able to understand and apply so they will be prepared as contributing members of society. Wiles and Bondi (2010) stated that curriculum may be considered as a cyclic system of development, whereby needs analysis leads to design and implementation, which is evaluated and modified. They thus defined curriculum development as "a process where the choices of designing a learning experience for clients (students) are made and then activated through a series of coordinated activities" (p. 2).

Chartock (2010: 65) defined curriculum in terms of its orientation, which can be reflected in online environments:

1. Teacher-centered (traditional)
2. Student-centered (humanistic)

3. Subject-centered (academic domains)
4. Broad fields (interdisciplinary)
5. Technology-based (behavioral)
6. Society-based (meeting social needs)

Curriculum and its development can occur on several levels: from an international curriculum, such as media literacy, to a single-incident training about one skill. PK–12 education is the most likely to have a standard curriculum at the state or national level. Professional pre-service curriculum for medicine and teaching are also likely to have standardized student learning outcomes because of licensure requirements. The institutions with which curriculum is affiliated also vary in scope: from a one-person operation to an international consortium. Within each institution, curriculum development needs to address every level of the experience:

- **Students**: grouped and individual
- **Learning activity**: a student outcome that is contextualized within a time frame and learning environment, a teaching approach, relevant resources, and student task that can be assessed
- **Course**: term-long set of sessions of closely related student outcomes (such as Clinical Electrophysiology, Nineteenth-Century French Poets)
- **Program**: curriculum for a well-defined, specific academic domain (such as Physical Therapy, Educational Administration)
- **College**: usually broad-based academic domains (such as Liberal Arts) within which departments house separate related programs (such as Languages, Social Sciences)
- **Institutional mission and vision**: from a comprehensive university to a bartending school
- **System or consortium**: overarching goal and agreements

It should be noted that Posner (2003) asserted that three realities of curriculum exist: the official (what is listed on the books), the operational (what is actually taught), and the hidden. Particularly if curriculum is thought to include the social and emotional learning experiences, hidden agendas that transfer underlying cultural values may result in biased teaching and learning. Online education, by its own existence, communicates certain biases such as the value and privilege of technology, and potentially the lesser status of face-to-face interaction.

Regardless of agenda, curriculum with its specific student outcomes, indicators, and standards is usually developed at the program level. Professional accreditation agencies, such as the National Council for Accreditation of Teacher Education (NCATE), formed in an effort to provide high-quality curriculum that attracts top faculty and students, and educational institutions often developed curricula that aligned and met those accreditation agencies' standards. Another approach to national standards is outcomes based, such as information literacy; both the Association of College and Research Libraries (ACRL) and the American Association of School Librarians (AASL) have developed standards and indicators. At this level, too, enough capacity exists to assess needs in light of desired outcomes and identify effective resources and instruction to ensure student success for a substantial level of expertise.

You could consider the library's program of resources and services as the basis for their curriculum. When existing as part of a larger entity, be it an educational institution or a corporation, the library program needs to align with and support that entity, and the accompanying curriculum needs to intersect and support that entity's goals, such as knowledge about the Vietnam War or cutting-edge chemical processes.

Contextual forces in curriculum design

As you design and develop curriculum, you must consider the human context of knowledge (human ideas and their representation) and social forces (society as a whole).

Knowledge

What should be taught? Obviously, social forces drive the answer; what knowledge and skills do people need in order to survive and succeed? Social and educational values generally define success. They also indicate the goal of education, be it to develop a "well-rounded, educated person" or to ensure a responsible and information citizenry that contributes to society. These two sample goals reflect attitudes about the role of education—and of individuals within society. At this point in history, knowledge is generally not considered a good in itself, but assumes value as it is applied (Wiles and Bondi, 2010).

No longer can one expect to know everything or to learn merely what the prior generation learned. Knowledge is not a closed universe, and society is not static. Not only do people now have access to remote resources around the world because of technology, but new knowledge is being generated every hour—or minute. Furthermore, knowledge is represented in more formats (such as podcasts and holographs) than ever before. How can you make sense of all the available information, and organize it into a manageable curriculum, especially since the shape of any body of knowledge impacts how it is perceived and used? Curriculum design, in preparing for an unknown future that calls for creative innovation and timely response to whatever crises or opportunities that might arise, challenges the hardiest instructional designer.

Social forces

The process of developing, approving, and delivering the curriculum reflects the social norms of the organization in particular, and the larger community in terms of societal influences. These social factors exist on several levels, each of which impact curriculum design.

- **Local**: Despite social trends and layers of legislation, U.S. education remains a local entity, especially in PK–12 public education. School and library boards, which make and oversee policy and resource allocation, are elected locally and are answerable to the local community. This situation can significantly impact online education, which often originates outside of the locale in which it is delivered. Developers of online curriculum must somehow bridge local needs and broader-based sources of resources.
- **State**: State legislation and boards generally set curriculum standards such as content frameworks to college requirements, and regulate technological infrastructures and resource allocation, such as subscription database licensing.
- **Regional**: The most telling social dichotomy exists between rural and urban settings, such as agriculture versus urban factories. As socioeconomic bases differ vastly, they impact educational priorities. In addition, the digital divide remains as the "last mile" syndrome continues to constrain technology access to remote homes and rural libraries.
- **National**: National standards and accountability issues increasingly impact U.S.PK–20 education and its curriculum design. More generically, the national economy impacts curriculum design, not only in terms of preparing future employees and retooling current workers, but also in terms of supporting and sustaining educational institutions and their infrastructures themselves. The increasing diversity of the U.S. population also impacts curriculum, as globalization issues trickle down to national and local levels.
- **International**: In his seminal 2005 book *A Whole New Mind*, Daniel Pink posited three social trends impacting the economy: abundance (of information and resources), globalization (which impacts allocation of human resources), and technology (which impacts access and processing of information). As a result, curriculum must meet the demands of international employers and students. Resources and instruction need to address specific language and cultural issues.

How do current knowledge and social forces play out in curriculum design? What social values are being transmitted through the curriculum? Does content itself address socioeconomic issues such as sexual identity, health and fitness, and cultural differences? Does a wide range of courses enable students to explore career possibilities based on their interests, such as fashion or construction? Do today's economic realities drive curriculum decisions, or are longer-term philosophies of lifelong learning and change adaptation addressed? As a librarian, you bring a broad perspective to these factors, and yet you may need to negotiate with the stakeholders who have specific agendas and learning needs.

Cultural sensitivity

Just as information and education are culturally contextualized, so, too, are the conditions for culturally sensitive curriculum. As you design culturally sensitive curriculum, examine the cultural landscape in order to discern—and align with—shared values and expectations. In his adult training handbook, Craig (1996) asserted that ignorance or denial of cultural norms will spell disaster for cross-cultural initiatives. If the most influential culture shares the goals and strategies of cultural sensitivity, then you have a natural "in." If the culture is strong, then the path to success is even better paved. On the other hand, a strong culture that discounts cultural sensitivity and has a closed attitude can pose challenges. A culture that undervalues cultural sensitivity may be won over if they have a more accepting nature—and can be persuaded by an overlapping stronger culture to join in the overarching goal. Ideally, culturally sensitive instructional design should be explicitly addressed and integrated throughout the organization rather than isolated in some sort of parallel universe of learning. In any case, both the dominant and minority cultures should learn about each other's cultural knowledge and values so they can promote mutual respect and understanding.

Information literacy as curriculum

One of the goals of education is to help individuals become functionally literate, which involves a continuum of skills that enables students to be able to *do* something: procedural knowledge. Students need to access, comprehend, and respond to information. In the United States, reading and writing ability are core competencies in that process. However, other skills such as numeracy and visual acuity are also implicated because knowledge can be represented in so many forms.

More recently, the paradigm has shifted from literacy to learning, as reflected in the 2009 American Association of School Librarians' *Standards for the 21st-Century Learner*. Likewise, a consortium of educational, nonprofit, and commercial entities (Partnership for 21st Century Skills, 2004) developed a framework for twenty-first-century learning.

Defining information literacy

Information literacy, as defined by the Association of College and Research Libraries (ACRL), includes a set of abilities "requiring individuals to recognize when information is needed and have the ability to locate, evaluate, and use effectively the needed information. Information literacy also is increasingly important in the contemporary environment of rapid technological change and proliferating information resources" (ACRL, 2000: 2). ACRL continues: "Information literacy forms the basis for lifelong learning. It is common to all disciplines, to all learning environments, and to all levels of education. It enables learners to master content and extend their investigations, become more self-directed, and assume greater control over their own learning" (p. 3).

At one time, these competencies were typically labeled "library skills" or "research process skills," but they now encompass much more than a physical library, incorporate many more formats of information, and address the issues of generating new knowledge as much as verifying and applying existing knowledge. Particularly with the advent of electronic information, information literacy also deals with social learning and responsibility.

In this light, information literacy facilitates a major facet of education: providing students the means to become critical lifelong learners. Indeed, as students develop and practice these skills, their learning increases across subject domains. Testing a hypothesis can transfer to justifying a thesis statement, for instance. In addition, information literacy competency standards provide a framework for assessing student achievement.

Technology literacy

Technology literacy refers to a person's ability to access and use technology responsibly and effectively. The International Society for Technology in Education (ISTE) developed technology literacy standards that apply to young students (2007) as well as to experienced teachers (2008). Their six areas of competency include:

1. creativity and innovation,
2. communication and collaboration,
3. research and information fluency,
4. critical thinking, problem solving, and decision making,
5. digital citizenship, and
6. technology operations and concepts.

The International Technology Education Association (2000) has also developed technology literacy standards for students, but these focus more on learning *about and for* technology rather than *using* technology as an intellectual tool. Their foci include:

• the nature of technology,
• technology and society,

- design (specifically, engineering design for problem solving),
- abilities for a technological world (creating technological products), and
- the designed world (i.e., agriculture, energy, medicine, transportation, manufacturing construction, communication).

In other areas of the world, technology literacy is frequently reconfigured as Information and Communications Technology or as Information and Technology Literacy, which recognizes the overlapping concepts. The ISTE standards, while rather tool based, offer the most delineated and most easily applicable set that can be expected for U.S. education.

Information literacy is linked to information technology but has a broader base and implication. "Information technology skills enable an individual to use computers, software applications, databases, and other technologies to achieve a wide variety of academic, work-related, and personal goals" (ACRL, 2000: 3). Technology also makes information literacy more complex so that adult education needs to consider information literacy as an underlying principle of lifelong learning. While information transcends technology, as evidenced when individuals interview experts, technology certainly impacts information literacy. Thus, technology is used as a learning and productivity tool while information literacy is, in effect, an intellectual framework.

Other supporting literacies

Just as information exists in many formats, so information literacy can be parsed into several overlapping literacies. Besides technology literacy, some other categories include visual, media, aural, and numeracy.

Visual literacy deals with the ability to understand, use, and create images. The International Visual Literacy Association (Griffin, Pettersson, and Johnson, 1996) developed the following visual literacy indicators:

- Interpret, understand, and appreciate meanings of visual messages.
- Communicate effectively by applying visual design principles.
- Produce visual messages using technology.
- Use visual thinking to conceptualize solutions to problems.

Aural literacy focuses on meaningful sounds: speech, music, environmental. Furthermore, sounds may be categorized in terms of source, quality, and type of information (Brazil, 2001). Thus, aural literacy may be defined as the ability to distinguish, process, and deduce meaning from a variety and sounds, and communicate meaningfully using sound (Project Slate, 2002). Musical literacy overlaps aural literacy in that it also involves musical notation, which might be considered a form of reading literacy.

Related to these literacies that focus on one sense, media literacy focuses on the messages conveyed by mass media. The Center for Mass Media developed five core concepts related to media messages (Thoman and Jolls, 2010):

1. All media messages are constructed.
2. Media message construction uses a creative language with its own rules; form and content are closely related.
3. Media have commercial implications; messages are constructed to gain profit or power.
4. Media have embedded values and points of view.
5. Different people experience the same media message differently. The audience negotiates meaning.

Numeracy is mathematical thinking. Steen (2001) defined numeracy as the ability to understand, analyze, critically respond to, and use mathematics in various social contexts. He also contended that a quantitatively literate individual can apply numerical ideas, appreciate the nature and history of mathematics, and its role in scientific inquiry and technological progress.

Furthermore, each academic domain has its own information universe. Kuhn (1962) posited that each domain has a unique set of artifacts and praxes, which rest on specific theories. Meta-theoretical frameworks, or paradigms, are built on domain-specific philosophical assumptions.

Each of these literacies has its own set of indicators. For instance, the aurally literate person can determine specific characteristics of a sound (such as volume, tone, pitch), and give a sound a specific meaning within a specific context. Therefore, when designing instruction, you must understand these literacies, and incorporate their indicators.

Librarians as information literacy experts

The core knowledge and skills of librarians focus on information literacy: the effective access, evaluation, manipulation, communication, and sharing of information. Be it during a reference interview or part of an online course, you draw upon your knowledge as you guide clientele to become more effective users of information. You can leverage information theory and practice as you make instructional design decisions about content that leads to several kinds of knowledge. These processes may be applied to any subject matter, which enables you to help people have intellectual access to information. Because librarians have additional academic preparation in specific academic disciplines, you can "think like a scientist" or other professional, bringing an understanding of how a specific discipline shapes and shares knowledge. Thus, you can teach these literacies autonomously, but you are also uniquely positioned to collaborate with other instructors, and help bridge different domains of knowledge in support of life-long learning (Grassian and Kaplowitz, 2009).

Collaboration in curriculum choices

Sometimes librarians consider information literacy as "their" curriculum. These set of processes may be considered procedural knowledge that interact with declarative knowledge. Thus, you can think of information literacy as an educational *lingua franca* that helps the learning community communicate and learn together. In this spirit, information literacy can be taught within the context of subject matter: true informational needs.

For this reason, besides the fact that good teaching often arises out of a community of practice, you and stakeholders should collaboratively design curriculum that fosters both subject-based knowledge as well as literacies. Many content frameworks include information literacy components, but they are not always explicitly labeled as such. Therefore, you and stakeholders should look at content standards and information literacy standards simultaneously together as you make curricular decisions, taking into consideration learners' prerequisite information literacy skills and available resources.

Differing degrees of collaboration exist in each education program depending upon status of the stakeholders and faculty culture. Nevertheless, before instructional design collaboration can exist, stakeholders have to understand and value information literacy—and your role in instructional design.

Overview of resources

Instructional design explicitly addresses curriculum material. It is not enough for the instructor to refer to textbook pages while learners take lecture notes. Particularly since instructional design is predicated on needs assessment, standardized texts seldom provide the contextualized information.

Providing resources in support of curriculum is the most basic function done by librarians. Research guides, in-class assignments, and print handouts are established methods of assistance. Technology gives opportunity to expand the role of librarians as a partner in the educational process. Consultation has been expanding from the role of a resource consultant to that of a joint creator of course content and delivery.

Whether you are selecting, adapting, or developing curricular materials, consider the appropriate format to convey information effectively. Marshall McLuhan's 1964 principles of form and function point out how format shapes the information message and the audience's cognitive processes. McLuhan asserted that print tends to be a solitary medium while aural presentation lends itself to a public audience. However, with the advent of digital technology, especially

Web 2.0, such concepts may be overturned. For instance, wikis make generating information a collaborative effort, and podcasts can be appreciated in private. Nevertheless, McLuhan was right in thinking that technology shapes individual and societal self-concepts and interaction.

While content constitutes the main factor in format decisions, McLuhan would agree that interaction between the learner and the content is also key. Instructional design points include selecting appropriate resources to incorporate: from needs assessment through to learning activities. In each instance, consider resources not only for their content but also their use (Tynjala and Hakkinen, 2005).

- **Cognitive tools to organize and externalize knowledge**: Students can learn how to use utility software applications (such as spreadsheets and databases) and graphic organizers to structure knowledge linearly and nonlinearly; incorporating simulations and other models to represent knowledge.
- **Scaffolding**: Programmed texts and hypermedia with branching options enable learners to decide what content to access; shared learning spaces facilitate peer tutoring.
- **Expertise development**: Simulations and other interactive models allow learners to test and practice content knowledge.
- **Social construction of knowledge**: Web 2.0 social networking features facilitate online collaboration; instructors can assign tasks that require collaboration, such as dramatizations.
- **Integrating face-to-face and online delivery**: Supplementing class-time activity with online resources, and following up in-class discussion with online chat, expands time for processing and sharing course information.

Not only should resources support the curriculum, but they also must take into account the learner and the learning environment. To that end, consider the following factors when choosing the most appropriate resource:

- Language: reading level, specialized vocabulary
- Learning preferences: different ways of processing information
- Images: style, quality, usefulness, and relevance
- Stereotypes: gender, ethnicity, lifestyle
- Availability
- Ease of use, which applies especially to technology-based resources
- Cost

While applications are emphasized here, it should be mentioned that you need equipment to use digital resources, so check availability and ease of operability before choosing digital resources. Learners not only have to comprehend the information, but they also have to know how to operate the equipment since they must physically access the resource before they can comprehend it. In terms of physical access to technology, consider the following factors:

- **Site access:** Is technology available to classes and individuals throughout the day and evening to accommodate adult working hours?
- **Remote access:** Can learners get to technology resources from home or public buildings?
- **Equipment circulation:** Does the site lend computers to learners or families? These days, a variety of options are feasible: low-end word processors and Internet devices; mobile devices; older donated computer systems that can be checked out for the year in a fashion similar to textbook circulation.
- **Physical accommodations:** Does the site have computers with larger monitors for visually impaired users, trackballs for physically limited motion, scanners to read text, adjustable desks to accommodate wheelchairs or other seating?

Discrete portions of resources may be selected and edited to demonstrate one specific concept or insight, and may be used for another course for another purpose. For example, a video clip of a lung surgery detail may be used in an anatomy class as well as in a drug-prevention course. These learning objects serve as instructional design blocks. They can consist of presentations, simulations, tutorials, assessments, or even readings. Each learning object can be embedded into an existing instructional session or learning activity to provide a variety of ways to experience a concept or deepen understanding.

Content-centric resources

Content-rich resources include subject-specific information, which may be packaged in print, nonprint, and digital format. Each format has its unique features, which optimize the representation of knowledge. For instance, a digital simulation models interactive factors of a process. A globe gives a realistic concept of a spherical world and distances between places. A short story can provide a compelling and nuanced psychological perspective on a social issue.

The world of print alone offers a myriad of possible relevant content-centric resources. Here is a sampling of scientific resources that librarians can offer (Farmer, 2009: 40): experiment handbooks, tutorials and textbooks, illustrated books on scientific phenomena, identification guides, specialized dictionaries, geographic atlases, medical manuals, health pamphlets, current science news clippings, scientific journals, science posters, teaching transparencies.

Digital resources are becoming a mainstay in education. Some advantages of these technology tools include combination of media, currency, multiple access points, user control, and capability to be repurposed. These features are particularly useful to meet the needs of learners with different learning styles and English-language barriers. In addition, when you transmit information via content-rich tools, they facilitate learning anytime and anywhere in a standardized way, which can provide large-scale instruction.

Learners can access these resources independently or as part of face-to-face classroom course delivery. In the latter situation, resources provide immediate exploration of relevant information. For instance, you might talk about copyright and then have learners take an online copyright test; afterward, the class can discuss the answers and implications. Resources can be easily inserted into multimedia and online presentations to offer a quick, clear explanation or to serve as an open-ended, generative learning prompt.

Production-centric resources

Other resources facilitate content manipulation and presentation. Such resources could be as basic as paper and glue, or as sophisticated as 3-D virtual reality programs. To varying extents, libraries support the production of information via tools and facilities; school libraries are probably the most active in this function because they are likely to have a centralized facility to circulate and use production resources. In general, libraries are most likely to provide technology-based production resources, as detailed below. In addition, application suites such as Microsoft Office and Google Docs enable individuals to easily transform digital information from one format to another. Implications for you as a librarian instructional designer are italicized.

- **Word processing/desktop publishing**: Easy to use and repurpose, and other applications can often be inserted. *You can create learning guide sheets, and learners can present and share their findings.*
- **Spreadsheet**: Helps organize data and facilitates numerical analysis. *You can locate data sets for analysis; learners can test hypotheses about data.*
- **Database**: Helps sort and links data sets. A newer form of databases is social networking websites, as exemplified by delicious, Flickr, and Facebook. *You can locate data sets for analysis; learners can test hypotheses about existing data and collaboratively create their own social sharing database.*
- **Authoring/presentation**: Combines media to present content sequentially or in other structured order locally and online. *Both you and learners can present content, and reorder or combine presentations.*
- **Audio files/podcasting**: Presents aural information such as voice and music. *You and learners can record and archive explanations and sound clips for later use.*
- **Graphic programs**: Represents knowledge visually; some programs require hours of training. *You can diagnose learner knowledge as they create content*

|||||||||||||||||||||||||||||||||||||||||||||||||||||||||||||||||||||||||||||||||||||||||||||||||||||||||||||

concept maps; both you and learners can explain concepts with images.

- **Video editing**: Realistic, multimedia format for presenting concepts, particularly processes and persuading audiences; requires some training and equipment. *Both you and learners can demonstrate how the selection and sequencing of video information can impact perception.*

- **Simulations and games**: Promotes active learning through focused engagement within a predetermined universe with rules. Good simulation and game designers follow Vygotsky's (1978) zone of proximal development: providing a challenge (not just routine operations) that can feasibly be met (i.e., the outcome is doable); designers of games that build on community set up the conditions such that the player needs to work with the community effectively in order for the outcome to be achieved (Engeström, 1987). *You can incorporate research strategy games as tutorials.*

Process-based tools have been further enhanced by other hardware such as tablets, interactive whiteboards, and Personal Response Systems (PRSs). These tools make it possible for learners to contribute and control information, thereby improving their information and technology literacy while focusing on the subject matter at hand.

- Computer tablets are typically laptops with a touch screen. The laptop can be held in clipboard fashion with the user being able to "write" on the screen. If the tablet is electronically connected to a data projector, you can circulate the tablet among the class so that each learner can input on the tablet as they are ready to contribute information.

- Whiteboards use a surface that is linked electronically to the computer; the image projection is calibrated so that the user can move images on the board as if it were a touch screen and "write" on it as if it were a computer tablet. In effect, the person at the board "controls" the computer, and can add information to the board and open computer application.

- PRSs (personal response systems) use infrared technology so that when students click on the handheld device their inputs are collected statistically and can be shared via the instructor's computer, and projected for the class to see. This system is particularly effective in large classes because it facilitates instant checks for understanding so that you can clarify confusing information—or speed ahead because the students already know the information to be discussed.

- Mobile devices such as smartphones have ratcheted up m-learning and associated instructional strategies because of their many features: two-way communication, text messaging, photo capture, calendaring, calculating, Internet access, application downloading and operating options, geographic information system (GIS) or global positioning system (GPS) functions, and language support.

Task-specific resources

To demonstrate how the choice of resource impacts instructional strategies, the following outline of content matter to teach information literacy incorporates technology at each step.

1. Identify the need for information.
   a. Video: Learners brainstorm information needs for a Middle East peace summit simulation.
   b. Graphic organizer application: Learners create concept maps and other visual techniques to help learners identify information needs.
2. Access information effectively.
   a. Demonstration and hands-on computer activity: Learners identify various search strategies to locate information, such as generating keywords and using library indexes.
   b. Screen capture tutorial: Learners use online databases and university catalog; use of bibliographies, etc.; locate educational research and lesson plans.
3. Evaluate and select information.
   a. Wiki: Learners use web evaluation criteria to develop a class list of good resources.
   b. WebQuest: Learners evaluate educational research and learning activities.
4. Manipulate information to accomplish a specific purpose.
   a. Vidcast: Learners create spreadsheets and timelines to organize information.
   b. Simulation: Learners explore physics laws.
5. Communicate product or performance.
   a. Video: Learners create a PowerPoint presentation.
   b. Refworks: Learners collect and collate bibliographic citations.
6. Evaluate process and product.
   a. Rubric application: Learners generate and use rubrics to evaluate their learning experience.
   b. Word processing tracking: Learners review and comment on peers' work.

Adapting and creating resources

Because curricular material development often requires extensive time and effort, you will probably rely on existing sources. These resources need to be thoroughly scrutinized to guarantee their alignment with and support of the tentative instructional design; these products should not drive instruction. Sometimes available resources can be adapted to meet local needs; creative commons facilitates this process and contributes to other instructional efforts. Original documents may be the most viable solution, especially to meet very specific and localized training such as the use of customized electronic resources or to meet institutional standards.

Adaptation and fair use

While in-house resources offer unique support, they are also labor-intensive to produce, and might not communicate effectively. Therefore, it is usually better to adapt or customize an existing high-quality resource than to create it from scratch. You can locate resources that provide applicable content, and then add those unique elements that pertain to the specific learning setting. For example, an existing pathfinder research strategy guide can provide a good starting point, and you can add the local periodical and DVD holdings to the list.

Usually such resource adaptations do not require written permission from the author because the objective is education and research, not profit-making, and particularly for one-time use. Of course, it is best to obtain the relevant copyright permission, and such permission is certainly needed for multiple and long-term use. In general, though, you can follow fair use guidelines exemptions, which are listed in Section 107 of Title 17 United States Code 106:

1. the purpose and character of the use, including whether such use is of commercial nature or is for nonprofit educational purposes;
2. the nature of the copyrighted work;
3. amount and substantiality of the portion used in relation to the copyrighted work as a whole; and
4. the effect of the use upon the potential market for or value of the copyrighted work.

Tips on creating documents

If creating resources is necessary, follow these simple rules.

- Assume that the audience will use the resource independently, so make all content self-sufficient and obvious.
- Make nothing ambiguous.
- Write clearly and accurately. Use simple, straightforward sentences and vocabulary.
- Create a glossary for unfamiliar terms.
- Make it easy for the reader to follow. Use **boldface**, font size, and bullet points to make key points. Avoid ALL CAPS.

- Provide some white space for the user to make notes and to ease readability.
- Use images to clarify, such as screen dumps. Be sure that every image is relevant, and adds to the information.
- If writing steps, number each one. Make sure to write all the possible actions at steps where decisions are required.
- Put major steps on separate pages.
- If giving directions, explain what to do if the user makes a mistake.
- Test any document before publishing it; have a few learners "walk" through the document aloud to catch for possible misunderstandings or awkward phrasing.

More detailed guidelines are found at the following websites:

- http://desktoppub.about.com/
- http://www.allgraphicdesign.com/design101.html
- http://www.microsoft.com/education/howto.mspx

Rapid prototyping

Rapid prototyping is a technology design process that quickly facilitates high-quality, responsive implementation of resource creation. To start with, the design team of the stakeholders (usually the supervisor, content expert, instructional designer, and technician) meets to identify the learning objective and the target audience; at this programming phase the planning timetable is set, and the program is approved by management. At the schematic phase, the design team determines the training parameters, design criteria, technical requirements, and the cost; management and a user group review the plan. At the design development phase, potential materials are reviewed and chosen, and development documents are created, taking into account design principles and technology architecture, with feedback given from the user group again. The actual documents are prepared and reviewed at the construction documentation phase. At the integration and administration phase, on-site staff are prepared for the product and observe it; the materials are given a final inspection and integrated into the system.

By working with the stakeholders throughout the process, you get organizational buy-in, and the final resource is more likely to be accepted and used in training and application. Moreover, as learners constitute the user focus group, their learning experiences inform the development and deployment of the resource so that they, in essence, co-construct knowledge (Beguin, 2003).

Self-paced learning tools

Increasingly, librarians have developed instructional web tutorials or, at the least, create web portals that link to such learning resources. These resources offer

opportunities for learner choice so that they can control the content to explore—
and the pacing of that investigating—within predetermined parameters. Such
resources have to be very carefully constructed since an instructor is not immediately available to provide feedback; the learning objects themselves have to
support such information. A good list of peer-reviewed online library tutorials,
which may be applicable to high school settings, is found at http://www.ala.org/
ala/rusa/rusaourassoc/rusasections/mars/marspubs/marsinnovativerefgeneral
.htm. Other starting points follow:

- ICT Literacy (http://www.ictliteracy.info)
- Information Literacy for K–16 Settings (http://www.csulb.edu/~lfarmer/
  infolitwebstyle.htm)
- Educator's Reference Desk: Information Literacy (http://www.eduref.org/
  cgi-bin/print.cgi/Resources/Subjects/Information_Literacy/Information_
  Literacy.html)
- Library Research Guides (http://www.lib.berkeley.edu/TeachingLib/Guides)
- OASIS: Online Advancement of Student Information Skills (http://oasis
  .sfsu.edu/)

You can use these resources in guided practice with an entire class, incorporate
single sections of these materials into a learning activity, or encourage students to
use them independently or in small groups. Providing a choice of venues allows
students choice and recognizes different learning preferences.

Guidelines for developing effective websites are found at the following URLs:

- http://www.sldirectory.com/libsf/resf/wpages.html
- http://goodpractices.com/
- http://schoollibrarywebsites.wikispaces.com/

Learner-generated resources

Probably the most influential change in resources within instructional design thus
far has been the introduction and increasing acceptance of interactive Web 2.0
resources. Knowledge is collaboratively built and shared. Whereas earlier decades
focused more on instructor-produced content, which could involve high-level
technical expertise, Web 2.0 tools are often easy to use so that content can regain
intellectual focus, and learners can be cocreators of knowledge. Having learners
participate in the authoring of their own learning tools adds to the educational
concept of constructivism and results in practical applications of information
literacy and student-centered curriculum. Johnson (2009) suggests several Web
2.0 resources that can be integrated in instructional design across the curriculum.

- **Blogs**: 21classes (http://www.21classes.com/) enables instructors to develop a class blog portal, and supports subject "tagging" and full-text searching. Class Blogmeister (http://classblogmeister.com/) is a free product that enables you to set up and monitor student blog accounts.
- **Wikis**: PB Wiki (http://www.pbwiki.com/) is a free webpage creator application that can be used collaboratively, including options for comments. Wiki creators, such as instructors, can customize access options. WikiSpaces (http://www.wikispaces.com/) is another site that can be secured; K–12 educators can establish a free account.
- **Group writing**: Google Docs (http://docs.google.com/) allows learners to share and edit documents using a suite of productivity tools. Google Notebook (http://www.google.com/notebook) organizes text, images, and links that can be shared, even from cell phones. Whiteboard (http://www .whiteboard.com/) facilitates collaborative writing, and saves earlier versions.
- **Image sharing**: Flickr (http://www.flickr.com/) is a free photograph management system that operates on several digital platforms, including mobile devices.
- **Multimedia**: VoiceThread (http://www.voicethread.com/) is a free (or low-cost) program that enables users to develop and share online "albums" of mixed media; viewers can comment in several ways. Zoho (http://zoho .com/) is a free online collaborative environment that supports group projects in a variety of formats.
- **Networking**: Ning (http://www.ning.com/) is an online social networking environment that supports links, groups, and sharing of documents such as videos. LinkedIn (http://www.linkedin.com/) facilitates business and professional connections, and lends itself to mentoring opportunities.
- **Video**: Viddler (http://www.viddler.com/) supports uploading and sharing of videos within a browser. Vimeo (http://www.vimeo.com/) provides 500 MB of video storage and sharing capacity. YouTube (http://www.youtube .com/) is a free online video streaming service that allows users to upload and share videos.
- **Virtual environments**: Second Life (http://www.secondlife.com/) is an object-oriented online environment in which users can interact with artifacts and avatars (personalities). Microsoft and VMware have introduced virtual "machine" software that creates a "sandbox" for technical students to explore hardware without harming it.

Digital divides and digital inclusion

Most librarian instructional designers try to address the issue of the Digital Divide: that is, inequities in access to resources, with a focus on technology. Most

||||||||||||||||||||||||||||||||||||||||||||||||||||||||||||||||||||||||||||||||||||||||||||||||||||||||

people tend to think about this issue in socioeconomic terms. Libraries themselves help address the Digital Divide as they try to optimize physical access to technology through longer operating hours and the circulation of computers.

Yet another significant population is sometimes overlooked: individuals with physical disabilities. While the congenitally visually impaired or wheelchairbound might be the first images that come to mind, remember that an aging population brings a greater need for physical accommodations. When the issue of digital resources arises, these same populations tend to have less access and less knowledge than other populations.

Assistive technology is usually the first consideration for providing accommodations for physical access to resources. It may be defined as "any aid, device or tool, compensatory strategy, used in different environments, information and referral, evaluation and recommendation, resources for funding, designing, fabricating, repairing and filling, training, support and follow-through service that improves a person's functional capacity" (Special Needs Technology Assessment Resource Support Team, n.d.: 1). This list of physical differences and supportive assistive technology provides a beginning point for choosing resources:

- **Visual differences**: larger font on monitors, change in background color on monitors, audiotapes, screen-reading software (including SimpleText on Macs and Narrative option on PCs), scanners, oral-input devices
- **Hearing differences**: closed-caption materials, transcriptions
- **Mobility differences**: seating options, trackballs and joysticks, digital controls (switches, scanning), oral-input devices

Another major element in accessibility is universal design: incorporating resources for everyone's use to the greatest extent possible without need for adaptation (Higbee, Goff, and Minneapolis University Center for Research on Developmental Education and Urban Literacy, 2008). Thus, when selecting materials or thinking about instruction, consider the following principles (http://design-dev.ncsu.edu/openjournal/index.php/redlab/article/view/102):   flexible and intuitive use, low physical effort, tolerance of error (e.g., spelling suggestion), and size for access and use.

With the passage of new government and industry guidelines regulating web accessibility for disabled users, librarian instructional designers in public institutions need to comply with Section 508 of the Rehabilitation Act (http://www.section508.gov/) and priority-one standards of the World Wide Web Consortium's Web Content Accessibility Guidelines (http://www.w3.org/WAI). When incorporating the web into instruction and learning, be it in using websites or creating them, make sure to consider the following elements to ensure that websites are accessible.

- Caption or use the ALT attribute to describe images and functions.
- Summarize or use a LONGDESC attribute for graphs and charts. Make tables readable line by line.
- Label hyperlinks so the user can understand them out of context (avoid "click here").
- Use consistent layout features and headings. Avoid frames, or create a non-frame version of the website. In case Applets or plug-ins are not supported by visual-impairment "reader" software, provide alternative content.
- Check accessibility through technology-based guidelines: http://www.w3.org/WAI/intro/wcag.php and http://wave.webaim.org/.

Fortunately, librarians have been working on access issues for decades, so the technology aspects can build on solid foundations. Cornell's website on disability laws discusses the rights of people with disabilities (http://www.law.cornell.edu/topics/disability.html). State services for the blind and visually impaired are well-known. WestEd in San Francisco lists several good website on access and equity, with particular attention to assistive technology; this is a good starting point: http://rtecexchange.edgateway.net/cs/rtecp/view/rtec_str/2.

Curriculum programs

Curriculum design as a whole is typically labeled as a "program." Within that framework, content is king; it determines what is taught. As mentioned in Chapter 4, the curriculum should be based on need, both in terms of what to learn and how to learn it. As an information specialist, you can leverage your expertise by incorporating literacies into the curriculum. Such knowledge gives you more credibility when teaching autonomously or collaborating with colleagues to design meaningful curriculum, particularly in support of lifelong learning.

Resources, then, provide the documentation for learners to consult and use. Again, you are uniquely positioned to locate relevant resources that meet the needs of learners. As a librarian, you are keenly aware that learners should have choice in the resources they use, and this option should be built into most instructional designs.

Indeed, the learner should be considered as a partner in curriculum and supporting resources. Whatever resources are selected, they should be used actively by the learner. As they gain knowledge, learners can suggest additional resources and create their own resources, which can be used by peer and future learners.

You can even think of the learning space itself as a resource, enabling the learner to interact with the curriculum in a social space. Of course, human resources such as instructors are needed to deliver the curriculum, either through direct instruction or by providing a learning environment: the conditions for learning. The library is a wonderful example of this meta-resource, which you oversee and support. These two factors are detailed in the following chapter, which focuses on the delivery of instruction.

Sample research project for high school students

The following lesson exemplifies the importance of preselecting developmentally appropriate resources for a learning activity (in this case, high school civics seniors), and providing choice for learners so they can practice evaluation skills. The lesson also contains all the elements of information literacy, including applying new knowledge for authentic purposes. In this case, teen rights resonate with the learners. Collaboration with the classroom teacher is a core component of the learning experience.

Lesson

Title: Teen Rights

Lesson overview: Students are usually aware that they do not have the same rights as adults. However, they might not know details about rights: the level of government, rights of drop-outs or emancipated youth, differences over time. In this lesson, learners explore age-linked Constitutional rights.

Time frame: 3–5 class periods

Learning objectives: Learners will:
- Interpret Constitutional rights in light of minors.
- Debate Constitutional rights as they apply to minors.

Curriculum standards
- Evaluate and take and defend positions on the scope and limits of rights and obligations as democratic citizens, the relationships among them, and how they are secured.
- Students summarize landmark U.S. Supreme Court interpretations of the Constitution and its amendments. Understand the changing interpretations of the Bill of Rights over time, including interpretations of the basic freedoms (religion, speech, press, petition, and assembly).
- Identify topics; broaden or narrow topic and develop ideas to direct the focus of an inquiry.
- Generate research questions based on interests, observations, information, stories, and issues or on an assigned topic.

- Identify and locate a variety of resources online and in other formats using effective search strategies.
- Evaluate and analyze information to determine appropriateness in addressing the scope of inquiry.
- Organize, synthesize, create, and communicate information.

Resources

- A variety of resources on the U.S. Constitution and its amendments
- Technology: Internet-connected computers; subscription databases if possible (especially SIRS); demonstration Internet-connected computer and projector/screen

Planning for diverse learners

- Text can be translated using an online translator, or read aloud using a computer reader.
- The difficulty of text can vary.

Instructional strategies and study activities

0. Before the lesson, librarian creates and posts a social bookmark of U.S. Constitutional resources. Here is a beginning list:

    Supreme Court of the United States: http://www.supremecourtus .gov/

    Oyez Oyez Oyez: U.S. Supreme Court Database: http://www.oyez .org/oyez/frontpage

    Cornell Law School resources: http://supct.law.cornell.edu/supct/

    Rominger Legal Links: http://www.romingerlegal.com/index.html

    Free law site: http://www.lexisone.com/

    Law reviews, journals, and periodicals: http://law.com/

    Infoplease almanac—SupremeCourt: http://www.infoplease.com/ ipa/A0873869.html

    GPO Access: http://www.gpoaccess.gov/

    FindLaw: Supreme Court Decisions: http://www.findlaw.com/ casecode/supreme.html

    Landmark Supreme Court Cases: http://www.landmarkcases.org/

    Fifteen cases with summaries, diagrams of how the cases moved through the system: http://dir.yahoo.com/Government/U_S__ Government/Judicial_Branch/Supreme_Court/

III

American Lawyer Media's Law.com—United States Supreme Court Monitor: http://www.courttv.com/archive/multimedia/supremecourt/

American Library Association Notable First Amendment Court Cases: http://www.ala.org/ala/aboutala/offices/oif/firstamendment/courtcases/courtcases.cfm

Constitutional rights, powers, and responsibilities: http://www.constitution.org/powright.htm

Student rights and the US Constitution: http://www.usconstitution.net/consttop_stud.html

1. Librarian and social studies teacher introduce the lesson by asking the class how age is mentioned in the U.S. Constitution and its amendments. Under the supervision of an instructor, a student can link onto http://www.constitution.org/constit_.htm and use "FIND: age" to locate relevant passages. Librarian or social studies teacher asks the class to orally identify rights (or lack of rights) that they think apply strictly to minors (such as filtering software, searching lockers, drinking laws).

2. Librarian or social studies teacher divides class into groups of four. Each group researches one amendment (or one aspect of an amendment, such as the First Amendment, which addresses free speech, free press, free expression) that has implications for minors. The following sites are good starters: http://www.usconstitution.net/consttop_stud.html and http://www.constitution.org/powright.htm. The group researches the right as it applies to minors, drawing upon the U.S. Constitution and Supreme Court cases. Two learners argue for distinction between minor and adult, and two argue for no age distinction. For each pair, one learner writes up the argument "brief," and the other orally defends the case. All learners must cite their sources. As needed, the librarian and social studies teacher give help in terms of locating and using resources, understanding the content, writing a brief, or conducting a debate.

3. Each group debates and the rest of the class votes for one side or the other. In each case, the social studies teacher asks one learner from each side to state the basis for their vote.

4. The social studies teacher assigns each group another group to assess (both the oral debate and the written brief) in terms of the debate rubric.

5. Librarian and the social studies teacher debrief the class in terms of concepts and skills learned.

Variations

- The topic can be limited to one constitutional right, with more variations (as follows).
- Learners can compare state and federal rights.
- Leaders can trace how rights have changed over time.
- Learners can compare rights for different youth populations (such as drop-outs, militia, pre-teens, teenage parents, emancipated youth).
- Learners can develop a new teen right, based on constitutional law.
- Learners can create a Supreme Court case simulation.
- Debates can be videotaped.
- Briefs may be done collaboratively using a wiki.
- Learners can begin the lesson by exploring http://www.angelfire.com/mn3/andymn/P3.html.

Student assessment

- Learners are assessed in terms of their research and debating skills.
- Debate rubric: http://writesmart.niceboard.org/t84-classroom-debate-rubric
- Research rubric: http://rhsweb.org/library/research_rubric.htm

Additional resources

http://cfbstaff.cfbisd.edu/davidj/Special%20Events/Constitution%20Day/constitution_day.htm#Lessons%20and%20Activities

http://www.atozteacherstuff.com/Themes/Constitution_Day/

http://www.educationworld.com/a_lesson/lesson/lesson347.shtml

http://www.teach-nology.com/teachers/lesson_plans/history/us_history/constitution/

‖‖

References

American Association of School Librarians. 2009. *Standards for the 21st-Century Learner.* Chicago: American Library Association.

Association of College and Research Libraries. 2000. *Information Literacy Competency Standards for Higher Education.* Chicago: American Library Association.

Beguin, P. 2003. "Design as a Mutual Learning Process between Users and Designers." *Interacting with Computers* 15, no. 5: 709–730.

Brazil, E. 2001. *Cue Points: An Examination of Common Sound File Formats.* Limerick, Ireland: University of Limerick.

Chartock, R. 2010. *Educational Foundations: An Anthology.* 2nd ed. Ventura, CA: Academic Internet Publishers.

Craig, R., ed. 1996. *ASTD Training and Development Handbook.* New York: McGraw-Hill.

Engeström, Y. 1987. *Learning by Expanding: An Activity-Theoretical Approach to Developmental Research.* Helsinki, Finland: Orienta-Konsultit.

Farmer, L. 2009. *Your School Library: Check It Out!* Westport, CT: Libraries Unlimited.

Grassian, E., and J. Kaplowitz. 2009. *Information Literacy Instruction.* 2nd ed. New York: Neal-Schuman.

Griffin, R., R. Pettersson, and R. Johnson, eds. 1996. *Eyes on the Future: Converging Images, Ideas and Instruction.* Sugar Grove, IL: International Visual Literacy Association.

Higbee, Jeanne L., Emily Goff, and Minneapolis University Center for Research on Developmental Education and Urban Literacy. 2008. *Pedagogy and Student Services for Institutional Transformation: Implementing Universal Design in Higher Education.* Minneapolis, MN: Minneapolis University.

International Society for Technology in Education. 2007. *National Educational Technology Standards for Students.* Eugene, OR: International Society for Technology in Education.

International Society for Technology in Education. 2008. *National Educational Technology Standards for Teachers.* Eugene, OR: International Society for Technology in Education.

International Technology Education Association. 2000. *Standards for Technological Literacy.* Reston, VA: International Technology Education Association.

Johnson, M. 2009. *Primary Source Teaching the Web 2.0 Way, K12.* Worthington, OH: Linworth.

Kuhn, T. 1962. *The Structure of Scientific Revolutions.* Chicago: University of Chicago Press.

McLuhan, M. 1964. *Understanding Media.* New York: McGraw-Hill.

Partnership for 21st Century Skills. 2004. *Framework for 21st Century Learning.* Washington, DC: Partnership for 21st Century Skills. http://www.p21.org/index. php?option=com_content&task=view&id=254&Itemid=120.

Pink, D. 2005. *A Whole New Mind.* New York: Riverhead Books.

Posner, G. 2003. *Analyzing the Curriculum.* 3rd ed. New York: McGraw-Hill.

Project Slate. 2002. *Listening, Aural Reading, and Live Reader Skills.* Lubbock, TX: Texas Tech University.

Special Needs Technology Assessment Resource Support Team. n.d. *Assistive Technology Guide.* Annapolis, MD: Annapolis Valley Regional School Board.

Steen, E. 2001. *Mathematics and Democracy.* Princeton, NJ: National Council on Education and the Discipline.

Thoman, E., and T. Jolls. 2010. *Literacy for the 21st Century.* 2nd ed. Malibu, CA: Center for Media Literacy.

Tynjala, P., and P. Hakkinen. 2005. "E-learning at Work: Theoretical Underpinnings and Pedagogical Challenges." *Journal of Workplace Learning* 17, no. 5/6: 318–336.

Vygotsky, L. 1978. *Mind in Society*. Cambridge, MA: Harvard University Press.

Wiles, J., and J. Bondi. 2010. *Curriculum Development*. 8th ed. Upper Saddle River, NJ: Pearson Education.

6

Instructional
delivery

Planning for the actual delivery of the curriculum usually focuses on instruction and its supporting factors. Ideally, the content provider and you should design instruction together, determining each person's role throughout the design process: from needs assessment through final evaluation analysis. As soon as you and your counterparts agree to participate in the instructional design, you should negotiate your roles and responsibilities.

Synchronous group instruction remains a typical instructional design delivery mode, although just-in-time coaching also exemplifies synchronous instruction. Furthermore, virtual synchronous instruction constitutes a growing delivery model. Prior to the event, you need to arrange facilities and resources, market the event, and set up the conditions for learning. Learning events normally should include follow-up activities and assessments; tips for sustaining learning are given. This chapter gives general principles for such educational events.

Asynchronous instruction speaks to the learner's desire for convenience. Printed materials have traditionally provided content and exercises for self-paced learning. Technology has greatly enhanced asynchronous instruction, making it more sensory and interactive. Since learner time often drives such instructional delivery, effective and convenient storage and retrieval of curricular materials must be in place. Issues regarding universal design and the instructional needs of special populations conclude this chapter.

A word about instructional theories

The basic focus of this book is instructional design: a systematic process for developing education programs. Chapter 2 discussed educational philosophy, and Chapter 3 focused on learning theories. Instructional theories describe how to facilitate meeting identified outcomes. Bruner (1956), one of the earliest researchers to synthesize instruction, stated that instructional theory should address four aspects:

1. Predisposition toward learning
2. Ways in which a body of knowledge can be structured so that it is most easily understood by learners
3. The most effective sequences in which to present material
4. Nature and pacing of rewards and punishment

Building on Bruner, Gagne (1985) stated that instructional theory should be able to predict the effectiveness of instructional conditions on learner cognitive processing.

Instructional theories reflect philosophies of education and learning, and tend to fall into one of three categories (Table 6.1). Basic characteristics are followed by representative instructional models, as identified by Ryder (2006).

In general, librarians tend to adhere to a constructivist instructional approach, reflecting their belief in individual choice and use of resources based on a rich collection of information in various formats. In implementing any instructional theory, you need to consider the learner, the learning environment, and the content. A number of factors that shape instruction are detailed in the following pages.

Time issues

A central factor of curriculum design is its organization and treatment. Time is a vital factor in that process, even in asynchronous situations.

Structure

At the most basic level, decision makers must schedule curriculum within a time frame, which may be internally or externally determined. For instance, a university system may require that a degree program must be completed within a certain number of credits, so the curriculum has to fit within that amount of time. A conference might need to be held at a certain time for a specified number of days because of facilities contracts. A training session might need to be accomplished by a certain date when new management software is to be installed.

Table 6.1 Instructional theories

Instructional theory	Objectivism/ behaviorism	Cognitivism/ pragmatism	Constructivism/ interpretivism
Characteristics	Emphasize observable and measurable behaviors, relate behavior and environmental variables, cue behavior and set conditions for it to occur, transfer behaviors representing knowledge, use consequences and reinforce learned behaviors.	Identify prerequisite relationships of content, structure information to facilitate cognitive processing, address mental structures and processes.	Contextualize knowledge, assemble knowledge from diverse sources to address problem at hand, support knowledge construction and reflective thinking.
Representative models	Skinner's programmed instruction, information processing, systems approach	Keller's ARCS model of motivation, Collins and Stevens inquiry teaching model, Merrill's component display model	Discovery learning, situated learning, problem-based learning, inquiry-based learning
Guides for instruction	Identify learning outcomes. Align assessment to outcomes. Divide content into small units. Sequence units. Give rules for learning content. Check that learning responds. Provide frequent feedback. Reinforce with immediate rewards. (Carlile, Jordan, and Stack, 2004: 10)	Encourage active learning. Avoid cognitive overload. Chunk materials to facilitate retention. Make structure of content explicit. Present content in more than one way to optimize retention. Outline metacognitive strategies. (Carlile and Jordan, 2005: 19)	Align objectives, strategies, and assessment. Approach content from learner's perspective. Accommodate learner diversity. Foster learner logs. Overview topic, purpose, objectives, rationale. Encourage active learning and discovery. Provide frequent feedback on performs. (Carlile, Jordan, and Stack, 2004: 17)

Whatever the scope and level of the curriculum program, the curriculum needs to be structured in terms of time: by program, course, unit, lesson, learning activity. A diagram provides clarity (Table 6.2).

Concomitantly, the amount of content also drives the amount of time needed to cover that content. For instance, it takes less time to understand the difference

Table 6.2 Curriculum schedule					
Month 1	Month 2	Month 3	Month 4	Month 5	Month 6
Program					
Course I			Course II		
Unit A	Unit B	Unit C	Unit X	Unit Y	Unit Z
Lesson i					
Activity a					

between a primary and a secondary source than it does to locate and evaluate a variety of primary and secondary sources. Thus, quantity of content and quantity of time have a symbiotic relationship.

In addition, the time *between* each instruction also needs to be calculated, often in light of other time demands. For example, a series of workshops might be offered weekly or monthly, depending on the schedule of the learners, the instructors, and the organization as a whole. The decision about scheduling also has to take into consideration retention of the content between workshop session; too short of time in between might not give learners enough mental time to process the information, but too long of time between might result in learners forgetting the content matter so that they have a difficult time linking content from one session to another.

Sequencing

Sequencing content is another time-linked decision. Sequencing can follow several patterns: chronological, developmental, relational, thematic, from easy to difficult, from overview to specifics, from specific to general, step-by-step of a process, spiral with growing sophistication, and so on. The structure of the academic discipline, the overall goal of the curriculum, and the educational philosophy tends to drive these sequencing decisions. For instance, librarians would discuss task definition before explaining keywords. History may be handled chronologically or thematically. A pragmatic educational philosophy is likely to start with concrete experience between making generalizations.

In addition, a set of prerequisite skills might need to be taught before the intended content is delivered. For example, addition and multiplication skills must be mastered before fractions can be taught. Such prerequisite skills might cross disciplines; for instance, students might need to take geometry before they take physics. With such cross-discipline interdependence, scope-and-sequence curriculum mapping is a good idea so that all the curricular areas can be efficiently sequenced. This practice is particularly useful for school librarians who want to make sure that all students become information literate. For instance, ninth-graders might learn how to locate science articles for a science fair project, which would apply as they evaluate websites in a second-semester social issues course. Tenth-grade language arts students might do an I-Search paper, which would prepare them for a junior American history research paper.

Nonlinear sequencing

It should be noted that in a class, learners may well have different levels of skill or prior experience, so one sequence might not be effective for all learners. In that respect, differentiated or personalized curriculum sequencing is ideal, although it can be difficult for the instructor to manage.

One way to deal with curriculum sequencing is to provide an overall set of learning modules, be they at the course or learning activity level, that need to be mastered in order to complete the program. Some modules may need to be taken in a specific order, such as orientation at the beginning and a service project at the end.

Technology can facilitate nontraditional curriculum sequencing. For example, a tutorial can be organized with branching options, which can be accessed based on interest or need. Hypermedia enables learners to explore a topic in more depth, linking to relevant information such as glossaries or supporting articles. Based on a digitized diagnostic test, learners can be directed to content needed to master a concept. Alternatively, content can be represented as a map or picture, with "hot" links that the learner can explore in the order that he or she chooses. In some cases, the learners' actions dictate the content to be used next; in other cases, the learner explicitly chooses which content to explore. In either situation, the learner's actions impact what content is used, so that the learner is not only more likely to be engaged but is more responsible for his or her learning. It should be noted that such nonlinear sequencing means that as an instructional designer, you have to make an extra effort to ensure that the learner interacts with the relevant content at the appropriate time.

Staffing issues

Who will serve as instructor? This is a central issue for librarians because they often have to negotiate that role with content providers, be they industry supervisors, staff development coordinators, or academic faculty. Within the library, librarians usually do the instruction because the curriculum is also usually library-bound or at least depends on the library's resources. The most obvious example of library curriculum and corresponding instruction is library orientation.

Information literacy may be taught as a separate course or a series of workshops. In some cases, information literacy units may be embedded in an academic course, taught in tandem. However, in many cases, librarians instruct learners because some other person is delivering a curriculum that includes an information task for which the librarian has some expertise, either as a resource manager or as a skilled researcher. The most usual scenario is a combination of curricula: that of some domain of knowledge (such as business practice, early reading, career exploration) and some kind of literacy, which may be under the authorization of another department or part of the library program. Unfortunately, what also happens is that the two curricula work in parallel rather than in tandem, occasionally intersecting as the need for using resources arises.

For this reason, instructional responsibility is sometimes determined separately rather than in negotiation, which can lead to less than optimal human resource allocation. If possible, try to work with your counterparts early on in the instructional design process in order to determine who should deliver the curriculum. Here are several instructor configurations:

- The classroom teacher and librarian co-introduce the information task, with the teacher focusing on the academic content and the librarian focusing on information processing. The two co-teach research strategies and evaluation methods, and both assess student work: the teacher focusing on the content, and the librarian focusing on resource use.
- The classroom teacher is bringing in his class for the same assignment as last year, which was done by another teacher. The librarian shares the prior experience, and suggests ways to make the learning activity more effective. The two people create a rubric that includes information literacy skills, and the librarian leads a session on using library reference materials in the library. Both people help students on a one-to-one basis in the library.
- The classroom teacher visits the library to see what resources are available for an upcoming unit. The librarian reviews the learning activity, and suggests a few alterations based on the available materials. The library assistant creates a cart of relevant items, and the librarian creates a webliography of relevant websites, which is posted on the library web portal. The teacher explains the assignment in the classroom, and has the students use the library on their own time. The librarian provides one-on-one student help.
- The classroom teacher asks the librarian to teach students how to locate articles using an online database aggregator. The librarian teaches in the classroom, to which the students have brought their laptops.
- The elementary school librarian develops a scope and sequence of information and digital literacy skills along with her counterparts within the district.

She works with the principal to make sure that the library curriculum aligns with the rest of the school's curriculum. The instruction is provided during the teachers' preparation period, and reports are given to the grade-level teacher to facilitate bridging the curricula.

- The university library contains the thesis office. The office director and departmental libraries develop a series of thesis workshops, which they offer in the library for all seniors and graduate students. They also develop a video tutorial, which is streamed from the library's web portal.
- A classroom teacher wants her students to produce a video. She schedules a session for a small group of students with the librarian, who trains the students in camera operation and editing. These students will serve as the video cadre for the class. The teacher provides the librarian with the final videos, to be added to the library collection.
- The librarian serves as an embedded instructional consultant for an instructor. In consultation with the instructor, the librarian produces bibliographies and online tutorials to be posted on the course management system, and conducts virtual reference interviews. During and after the course, the librarian and instructor assess the usefulness of the librarian products and services, and adjust them for the next semester. The instructor also shares his experiences with the members of his department, who decide to establish a department website with library links.
- A librarian is a member of an industry research team. She explains to her teammates how to use Skype and wikis to communicate when out in the field remotely.

As the previous examples demonstrate, you might delegate work to other library staff and can even enlist the help of trained volunteers, particularly for individual coaching. Likewise, the extent and follow-up of collaborative efforts can vary greatly. The more systematically that staffing decisions can be made, the more predictable and efficient will be the instruction, and the easier it will be to assess and adjust the implementation. Moreover, the more consistently that you work with the same personnel, the easier it is to make needed adjustments and build on success.

Space issues

Space impacts teaching and learning, whether that space is explicitly considered or not (Strange and Banning, 2001). Indeed, educator John Dewey stated back in 1933 that "whether we permit chance environments to do the work, or whether we design environments for the purpose makes a great difference" (22), asserting that educational settings are better served by specificity rather than serendipity.

Current literature about learning spaces refers to building pedagogy as "architectural embodiments of educational philosophies" and "layout, location and arrangement of space" as it impacts behavior (Strange and Banning, 2001: 15). Strange and Banning also contrasted the terms "formal learning" (curriculum based, which is often classroom-based intentional opportunities for learning) and "informal learning" (serendipitous human interaction that involves learning, and often occurs outside the typical classroom).

Cannon's 1988 extensive synthesis of research on the impact of the environment on learning provides a starting point for learning space discussion. Basically, contemporary design of learning spaces builds upon an educational philosophy of active and social learning. This approach starts with the student, examines desired outcomes, and plans the physical conditions for an optimum learning environment. Keeping in mind instruction and learning style variances, learning spaces are designed to provide differentiated areas and grouping arrangements. In addition, items within these environments should support modification and customization to reflect users' interests and needs. Oblinger (2006) synthesizes many of the key features of effective learning spaces: flexibility, decentralization, ergonomic comfort, stimulating to the senses, ubiquitous technology.

With the incorporation of digital technology, the definition of learning spaces has changed. Increasingly, the space in which learning occurs has broadened to include cyberspace as well as physical space. Brown (2005) defined learning spaces as spaces that encompass the full range of places in which learning occurs, from real to virtual, from classroom to chat room (p. 12.4).

User needs

Based on learner and social realities, as well as research on effective education, learning spaces need to foster student engagement and active learning. Benchmarks and indicators include student interaction with peers outside class time on readings and assignments and student interaction with faculty outside class time about coursework, research, and other activities. Students find group study more important than do faculty, while faculty consider student-faculty communication more important than do students. Concurrently, students and faculty view learning spaces differently; for example, students view common spaces as more effective learning spaces than do faculty (Bennett, 2007).

Today's students also think that creating content is more important to learning than just consuming content, an attitude supported by current learning theory. To that end, learning spaces need to include production areas and tools (Milne, 2007). These perspectives impact the planning and implementation of learning spaces.

One of the main reasons for re-conceptualizing space is community-building. Increasingly, the notion of a community of learners and practitioners drives education and the business world; research finds that students learn best in community (Oblinger, 2006: 3). The underlying principle is that members with common values and norms can reflect upon their knowledge and improve their performance and impact by building upon one another's expertise. Physical features that foster community-based learning include the following:

- Communication surfaces (e.g., portable SMART Boards, powerwalls, wonder wall [http://wonderwall.msu.edu], tackable/writable walls)
- Open areas with flexible furniture/seating for impromptu meetings/study groups
- Joint work space, project area, and adjustable lighting

The community—and world—in which students live is changing. Major trends include globalization, urbanization, ever-changing technology, environmental issues, communication/information overload. Students must have learning experiences that help them prepare for these global challenges.

Technology trends

In education, technology plays a key role, both in terms of providing resources as well as integrating personal technology devices. Learning spaces also acknowledge the importance of cyberspace, and try to meld the virtual and the physical. Regardless of the learning space, technical requirements must be addressed: terminal/workstation requirements, system platform configurations, electrical demands, network hardware, Internet connectivity issues, and administrative software. Emerging learning area devices include teaching walls, convergent technologies, peripheral accessories and room-scale peripherals, transparent information-capture systems, spaces with memory (e.g., interactive memory wall), IP network videoconferencing, embedded-system versions of operating platforms, learning space systems, software middleware infrastructure, and pervasive computing infrastructure (Milne, 2007). Technology support must be available 24/7, in both physical and online environments, and this needs to be calculated as part of planning and implementation endeavors.

With the incorporation of social networking, another layer of considerations are required: cross-device sharing, parallel awareness, group archiving, and groupware in general. Even computer labs can be modified to meet a greater variety of learning needs, particularly in terms of social interactivity. Seating can be more flexible. More open spaces can be allocated for laptop and other mobile device use. Large screen systems with circular work areas can support group projects. Glass-enclosed tech conference spaces can ensure privacy while maintaining supervision. Production and project areas can be used for one-time and ongoing team endeavors. Additional security and privacy measures (including issues of remote access) also need to be taken with Web 2.0 incorporation.

On a grander scale, virtual worlds enable learners to experience situated learning in three dimensions, or a facsimile thereof. Visual immersion systems, from head-mounted visual systems to 3D "caves," enable learners to experience a visual simulated environment. These systems can sense the learners' movements, and adjust the visual components accordingly. Individuals with physical limitations can approximate movement in real situations (Roblyer and Doering, 2009).

Physical and virtual communities of practice are likely to have different learning experiences. You will need to reconcile these differences with the intent of optimizing each learning space; instructional design incorporating technology can offer successful solutions. Unique technology-enhanced instruction will be detailed in Chapter 7.

Planning and assessment

Think of designing learning spaces as a product to develop rather than a space to be changed. The product is based on the institution's values about learning. In terms of planning learning spaces, broad-based input and ownership have become accepted practice. Input may be done through photo surveys, not just committee meetings. Denison University also developed a set of guiding principles in planning learning spaces: support diverse learning styles, provide versatile space, comfort and attractiveness, information richness, technology reliability, continuous maintenance, continuous access, effective use, and sufficient resources.

Assessment of learning spaces should be an ongoing process but is often overlooked. Several factors need to be addressed in assessment endeavors: (1) determining the focus: cost analysis, facilities management, impact on teaching and/or learning (from individual or institutional level), interaction between people, human-physical space interaction, identifying the spaces to assess; (2) determining usage: formal versus informaal learning, frequency and timing of usage, demographics of users—and nonusers.

Libraries as learning spaces

Within many institutions, the chief service unit that has embraced the concept of intentional, redesigned learning space is the library, which is increasingly labeled an "information commons" or "learning commons." Because libraries cross curricular lines, and promote student-directed learning, these spaces serve as models for needs-based, flexible learning spaces. Some of the salient features include the following:

- Differentiated spaces for individual and group work, some with presentation/projection capabilities; some classrooms may also be available
- Mix of office- and leisure-style furniture (including beanbags and diner booths), much of which may be moved

- Pervasive technology, including hundreds of computers with a variety of software programs, WiFi capability, large-screen dynamic display/signage, multimedia consumption, and production areas
- Service centers: reference, technology, writing, thesis/research assistance, instructional design, faculty development
- Food and supply areas
- Recreation/entertainment venues

Librarians often bridge physical space and cyberspace through digital reference service, web tutorials, online repositories of learning objects, and links to course work. Further findings about library commons may be found in Henning's 2005 report (http://jhenning.law.uvic.ca/final_report.html).

The librarian is more likely to instruct in the library than elsewhere. If the library is heavily booked, then scheduling can be more difficult, possibly limiting instructional opportunities. Instructing in the library also facilitates the learners' use of the library's collection. A presentation area facilitates large-group instruction, and smaller conference rooms facilitate interactive, just-in-time targeted instruction. The number and quality of computers in the learning space determines how that technology will be incorporated into instruction, from having the librarian demonstrate online information using skills while the students watch to having each learner do hands-on online learning activities. Virtual learning spaces facilitate document sharing and can make it more convenient for all parties, especially those who live at a distance; however, everyone needs stable connectivity.

Reference interviews are an interesting case in that reference librarians usually do not determine the curriculum, although they try to align with and support the organization's curriculum. Especially in large institutions with several librarians, it is likely that each librarian is a subject specialist, and probably does not know other content area assignments or resources well. In these cases, reference consultations are more likely to be effective; the spaces for such consultations may include the traditional reference desk, the librarian's office, the classroom, or online. Usually for in-depth instruction, private space is preferable.

University libraries have tended to lead in library learning space innovations and best practice, largely because they have the capacity to so do, and because the nature of post-secondary education allows for more flexible learning venues. The following websites showcase representative efforts by university libraries as they reconfigure space for twenty-first-century learning.

- Eckerd College Armacost Library: http://www.eckerd.edu/librarydedication/
- Murdoch University Information Commons: http://wwwlib.murdoch.edu .au/
- Northwestern University Information Commons: http://www.library .northwestern.edu/ic/

- Oregon State University Libraries: http://osulibrary.oregonstate.edu/learning_spaces.html
- Oxford Brookes University Blended Learning Landscape: http://bejlt.brookes.ac.uk/vol1/volume1issue3/perspective/francis_raftery.pdf
- University of Georgia Student Learning Center: http://www.slc.uga.edu/

Overview of instructional strategies

The teaching aspect of instructional design focuses on *how* students gain that knowledge and skills: through the input of learning activities that set information within a learning environment in which students can actively engage with the material.

With these premises, the role of the instructor becomes more the role of a facilitator or change agent, guiding the process more than delivering the content. The newest term for instructional designer is "knowledge engineer." These procedures cross delivery methods, as they can be face-to-face role-plays or web-based tutorials. As an instructor, you provide a safe and positive learning climate, structure the setting to facilitate joint planning, assess the learners' needs and interests in order to identify objectives and craft learning activities, and then implement and assess the activities. In addition, instruction and learning should be considered as a self-reflective system. Both you and learners bring prior experience. All of you need to engage with one another and the content at hand. The learner must somehow change, hopefully in a manner that you can discern. This series of thoughts and actions is assessed in order to improve the system. Indeed, throughout instruction, you need to assess the process, the product, and the people involved.

Probably the most effective instructional strategy is one that most closely resembles the situation in which learners apply their new knowledge and skills. For this reason, apprenticeships continue as a popular method for learning a skill. The reference desk is a good example of this practice. However, such one-on-one or small-group training is labor- and time-intensive, and does not scale up well. In addition, when the consequences of poor performance by novices, such as neophyte surgeons and pilots, are costly, simulations provide approximate experiences without the dangers. Access to instruction can also pose problems and lead to educational inequalities.

Structuring instructional strategies

For any given learning outcome, a series of processes are needed to guide learners to accomplish that outcome. At the most fundamental level, you present the outcome and curriculum to be learned, show how to accomplish the outcome, provide opportunities for learners to understand and practice, monitor learning, and provide feedback (such as interventions or support) so that learners have a fair chance to succeed. To a certain extent, the interaction among you, the learner, and the curriculum resembles the fundamental process of engagement with information: an information cycle.

Pre-engagement

You—the instructor—and the learners come to the curriculum "table" with prior background, capabilities, and knowledge. All of you are also situated in some specific time-space continuum, which impacts the potential engagement.

Origin of need

What causes the parties to meet? The origin of need may be internally or externally motivated. K–12 schooling is required, so one might say that the need is societal and community based. Postsecondary education need might arise from a personal career choice that requires training or a desire to fulfill familial or social expectations. The workplace may require training, or an employee may self-identify a learning need. Informal education is usually personally motivated, such as planning for retirement or learning how to take better photos. Instructors are curriculum experts who want or need to share their expertise, and may be representatives of an organization or institution that wants to educate their constituents. Librarians are often both content and process experts.

Task determination

The learning task may be defined as the end product or a result that demonstrates the learner's competence. It is the result of a negotiated process by the relevant stakeholders. The curriculum leads to the outcome, with accompanying standards, indicators, and objectives, each of which involves stakeholders to some extent. The learning task and its standard usually focus on just one or two outcome objectives, and may be established externally to the organization (such as scoring 500 or better on the Test of English as a Foreign Language [TOEFL]) or internally determined at one of several levels: from one class session to an institutional graduation requirement. Nevertheless, a course within a program's curriculum is the normal level at which the learning task is stipulated, and is normally designed by the instructor or the curriculum coordinator.

Table 6.3 gives some representative learning objectives and learning tasks.

It is obvious that the learner's self-determination of the task might not align with the instructor or organization, in which case the results will probably be less than stellar. For instance, a person might define his learning task as "acing the exam" or "figuring out what the teacher wants" or "getting that cute girl to notice me." In that respect, you need to make sure to communicate the learning

Table 6.3	Learning objectives and learning tasks
Objectives	**Learning task**
Locate information about an artistic movement. Critically select information about an artistic movement. Identify the significance of a specific artistic movement, including its artists, achievements, and influences. Apply art principles in designing a brochure.	Design an exhibit brochure describing an artistic movement.
Identify and sequence steps to make a repair. Write clear directions.	Develop a set of instructions for a specific household repair procedure.
Locate textual and visual information about a significant young adult author. Critically select textual and visual information about a significant young adult author. Identify significant facts and major works of an author. Appropriately use the features of a graphic comic to communicate information. Correctly cite sources of information.	Create a graphic comic about a significant young adult author.
Locate information about a censorship issue. Critically select information about a censorship issue. Orally discuss pros and cons relative to censorship.	Debate censorship issues.
Locate foreign folktales. Recount a foreign folktale Transform a folktale into dramatic form. Communicate meaningfully in a foreign language.	Dramatize a foreign folktale in the original language.
Locate information about weight control. Critically select information about weight control. Accurately calculate percentages and ratios. Represent and manipulate data in spreadsheet form.	Develop a weight control plan.
Locate information about a musical instrument. Critically select information about a musical instrument. Compare characteristics of different musical instruments.	Develop a set of cards about a specific musical instrument, each card representing one aspect. Play "go fish" game using the cards.
Locate textual and visual information about dinosaurs. Critically select textual and visual information about dinosaurs. Identify and categorize characteristics of specific dinosaurs. Describe the characteristics and use of a nature field guide.	Create an interactive dinosaur field guide.

Table 6.3 Learning objectives and learning tasks *(continued)*	
Objectives	Learning task
Locate information about economics for a specific political region. Critically select information about economics for a specific political region. Identify factors that contribute to the economic conditions of a specific political region. Analyze and compare economic factors. Use map legends to describe geographic features.	Create a mashup linking geography and an economic factor.

task clearly, and motivate the learner to acknowledge and accept that learning task. The most obvious approach is to provide a rationale for doing the learning task at the start of the lesson. For example, several reasons undergird the learning task of citing sources of information correctly: to credit the idea's creator, to document the learner's research process, to make it easier for the learner and others to read the cited information, to foster responsible use of information, and to avoid accusations of plagiarism. Each reason may resonate for individual learners, depending on their attitude and motivation. Finding out the learner's perspective on the task, and looking for overarching mutual objectives, can foster engagement and cooperation.

First contact

The precursor to contact with the specific curriculum is the decision to participate in the curriculum as a whole. The learning task may be first in a series of sessions, or the learner may have experienced several activities prior to the one at hand. In the latter situation, the learner's attitude will be influenced by the previous experiences. If the learner joins a preexisting group of people that, too, will impact the first contact since socialization is part of the learning experience. The new learner will need to find his place with an established group dynamic.

In any case, the first contact with a specific learning task starts with awareness: gaining the learner's attention. In e-learning situations, the instructor sets up the structures that provide stimuli for the information-interaction process, but the student might have to proactively seek the stimulus, and can be distracted by other stimuli. As with any type of outside stimulus, the learner becomes aware of stimuli through his or her senses, and makes decisions as to whether to ignore the stimuli or pay attention to them. What causes the learner to pay attention? Novelty (such as an unknown sound) or impact (such as a protruding nail or changing sports rules for an athlete).

|||||||||||||||||||||||||||||||||||||||||||||||||||||||||||||||||||||||||||||||||||||||||||||||||||||||||||||||||||||||||

Processing the curriculum

Motivation is key at this point too; without it, persons will not engage with the curricular stimuli. Motivation draws from prior experience, and is contextually situated: what is happening to the person at the time that the stimulus is sensed. Motivation may be external (such as getting good grades or looking good in front of others) or internal. Motivation involves feelings; a pleasant surprise can stimulate the person to process the information and derive pleasure from figuring out the surprise. On the other hand, too much emotion, such as overwhelming fear, can paralyze a person's processing. Furthermore, even if the curriculum makes sense, the question remains: "Does it have meaning?" Is it relevant? The answer to this question is a personal judgment call, but can be influenced by your efforts to motivate the learner.

To help guide instruction and facilitate continuity of learning, you should ask learners to recall relevant prior knowledge. This process helps focus learner attention and connect with prior experience. It also helps you determine whether a quick review is needed before introducing new information. You also must establish a baseline of knowledge, diagnose learners to determine whether they have the prerequisite knowledge and skills, and then decide whether to: reshift the baseline, perhaps starting instruction at a lower level of knowledge; provide targeted remediation for those learners who do not meet that baseline (which is most likely to happen if technology constitutes part of the instructional strategy); or arrange learners into small collaborative groups in which learners can complement each others' knowledge and skills.

For persons to successfully process the curriculum, they must be able to intellectually access that curriculum (make sense of it), which entails both biological processes as well as mental and psychological processes. They have to decode it (that is, determine the communication protocols of linguistics, visual principles, etc.) and understand the content being communicated (that is, the vocabulary, semiotics, concepts, etc.). Some people can process abstract information more easily than concrete information, and vice versa. When information is novel, being able to build on well-developed processing methods can help individuals to pay more attention to the content. On the other hand, when the content is familiar, the person can focus attention on processing in novel ways. Part of the instructional strategy involves deciding what type of knowledge to focus on: declarative or procedural, for instance.

Table 6.4 shows representative instructional strategies to help learners process curricula (Smith and Ragan, 2005).

For you to assess whether learners have processed the information appropriately, you need to check for understanding by eliciting some kind of external expression of attitude or behavior. It is not enough to ask the question "Do you understand me?" The difficulty is that internal processing for comprehension

Table 6.4	Instructional strategies by type of knowledge	
Type of knowledge	**Instructional strategies**	**Evidence of learning**
Declarative knowledge	Link prior knowledge to new knowledge (e.g., concept maps). Organize information (e.g., graphic organizers). Elaborate/give details about the new knowledge (e.g., analogies, imagery).	Accurate and detailed concept map; correct paper-and-pencil test answers
Conceptual knowledge	Use a concept attainment model: provide matched examples and non-examples; learners make hypotheses about the underlying concept.	Increasingly accurate student-generated hypotheses and examples
Procedural knowledge	Chunk a process into stages or phases. Demonstrate one stage, and have learners practice it. Then demonstrate the next stage, and so on, until the entire process is covered.	Process listed, traced, or performed accurately and thoroughly
Problem solving	Simulate the problem. Principles may be presented at the beginning, with learners testing the principles via test cases (deductive learning), or learners may explore the simulation and figure out the principles (inductive learning).	Correctly solved problem with appropriate process
Cognitive strategy	Overview the strategy's specific steps, model the strategy (and think aloud), give examples/non-examples of applying the strategy. Guide the learner through a practice cognitive strategy (e.g., researching a topic).	Accurate and thorough flow chart; final product and self-reflection; I-Search paper
Attitude learning	Model desired behavior. Have learners role-play desired behavior, and process feelings, attitudes, behaviors, consequences. Reinforce desired behavior.	Self-assessment and peer assessment; observation of behavior
Psychomotor skills	1. Explain the skill and the sequence of steps. 2. Model skill, and have learners physically practice skill. 3. Coach learner practice until skills are done automatically and flawlessly.	1. Described skill and listed steps 2. Guided skill performance 3. Automatic skill performance

does not equate to performance. Only when you can find out what is happening internally for the learner can you adjust your instruction to optimize learning. Some ways to check for understanding include the following:

- Asking learners to identify concepts that are still unclear to them
- Pairing learners to verbally explain the content to each other, or ask each other questions about the content

- Having learners paraphrase the information
- Having learners read aloud a text, and do a "think aloud" about it
- Having learners ask questions about the content
- Using a cloze process, whereby learners fill in study guide blanks with the key terms

Information literacy processing can be easy to assess if the learner can demonstrate understanding by performing the information-using behavior: pointing to the call number, identifying an appropriate reference source to use, highlighting keywords in a sentence. Information literacy also involves metacognition: thinking about thinking, how one learns. When you model metacognitive processes such as talking aloud or jotting down notes as you encounter new information, you are showing learners how to externalize their thinking process.

In any group, capabilities and prior learning experiences vary, so you need to provide interventions that address individual processing needs. For instance, the cognitive load may overwhelm working memory so that learning suffers. Misanchuk (1992) provides several instructional strategies to lessen cognitive load:

- Spread the information across senses: complement text with visuals or auditory information.
- Segment the information into smaller chunks or steps.
- Eliminate extraneous information.
- Start by teaching the essential features/facts/rules. Later add details and exemptions.
- Provide advance cues, such as graphic organizers, for how to process information.

More generically, strategies that provide more of the structure and details so that the learner does not have to construct so much meaning himself or herself ameliorate cognitive load. However, extremes of this instructional approach can lead to rote or dependent learning, so they should be used only when prior knowledge and learning skills are limited. As learners become more competent, encourage them to add their own ideas or transfer the skill to other contexts.

Evaluating curricular information

Next, the learner relates the "new" information with his or her existing knowledge. Learning only happens when the curricular information is understandable as well as new/novel or contradicting existing knowledge; a disequilibrium exists. In response, the person tries to regain equilibrium by either rejecting or adding the new information, or reconciling it with current information (which might result in rejecting or modifying the existing information). In addition, the more relevant and important the curricular information (both mentally and psychologically), the greater impact the learning (or decision to *not* learn) has. Both cognitive and affective factors come into play. For instance, if the person dislikes the instructor, then the curriculum itself may be rejected. On the other hand, if a new discovery delights a person, old ideas might be easily shed.

As with the processing step, help learners grapple with new information intellectually and psychologically, and incorporate it into their long-term memory for later action. Include providing criteria for evaluation information, tools for comparing such as T-charts, and additional resources to reinforce the validity of the new information. When you know what is personally meaningful to learners, you can better understand why they might reject or have a difficult time accepting new information, and you can provide ways to negotiate and accept the new information. For instance, you might have to convince learners that using subscription databases instead of Wikipedia is worth the supposed extra time because of the higher quality and more in-depth nature of the retrieved information, and that it takes less time in the long run to find the most relevant information. You can also offer external incentives for accepting the new information, such as grades and career opportunities.

Manipulating curricular information

You should also provide opportunities for learners to *do* something with the curricular information. Typically, doing implies an externalization process: the next part of the information cycle as it applies to learning. If the person just parrots back that information, no change occurs. On the other hand, for learning to occur, that information needs to be transformed in some way: through interpretation, organization, synthesis, reformatting, relating. In any case, information manipulation consists of four procedural skills:

1. Extracting the information
2. Deciding how to represent it
3. Determining the method of manipulating it
4. Knowing how to do the manipulation

Throughout this surprisingly complex interaction with information, individuals need to make decisions that are based on prior knowledge—or lack thereof. They cannot continue to interact and act unless they have the prerequisite knowledge and skills to build upon.

In formal educational situations, instructors tend to stipulate the parameters for the learners to manipulate the information: the basis of the learning task. For any of the four procedural skills, you need to make sure that students have the intellectual and physical tools necessary to complete each task. As with processing information, finely targeted diagnostic abilities are called for, as well as interventions that help students gain those skills. In some cases, the focus of learning is actually in such manipulating skills. For instance, students may know about biomes, but now have to extract pertinent information about biomes from a given article about birds. You might need to explain how to take notes or locate key phrases in a text. Likewise, you might focus on showing students how to create a concept map as a way to represent their knowledge. Provide opportunities for learners to explore and practice these manipulation tasks so they can do them independently, and demonstrate their competence in achieving the ultimate learning task.

Technology provides many tools for manipulating information. In fact, computers were created originally to compute: to "crunch" or process numbers. Ideally, technology can do the "grunt" or mechanical work so that learners can focus on the cognitive work. It should be noted that technology can also help store and retrieve information for use. We also need to remember that additional time may be needed for learners to practice using the technology tool itself, regardless of the content to be manipulated. Here are just a few technological tools and ways that they help learners manipulate information.

- **Spreadsheets** enable one to organize and sort information data by category, create and use formulas, and generate charts. Spreadsheets can be used to test hypotheses and make predictions. For instance, students can determine if household income might be correlated to infant mortality or other health issues.
- **Databases** enable one to organize and sort information data by category, and link related databases of information such as demographics and politics. Databases help one test hypotheses and analyze groups of data. For instance, a database of plants and chemicals might lead to medicinal discoveries.
- **Presentation tools** (e.g., PowerPoint, Keynote, HyperStudio) enable one to organize and sequence information, and combine media to more effectively represent knowledge. Presentation tools can be used to outline information and relate ideas. For instance, a PowerPoint presentation can aid a person in reporting on an author's life.
- **Graphic programs** (e.g., PhotoShop, Illustrator, iPhoto) enable one to produce and modify images. Graphic programs foster visual literacy. For instance, students can see how different color schemes can affect perceptions about interior design.
- **Audio tools** (e.g., Audacity, GarageBand) enable one to record, capture, and manipulate sounds. Audio applications foster aural literacy so that one can be used to perceive poetic rhythm or distinguish linguistic features. For

instance, students can use different music to convey different interpretations of an advertisement.

- **Video tools** (e.g., Movie Maker, Photo Story, iMovie, Premiere) enable one to record, capture, and manipulate a combination of sound, image, and movement (image in space and time). Video tools help one process realistic information and procedures such as chemical reactions. For instance, students can make a video to explain how to repair a car.

Identifying which technology is the most appropriate to manipulate information requires learning about the technology itself. For instance, as learners make sense of a video and its visual language, they are better poised to use video to manipulate information. If the focus of learning is on creating a video, students experience what processes are involved, and how they impact the video product. They become fluent in the "language" and "grammar" of video (and sound and image) so that they can comprehend its meaning and ways to manipulate that meaning more subtly.

While students can explore different technologies on their own, testing which media work best, you can mandate appropriate technologies as you understand how each technology operates. In such situations, students can focus on the information manipulation rather than on the technology manipulation. However, you would be remiss if you did not point out the features of the technology on hand so that students can learn how to identify appropriate technologies independently. More details about incorporating technology are provided in Chapter 7.

Acting on information

Still another instructional decision needs to be made after the manipulation: how to have learners act upon that information, if at all. While curriculum may be meaningful and interesting in itself, such as the elegance of a mathematical proof, it derives power when contextualized and related to other information. Learners may apply the information to a familiar or novel situation, they might solve a problem or answer a question, or they might change their environment or themselves. In terms of the information cycle, the individual becomes the creator or initiator. Taking the curriculum that has been the focus of attention, the learner links it to other information or source of information, including other people. The act can also be the generation of new information. The cycle spirals. Not only does the information have meaning, but the learning itself gains meaning as it impacts the individual, who can then impact others.

As an instructor, you prime the action pump by identifying the learning task in the first place, which also motivates the student to engage with the information and resolve the underlying problem. You can also critique—and help learners self-critique—their efforts with the intent of reaching an optimal conclusion. For instance, a student might know how chemicals react, and might know how to use the appropriate equipment, but still might have a chemical spill that the instructor might need to address—and help students to learn how to deal with. Alternatively, a student might know how to create a webpage with relevant content, but might still need to submit the material for you to upload onto the server, or learn how to upload the information independently.

One of the most obvious ways to act upon curricular information is to communicate it. With the advent of digital technology, today's learners have many more opportunities to communicate with a wide and authentic audience. Students passing on their learning to others so that they, in turn, can learn is an empowering experience for all parties. That communication is usually in the form of a product: a letter, a research paper, a presentation, a skit, a timeline, and so on. Particularly if the product is targeted to an audience, an effective way to assess learning is to assess the reaction of the audience: Do they comprehend the message? Do they respond to the message? Are they persuaded by the message?

An extension of communicating the new learning is to teach it. This process requires not only that learners know the curriculum, but that they value it enough to want others to learn it. Such learners also have to use metacognitive processes in reflecting upon how they learned the curriculum so that they can optimize the learning experience for others. Provide opportunities for student teaching through peer coaching and service learning. Consider enlisting expert learners as library aides.

Acting on curricular information frequently involves solving problems, particularly for novel situations. Indeed, one model of instructional design is problem-based learning. The most obvious examples draw from sciences: solving a quadratic equation that the learner has not seen before, identifying the elements of an unknown chemical mixture, repairing a car. A research report can be construed as a problem-solving process as learners pose a question that involves gathering, analyzing, and organizing information in order to answer the question.

Another obvious way to act upon the new learning is to apply it, for example, to new situations or environments. One increasingly popular way to apply learning authentically is through service learning: learners volunteer to help community groups in their curricular area. As they experience the application of new knowledge in the concrete setting, learners can compare practice and theory throughout the experience. While such opportunities can be very powerful for both learners and the community, they can be very labor-intensive for instructors because they require good alignment with the curriculum, appropriate placement, possible travel to the service site, possible training of the community, as well as ongoing monitoring of the learner and the service setting. In that respect, you can control such service learning if it occurs at your own work site. You might also have good working relationships with other library settings, which facilitate placement and assessment.

Regardless of the action, it often constitutes the basis for the summative, or final, assessment. At that point, you determine the extent and quality of the learning, as well as assess your own instructional design. As noted in the preplanning stage, the summative assessment should already be in place so that the learners know ahead of time how they will be evaluated, and can use that assessment tool as a way to self-monitor their own learning along the way, and make adjustments accordingly. Use that same assessment tool to give formative feedback to the learner.

Grouping of instruction

When designing instructional strategies, you must determine how to group learners. This decision is based on the curriculum, the learning objective, the learners, and the learning environment.

Most curricula can support a variety of groupings. However, some curricula lend themselves to different scales. For instance, craftsmen may follow an individual learner apprenticeship (such as glassblowing), and mentoring engages an expert and one neophyte. At the other end of the spectrum, basic real estate training could be presented to hundreds of learners simultaneously.

Within a curriculum program, instruction is typically divided into courses, which may range in size from a handful to a large lecture room full of people. The type of course dictates the size of that group: individual, directed study and site-specific field experience, small group seminars that foster in-depth interaction, hands-on lab courses of a couple dozen learners using specialized equipment, large lecture courses with several study groups within.

For an individual learning task, you might arrange learners in different group configurations depending on the learning objective. For declarative knowledge or demonstrating, you would usually address the group as a whole. Other learning experiences are better suited to small groups of four to seven members: these include exploring an issue, role-playing, tutoring, case study, literature circles, and problem solving. When independent knowledge, such as writing, is needed, individual learning activities may be in order. Other group arrangements exist:

- Pair-share to exchange perspectives and facilitate peer review of student work
- Triads to pool ideas and develop leadership skills
- Panel to present different points of view
- Inner circle and outer observation circle (fish bowl) to reflect and listen actively

The most common way to learn socially is through collaboration: typically, small groups working together toward a common goal or solution. Other features of collaborative learning include group and individual accountability, distributed leadership, and group autonomy. Collaboration provides opportunities for individuals to think aloud and engage both intellectually and emotionally, and incorporates both academic and social objectives. Another basic tenet of collaborative learning is that students have significant control over learning through autonomy and key decision making.

It should be noted that collaboration is a set of learned skills in itself. For individuals to work together as a group effectively, all members need to share information, listen, follow directions, keep on track, clarify and check for information, share leadership and decision making, and show respect (Dishon and O'Leary, 1998). While collaboration can be learned informally, you should provide explicit instruction and feedback for each skill, and teach self-governing techniques. Monitoring is close and extensive, and groups spend significant time discussing group dynamics and brainstorming ways to improve group management. Each group member should have a specific function or role, and each group member needs to respect one another and their ideas. A good breakdown of member roles follows:

- Facilitator, who makes sure all members participate
- Reporter, who records the discussion
- Timekeeper, who keeps the group on task and watches the time
- Materials handler, who gets any resources needed and keeps track of them
- Assessor, who makes sure that social skills are used
- Checker, who makes sure that all members get the right information

During the activity, you should "float" between groups to monitor the class climate and be available to address group concerns as needed. At the end of the exercise, each group should "report out," that is, share their findings with the rest of the learners. You can then facilitate a large-group discussion to analyze the findings and the process.

Decisions about instructional grouping also involve the facility itself. For instance, a presentation of declarative knowledge might work better if peers do not interact, in which case a theater-style arrangement is effective. On the other hand, if social skills constitute part of the learning objective, then small groups around a circular table is more effective. For a small seminar in which all-group discussion facilitates learning, then a seating arrangement of one large circle, with the instructor sitting alongside, is preferable. In some cases, permanent seating, such as in a lecture hall, can constrain how you can group learning activities.

Scaffolding learning

As noted earlier, you must factor in learner variables, and provide scaffolding to bridge learning gaps. For instance, to deal with the English learner, you might provide relevant information that is written in the student's home language or is communicated visually rather than in text. If that class has several students with the same home language, you might well locate alternative texts in that language for the entire year. You can analyze prior instructional designs and delivery to identify probable problem areas in order to choose more understandable resources or demonstrate desired skills more clearly so that learners will be more likely to engage meaningfully in the task. For instance, if students are supposed to write a haiku about weather, but do not know what a haiku is, you can provide that information via an information sheet, book reference, online tutorial, or website. Depending on what access learners have to digital information, you can determine what format is more useful and accessible to the learner.

Determining what scaffold to use and how to provide it are complex decisions. Even if you thoughtfully set up instruction and the learning environment to include scaffolds to differentiate learning with an intent to provide universal instructional design, those scaffolds might not work with a specific student in a specific situation. For instance, a student might get distracted by blinking images. Perhaps the topic is a sensitive one for the student. For example, a student could be sensitive to the topic of cancer if her mother died from it. What if the student breaks her wrist and is supposed to type? In these unforeseen cases, scaffolding is usually called an intervention, and is done on a case-by-case situation. You need to have a deep understanding of subject matter and associated processes in order to bridge the gap between learners and the intended goal, to help learners demonstrate competence.

Fortunately, you are not alone in this process of scaffolding. For one thing, students themselves may be able to identify their own gaps. This process of being able to think about and articulate learning processes is called metacognition, and is another skill that students should learn. The more they can identify learning gaps and self-regulate their learning processes, the more able students are to take responsibility and control their learning. Along with identifying the learning gap, if students can identify a way to bridge that gap themselves, they can become self-sufficient learners.

Sometimes processing requires external scaffolding. In that respect, interaction is not just between the learner and the curriculum but also between learners as intermediaries or gap-bridgers. Learners may ask for help from other people: "What does this word mean?" "Can you open this file?" Learners might consult other sources, such as dictionaries or encyclopedias, to help them understand the information. They might use tools to highlight passages or draw diagrams to better comprehend the information. As a librarian, you are uniquely trained to make suggestions about external sources of help.

Differentiated instructional strategies

As you structure and monitor learning activities, diagnose the obstacles and facilitating factors of learning, which may apply to the entire learning group or may differ from individual to individual. Based on those diagnostic assessments, you can then optimize the learning situation.

To the degree that the learning group is homogeneous, you can design instruction from the start to address the group's needs, such as a neighborhood troop of ten-year-old Girl Scouts who want to earn the Books badge. Even within that group, reading interests and skills differ. When the group varies along several dimensions—such as age, physical differences, language, geography, values—then you have to use a more context-neutral, didactic instructional strategy; design small-group collaborative learning activities; or provide a rich set of resources, activities, and assessments from which learners can choose.

Taken to the nth degree, you could design instructional strategies that are individualized and personalized. This practice is not only time-consuming and labor-intensive, but may actually be less effective in the long run because it does not enable people to experience different ways of interacting and learning. It is more productive and effective to incorporate personalization at the feedback stage, giving each student specific recommendations for improving learning within the context of the specific action within a specific situation.

Universal instructional strategy design is a good practice to try to engage and support all learners. For instance, by showing an image, captioning it, and verbally describing it, you can address both physical differences and learning-style preferences.

- Provide clear information and expectations about content, technical aspects, procedures, participation, assessment, available support.
- Get to know the students, and help them learn about one another.
- Create a positive class climate. Make learning safe and comfortable.
- Make the structure of the class explicit. Structure learning for meaning. Bring in socio-cultural differences rather than masking them. Help students to connect content to their own environments.
- Explain the "big picture" and also show real-life concrete applications.
- Design authentic learning tasks that are personally meaningful.
- Provide learner choice in resources, activities, and ways to assess learning.
- Let learners assume differentiated roles within small-group activities.
- Incorporate both competitive and collaborative learning activities.
- Help learners clarify and justify their understanding. Encourage study groups.
- Emphasize the importance of both the process (means) and the product (ends).
- Foster curiosity, persistence, and pursuit of excellence.
- Address both the cognitive and affective domains of learning.
- Provide a safe learning environment in which students can take intellectual risks and take control of personal learning.

- Provide support and scaffolding for learners as needed.
- Give learners time to process and evaluate information.
- Give timely and specific feedback throughout instruction.
- Help students self-monitor and express their learning in several ways.
- Give learners a voice in helping shape instructional design and generating knowledge.

Nevertheless, your instructional strategies should take into account the needs of learner populations who differ from the majority or typical population. Some of these differences have already been mentioned in Chapter 3. In some cases, the entire learning group has a common characteristic, such as Spanish speakers who are learning English or sixth-grade students who have cerebral palsy. In other cases only a few learners within the class may have that characteristic, so you may need to differentiate instruction to accommodate those differences.

Instructional strategies for learners with disabilities

The University of Illinois at Urbana-Champaign's Center for Disability Resources and Educational Services offers technology-related instructional strategies that are disability specific (http://www.disability.uiuc.edu/page.php?id=38). Other organizations that focus on instruction to these populations include the Association for Persons in Supported Employment (http://apse.org/), Learning Disabilities Association of America (http://www.ldaamerica.org/), and the University of Washington's DO-IT website (http://www.washington.edu/doit/). With information from these and other experts, you can develop instructional strategies that can be accessed by *all* populations.

As an example of instructional strategies that are effective with specific populations, Akin and MacKinney (2004) provide an excellent introduction to the needs of children with autism—and ways you can help them. They assert that the ideal 30-minute session should include routine, repetition, and redundancy. Some of the instructional strategies they mentioned follow.

- Repeat related reading, particularly of storybooks.
- Use concrete social stories to help model appropriate behavior.
- Instruct using a variety of formats: comics, audiocassettes, software, puppets, toys, and manipulatives.
- Emphasize visual stimulation rather than auditory stimulation.
- Incorporate songs with motion.
- Incorporate computer technology, which extends children's attention span.
- Plan supplemental activities as a backup.
- Encourage peer tutoring, if tutors are well trained.
- Provide ending rituals.

Culture-sensitive instructional strategies

As learning populations become increasingly diverse, particularly in distance education, you need to factor cultural dimensions into your instructional strategies. Domer and Gorman (2006) offer several useful suggestions, which are described in the paragraphs that follow.

Student-Teacher Relations. Learners from high power-distance cultures expect formal, hierarchical relationships with their teachers. To ease their stress in more egalitarian or constructivist courses, clearly and explicitly define your role, and work with students to make clear decisions about course expectations. Personal acknowledgment rituals and relationships can also counterbalance power distance formality (Gurubatham, 2005). Tell students the how to address you (e.g., Professor Ramirez, Dr. R., Paulo). Traditional males may feel uncomfortable having a female instructor; providing information about the instructor's expertise and status, along with testimonials from high-status males, can further elevate a female teacher's credibility. Students who are shy about asking for help should have several options available: confidential e-mail, intermediation by a course student representative/ spokesperson, peer assistance, referrals to resources such as online tutorials. You can preemptively help this situation by frequently checking for understanding (e.g., short online quizzes and quick writes) and giving all students immediate feedback.

Topics of Discussion. Be aware of possible taboo subjects. This issue might emerge in health issues where gendered practices might inhibit student discussion. Consult your peers in relevant countries to find out ahead of time what topics might be sensitive to your learners. Provide accommodations for alternative topics, resources, or ways of learning so as not to disadvantage affected learners. In almost all cases, connecting course concepts with real-world context and applications helps all learners, not just field-dependent ones.

Choice of Resources. In most cases, instructors choose the material to be covered in a course or training. Craig's training handbook (1996) states that selection or filtering processes may reflect cultural bias that might disadvantage some international students; specific ideas might be supported and others omitted, thus shutting down opposing viewpoints. Even a simple factor of choosing examples reflecting only urban practice might ignore the needs of students working in rural areas. At the least, enable students to choose from a wide spectrum of reading materials reflecting a variety of perspectives. It should be noted that students tend to find and understand web-based information more quickly when the content is created by designers from their own cultures (Faiola and Matei, 2005). Alternatively, permit students to seek self-relevant sources. This latter approach might trouble some instructors who want to control students' reading materials, which, in itself, reflects a certain cultural value; however, most librarians relish this opportunity to provide choice and help students learn how to evaluate resources. Likewise, in some cultures, such as China, students typically read only what the instructor chooses, so self-determination of materials can be uncomfortable for them at first. Furthermore, as they seek relevant resources, many non-U.S. students have little experience using academic libraries and may hesitate before asking librarians for assistance (Laroche, 2003). Therefore, you may need to assure such students that your job is to help them.

Learner Participation. Again, clear expectations and course norms from the first contact will help reduce learner confusion and distress (Laroche, 2003). If the student population includes a mix of cultures, then a corresponding combination of individual and collaborative activities would be appropriate. Alternatively, you can provide students with options to do work independently or with others. To accommodate learners from collective cultures, you might need to initiate discussion or start groups off when introducing problem-based learning; step-by-step guidelines also facilitate field-dependent learners. In any case, the e-learning environment should be safe and comfortable for all learners.

Learning Activities. Probably the best solution for culturally sensitive activities is inclusive instructional design that accommodates *all* students. Here are some other specific suggestions, based on Rapoport's (2008) work:

- Some students are not used to self-directed learning. Rather than telling students the answer, provide process simulations that can be used to find answers.
- Students may be accustomed to rote learning facts, rather than applying skills. Help students apply general principles to a variety of research situations by integrating case studies.
- Students might not be used to critically evaluating information. Provide checklists or criteria for students to use in evaluating sources.
- Many students are only interested in what is needed to pass exams (achievement orientation). Invite online speakers who emphasize the importance of knowledge and skills for lifelong success as well as immediate career advancement.

In some cases, students need to adjust to the targeted culture, be it the specific workplace or teaching as a whole. Lopez-Valadez and colleagues (1985) offer the following ideas that can facilitate the transition: produce videotapes of appropriate and inappropriate workplace behavior, which can facilitate student discussion; enable students to listen to or read job interviews; and seek opportunities for students to combine course e-learning and internships.

Cultural adaptation process

In researching cross-cultural e-learning, Edmundson (2007) developed a two-pronged approach in her cultural adaptation process (CAP) model of instructional design accommodation in order to address cultural differences both between the instructor and students as well as among the student population. One prong focuses on the learner, and the other prong analyzes the course. Edmundson posits a four-step process, aligned with the complexity of the content.

1. Evaluate the content along a continuum from simple, core information (such as basic procedures and products) to complex knowledge and soft skills (such as project management and conflict resolution). The e-learning delivery dimension can range from one-way lectures and handouts to social networking.
2. Identify instructional methods and activities along the spectrum from objectivist/rote to constructivist-cognitive/high context communication.
3. Identify cross-cultural dimensions relative to learning.
   a. Cooperative learning: from unsupported to integral
   b. Origin of motivation: from extrinsic to intrinsic
   c. Learner control: from nonexistent to unrestricted
   d. Teacher role: from didactic to facilitative
   e. Value of errors: from errorless learning to learning from experience
4. Identify culturally contextualized e-learner preferences.
   a. User activity: from multiple access methods to the same content to learner-generative processing
   b. Experiential value: from abstract to concrete
   c. Accommodating individual differences: from nonexistent to multifaceted

In e-learning environments, the degree of cooperative learning and the origin of motivation are particularly culturally sensitive, and need to be addressed when designing instruction.

For basic, objective learner outcomes in low-context cultural norms, materials just need to be translated, typically using global English with simple grammar and standard phrases. Use examples that are culturally neutral, such as climate and mathematics. The only cultural dimension that may impact e-learning would be orientation to time, so make culture-sensitive accommodations for synchronicity and sequencing.

With increasing complexity and culture sensitivity, courses need localization where resources and examples reflect the daily life and cultural context of the target learner. Sometimes learners, particularly adults, can locate or generate such examples. The burden is on you to determine if the learners' selections are relevant and appropriate.

Modularize complex and socially constructed courses with culture-specific learning objects. When cultural soft skills constitute the central learning outcome, it is probably best for that culture to originate the instruction design and delivery, even for e-learning environments.

Solutions to language problems

Increasingly, students from different cultures and language backgrounds are found in the same course, especially in online education. Focusing on cross-cultural technical education, Laroche (2003) noted that international students usually have taken English courses before they start teacher education, but that instruction is typically provided by teachers whose primary language is not English. British English (with a British accent) is more likely to be taught than American English, which can also impact the meaning of common terms, such as "bonnet" for car hood. In addition, the English taught is unlikely to address technical vocabulary; for example, the term *literacy* has different connotations in different languages.

The following specific instructional strategies, largely based on Sarkodie-Manash's (2000) work, apply to many learning situations, even those where everyone uses the same language.

- In all communication, use plain English and short sentences, and avoid idioms. Rephrase and simplify statements. Define new terms. Use meaningful gestures.
- If using audio files or online speech, speak clearly and slowly without accent.
- Use repetition, paraphrasing, and summaries.
- Focus attention on essential vocabulary needed for the specific training or profession. Provide bilingual glossaries and visual references.
- Use visual aids and graphic organizers to help learners understand content organization and relationships.
- Include frequent comprehension checks and clarification questions, such as online quizzes.
- If possible, provide instruction in the learner's primary language (unless learners represent several native languages). Pair students linguistically. Consider providing resources in primary languages. Check the readability of documents, and locate materials that include visual or aural cues. It should be noted that some images may be unrecognizable, demeaning, or have different meanings to different cultures.

Differentiated assessment

Many factors—age, gender, culture, disabilities—impact student performance. In terms of language, even simple tasks such as following directions can disadvantage some learners. Some of the measures that can be taken to mitigate cultural discrepancies include the following:

- Giving shorter tests and recall items rather than tasks that require high-level language and literacy skills (Teresi et al., 2001)

- Providing accurate translations in those cases where language ability is not the element being tested
- Providing bilingual glossaries
- Considering the option of having students demonstrate their skill kinesthetically (e.g., video-recording their performance or having a local expert verify their ability)

Make sure that the test is not culturally biased, that is, one cultural group does not outperform others systemically. Bias usually occurs when cultural knowledge is assumed (e.g., use of bidets, knowledge of July 4, eating habits). Images, too, may have culturally defined meanings or connotations (for example, owls connote different attributes in different cultures). The easiest approach is to check with learners via non-test activities about their understanding of textual and visual information.

The writing process is another area of possible cultural misunderstanding. While U.S. students are taught to write sequentially, often relying on an outline, other cultures prefer that writers build arguments starting with a general stance and arriving at the specific issue only at the end, and still other cultures use an argument/counterargument structure. Therefore, you should focus on the content more than the presentation, or specify how a report is to be written—and provide the support needed for students to succeed in writing in a particular style. Furthermore, non-U.S. cultures sometimes have a different attitude about intellectual property. Many students are not used to crediting their sources, and do not know about citation styles. A blanket punishment for plagiarism is obstructive without explicit instruction and support to help students comply with U.S. copyright laws.

Assessment also needs to take into consideration affective elements. For instance, non-cognitive variables accounted for about one-quarter of the variance in grade point averages for African Americans at predominately white universities; at black universities, noncognitive variables accounted for about 18 percent of grade point average variation (Lockett and Harrell, 2003). The authors concluded that the relationship between students and faculty influence self-confidence and self-efficacy. Although e-learning might mitigate such differences in perception, language use in written and oral communication may indicate a person's cultural background, and might influence some parties' perceptions either of the instructor or the interaction.

Sample instructional design resources

Librarians and other educators have published numerous teaching guides, some of which have been cited in this book. Although few focus specifically on instructional design, most have worthwhile learning activities that can be consulted during the design and delivery, especially for information and technology literacy. Here are ten representative recent materials. "Instructional Design Resources" at the end of the book includes a variety of instructional web resources.

Bell, S., and J. Shank. 2007. *Academic Librarianship by Design: A Blended Librarian's Guide to the Tools and Techniques.* Chicago: American Library Association.

Bonk, C., and K. Zhang. 2008. *Empowering Online Learning: 100+ Activities for Reading, Reflecting, Displaying, and Doing.* San Francisco: Jossey-Bass.

Booth, C. 2011. *Reflective Teaching, Effective Learning: Instructional Literacy for Library Educators.* Chicago: American Library Association.

Burkhardt, J., M. MacDonald, and A. Rathemacher. 2010. *Teaching Information Literacy: 50 Standards-Based Exercises for College Students.* Chicago: American Library Association.

Carliner, J., and P. Shank. 2008. *The E-Learning Handbook: Past Promises, Present Challenges.* San Francisco: Pfeiffer.

Cook, D., and R. Sittler. 2008. *Practical Pedagogy for Library Instructors: 17 Innovative Strategies to Improve Student Learning.* Chicago: American Library Association.

Hollister, C., ed. 2011. *Best Practice for Credit-Bearing Information Literacy Courses.* Chicago: American Library Association.

Shank, P. 2007. *The Online Learning Idea Book.* San Francisco: Pfeiffer.

Sittler, R., and D. Cook, eds. 2009. *The Library Instruction Cookbook.* Chicago: American Library Association.

Smith, S. 2006. *Web-Based Instruction: A Guide for Libraries.* Chicago: American Library Association.

Context of instructional delivery

Social context impacts curriculum delivery effectiveness. For instance, social development norms and self-identity experimentation contextualize collaborative learning activities. Millennials and senior citizens tend to have different learning attitudes and experiences, and individuals with physical disabilities need to be accommodated in terms of accessing and processing information. In addition, gender-linked development impacts student interaction. For example, with the offset of puberty through adulthood, females tend to underperform in technology-related tasks when they act in coed settings (Cooper and Weaver, 2003). On the other hand, when technology leverages females' interests and facilitates interaction between players, then girls are just as engaged and successful as boys (Gee and Hayes, 2010).

Furthermore, each person has to negotiate his or her learning experience and the rest of daily life. If the curriculum espouses one set of values, such as evolution in a biology course, and the learner's family is Protestant fundamentalist, then the learner will probably feel conflicted and need to resolve that conflict in one of several ways: rejecting the scientific explanation, rejecting the familial value, persuading the family to change, or "siloing" learning into a situation-specific stance. If you instruct diverse students, you need to help those learners navigate within the educational and family or workplace cultures successfully. These skills might include learning social expectations and norms, identifying the cultural assumptions being made about presented (and missing) content, and communicating in socially acceptable ways (e.g., avoiding jargon, understanding social space). For instance, "school" talk might be more formal than discussions at home. At school, females might be taught to speak up, but at home they might be expected to be passively quiet.

Formal education may align with or vary from workplace practice, which especially impacts in-house professional development and internships. In the former case, instruction can usually be applied immediately. In the latter case, advanced-degree intern students may learn cutting-edge techniques that contradict workplace ones, either because employers have not kept current or because the associated resources are not available in the workplace. On the other hand, employees can learn about a technology that will improve their work quality and job security. Remember, though, that the time used for training takes away from the regular work time, and improved technological skill may result in more work but no additional pay. Instead, just the workload and responsibility increase (Petrina, Feng, and Kim, 2008). Distance education is another situation in which the curriculum might not align with local practice because some functions are locally contextualized; for instance, health education differs greatly between Chicago and a rural Middle East setting. In advising library staff, McMahon and Bruce (2002) recommended that librarians take care to respect each student's cultural stance while noting the importance of learning about the social climate to be experienced as a potential employee. In any case, the more opportunities that you can provide to share the context of their learning, the easier it is for you to plan learning activities that link curriculum to other parts of learners' lives. Some ways that such linking can be integrated include student identification with relevant course material, use of workplace experts, class-generated wikis, service learning, and external evaluation of student work.

Further instructional delivery implications for you

Librarians may instruct without knowing the full context of learning. Other instructional designers tend to think about librarians as resource specialists rather than instructors. To a certain extent, this situation is ironic because, frankly, much instruction requires explicit incorporation of librarians; on the other hand, school and academic librarians are not likely to exist without classroom instructors.

Librarians usually recognize the importance of context when instructing their clientele, and wish to gain access to that information. For that reason, the extent of collaborative instructional design impacts the effectiveness of librarian instruction. Typically, librarians have to take the initiative in that collaboration. But like the instructors who need to consider the motivation of their learners as they communicate and monitor the learning task, so too do librarians need to motivate instructional designers to engage in instructional tasks together.

In those situations where you collaborate with other instructors to deliver curriculum, plan its various aspects. The Learning Activity Collaborative Planning Checklist (p. 144) can guide discussion.

Sample project-based lesson for middle school students

The following face-to-face lesson for eighth-grade physical education students incorporates several points discussed in this chapter: collaborative instruction, grouping of learners, choice of resources, incorporation of information literacy, metacognition, social aspects of learning, and differentiated learning. Specifically, this lesson builds on middle schoolers' concerns about body images and self-identity, and teaches important proactive applications of information literacy.

Lesson

Title: Exercise Cycles

Lesson overview: As teens make decisions about physical fitness and exercise, they need to know how to locate and evaluate relevant information. They also need to think about their privacy as they seek such information. This lesson examines the communication cycle, and notes how information technology impacts it. It also addresses how communication is recorded and shared, which can impact privacy. Both legal and ethical issues are addressed.

Time frame: 2 class periods

Learning objectives: Learners will:
- Describe how to find information about exercise issues.
- Evaluate sources of information.
- Explain the impact of technology on locating and sharing information.

(continued on page 145)

Learning Activity Collaborative Planning Checklist

❑   What are the desired student outcomes in terms of knowledge, skills, and attitudes? What evidence will indicate their ability? How will they be assessed?

❑   What content and information literacy standards are being addressed? In terms of information literacy, do students need to locate and evaluate information, or do they need to focus on extracting information from preselected sources?

❑   What prerequisite knowledge and skills do students need to accomplish the desired outcome? Who will determine those prerequisites? How will students gain that knowledge?

❑   What resources are needed? How do they address content and student needs?

❑   What resources are available in the library or accessed from the library? If resources need to be gathered from another location, what conditions and deadlines must be met?

❑   What resources, including teaching and learning aids, need to be created or modified? Under what conditions and timelines must they be made?

❑   What instruction is needed? Is introduction, review, or extension needed? Who will provide it—and under what conditions?

❑   What learning tasks will students be doing? What activities will they practice in order to accomplish their assignment independently? Who will check for understanding and provide feedback?

❑   What information and directions (for example, handouts) will be given to students? Who will produce and disseminate them?

❑   Where will teaching and learning occur? What arrangements need to be made in order to ensure the appropriate learning environment?

❑   What is the time frame for the teaching and learning? Do students need extra time to learn prerequisite skills, such as scanning images? Will some students need more time in the library than others; if so, how will they be supervised?

❑   How will students be grouped for learning: the whole class, small collaborative groups, or individual efforts?

❑   How will differentiation be addressed? What resources and instruction need to be added or modified to accommodate diverse populations (for example, different learning styles, gender differences, English-language learners, students with special needs, and the gifted and talented)? What physical changes need to be made? What interpersonal factors need to be addressed?

❑   How will teaching and learning be assessed? Who will do it? When? How will that information be used to inform future teaching and learning?

(Reprinted with permission from Farmer, 2009: 72.)

Curriculum standards

- Analyze the validity of exercise information, products, and services.
- Use a decision-making process to examine barriers to making healthy decisions about exercise and exercise products.
- Use a decision-making process to analyze when it is necessary to seek help with or avoid an unhealthy situation.
- Support others in making positive and healthful choices about exercise.
- Select and use appropriate tools and technology to locate resources.
- Use a variety of print, media, and online resources to locate information including encyclopedias and other reference materials.
- Analyze media for purpose, message, accuracy, bias, and intended audience.
- Determine whether resources are designed to persuade, educate, inform, or sell.
- Recognize and protect the private information of oneself and others.

Resources

- Technology: Internet-connected computers, demonstration computer with projector/screen
- Worksheet:

---

1. Issue:
   _____

2. Communications channel:
   Public or private? Likely to be recorded/archived?
   _____

   Potential number of people who could access/receive the message: _____

3. Audience/receiver:
   Likely type of information to be provided:
   _____

   Likelihood of keeping communication private:
   _____

   Likelihood of sharing communication (making it public):
   _____

4. Consequences of interloping (to interloper and target person):
   _____

5. Recommendations for locating and sharing information:
   _____

Planning for diverse learners

- Learners can work in same-sex pairs.
- Choice of information sources varies by reading level and language ability.
- Second-language materials should be made available.
- Topics of discussion might be culturally sensitive, or might reflect different personal values, so learners should have a safe way to choose or "opt out" of certain topics.
- Librarians provide more structure for the task or divide the steps into substeps.

Instructional strategies and study activities

0. Before the lesson, librarian sets up computers. Librarian prints worksheet.
1. Librarian explains the communication cycle. The communication cycle begins with an idea that someone tries to communicate to another person, usually with the intent that the receiving party responds. The communication channel can impact the message and its receiver/audience. While a response to the sender typically completes the loop, the audience could communicate to other parties. An image of the communication cycle is found at the website http://www.media-visions.com/communication.html.

   This model also works for seeking information, with the intent that the receiver provides the sender with the needed information. The sender's choice of communications channel impacts who will receive the query. The communications channel may be public (open to anyone) or private (directed to an intended receiver), and the message may be documented or not. The sender also needs to think about the receiver in terms of whether the message will be sent only to the sender (a closed cycle) or might be communicated to others (an open cycle).

   Learners as information seekers/senders need to think about the communication channel, the receiver, and privacy factors. Particularly since issues of relationships and sexual health may be sensitive in nature, learners often do not want their communication to be made public. Furthermore, they might not realize the consequences of sharing such information. This lesson helps them understand these issues.
2. Librarian and physical education (PE) teacher ask learners to brainstorm exercise plans, products, and services that require information seeking. Here is a beginning list (which may be used as the lesson topics):
   - A middle school boy wants to build up muscle. He wants to know what exercises he can do at home without buying equipment.

- Friends tell a middle school girl she has baby fat. She wants to lose it immediately, and is thinking of buying pills to speed up the process.
- A family is going to buy some home exercise equipment, and the middle schooler wants to research what would be appropriate for his age.

3. Librarian asks learners to brainstorm technology-based communication channels that could be used to get the desired information. Alternatively, the following list may be used as a guiding or final list.
   - telephone conversation
   - smartphone texting
   - e-mail
   - Internet searching
   - Facebook/social network query

4. Librarian and PE teacher split the class into groups according to communication channel. Have each group identify if their channel is public or private. Have student groups also identify whether their channel records/archives the information. Have them research how many people might potentially access the information (e.g., http://www.facebook.com/press/info .php?statistics).

5. Librarian and PE ask learners to brainstorm likely receivers/audience of the query. Examples include the following: parent, teacher, friend, recreation center, doctor, commercial gym, social agency. Have each student within each group choose to be one receiver. Have each identify the likely kind of information that they would give (e.g., clergy would advise abstinence, doctor would give medical information, etc.). If learners are unsure about what kind of information that would be given, have them research it (e.g., using Internet search engine or database aggregator keyword combinations such as "exercise OR fitness" and "equipment"). Have each group discuss their findings.

6. Librarian and PE ask learners to predict whether their source of information (receiver/respondent) would be likely to (1) respond directly to them; (2) tell others about the communication. If learners are unsure about what kind of information that would be given, have them research the answer.

7. Librarian and PE teacher ask learners to discuss within their group about the consequences of the communications cycle being open/public.

8. Librarian poses the question "What if someone were to overhear/access the query?" What might be the consequences? For instance, if someone saw a teenage girl walking into a Jenny Craig center, and told others that the girl was a fatty when she really was waiting for her mother, what would be the consequences for the (1) girl who visited, and (2) person/

interloper who told others untrue gossip? Have groups discuss the issue and ramifications. Some of the terminology that might arise includes: libel, slander, false representation; these terms can be researched by the groups.

9. Librarian and PE teacher ask each group to report out their findings and predictions about consequences of actions. If the class is large, split them into two or three groups, each with a separate issue.

10. Librarian and PE teacher conduct a class debriefing about locating and sharing information via technology about exercise issues. Have the class develop guidelines for behaviors relative to technology use.

Variations
- Another health topic can be addressed.
- Boys and girls can compare their perspectives and information found.
- The class can focus on just one aspect of exercise: one part of the body, one reason for exercising (muscle versus weight).
- The class can focus on exercise equipment.
- The class can locate information on the Internet, comparing sources of information.
- The class can compare information found on the "free" Internet versus subscription databases.
- The class can start by doing the following WebQuest on diet and exercise: http://www.viterbo.edu/academic/ug/education/edu250/vawall/

Student assessment
Learners are assessed according to their communication thoroughness, validity, and justification for the following criteria:
- Following directions
- Documenting work
- Collecting information/conducting research
- Understanding the communication cycle
- Understanding the impact of technology
- Understanding issues of privacy
- Making recommendations for decision making

Additional resources
- http://kidshealth.org/kid/
- http://www.bam.gov/index.html
- http://www.lensaunders.com/aces/aces.html
- http://www.presidentschallenge.org/challenge/active/index.shtml
- http://www.shapeup.org/

References

Akin, L., and D. MacKinney. 2004. "Autism, Literacy, and Libraries." *Children & Libraries* 2, no. 2: 35–43.

Bennett, S. 2007. "First Questions for Designing Higher Education Learning Spaces." *Journal of Academic Librarianship* 33, no. 1: 14–26.

Brown, M. 2005. "Learning Spaces." In *Educating the Net Gen,* edited by D. Oblinger and J. Oblinger, 12.1–12.22. Boulder, CO: Educause.

Bruner, J. 1956. *Toward a Theory of Instruction.* Cambridge, MA: Belknap Press.

Cannon, R. 1988. "Learning Environment." In *Encyclopedia of Educational Media Communications and Technology,* edited by D. Unwin and R. McAlees, 342–358. New York: Greenwood Press.

Carlile, O., and A. Jordan. 2005. "It Works in Practice but Will It Work in Theory? The Theoretical Underpinnings of Pedagogy." In *Emerging Issues in the Practice of University Learning and Teaching,* edited by G. O'Neill, S. Moore, and B. McMullin, 11–26. Dublin, Ireland: AISHE.

Carlile, O., A. Jordan, and A. Stack. 2004. *Learning by Design.* Waterford, UK: WIT/BBC Online.

Cooper, J., and K. Weaver. 2003. *Gender and Computers: Understanding the Digital Divide.* Mahwah, NJ: Lawrence Erlbaum.

Craig, R. 1996. *The ASTD Training and Development Handbook.* 4th ed. New York: McGraw Hill.

Denison University. 2011. Denison University Learning Space Project. Granville, OH: Denison University. Accessed April 15. http://www.denison.edu/academics/learningspaces/checkl.pdf.

Dewey, J. 1933. *How We Think.* New York: D. C. Heath.

Dishon, D., and P. O'Leary. 1998. *Guidebook for Cooperative Learning.* Holmes Beach, FL: Learning Publications.

Domer, D., and G. Gorman, G. 2006. "Information Literacy Education in Asian Developing Countries: Cultural Factors Affecting Curriculum Development and Programme Delivery." *IFLA Journal* 32, no. 4: 281–293.

Edmundson, A. 2007. "The Cultural Adaptation Process (Cap) Model: Designing E-learning for Another Culture." In *Globalized E-learning Cultural Challenges,* edited by A. Edmundson, 267–290. Hershey, PA: Idea Group.

Faiola, A., and S. Matei. 2005. "Cultural Cognitive Style and Web Design." *Journal of Computer-Mediated Communication* 11, no. 1. http://jcmc.indiana.edu/vol11/issue1/faiola.html.

Farmer, L. 2009. *Your School Library: Check It Out!* Westport, CT: Libraries Unlimited.

Gagne, E. 1985. *The Cognitive Psychology of School Learning.* Boston: Little, Brown.

Gee, J., and E. Hayes. 2010. *Women and Gaming: The Sims and 21st Century Learning.* Palgrave, UK: Macmillan.

Gurubatham, M. 2005. "Cognition, Culture and Effective E-praxis Guiding Principles." In *E-training Practices for Professional Organizations,* edited by P. Nicholson, 121–128. Boston: Kluwer Academic Publishers.

Laroche, L. 2003. *Managing Cultural Diversity in Technical Professions.* Boston: Butterworth Heinemann.

Lockett, C., and J. Harrell. 2003. "Racial Identity, Self-Esteem, and Academic Achievement." *Journal of Black Psychology* 29, no. 3: 325–336.

Lopez-Valadez, J., J. Friedenberg, N. Lucas, N. Kremer, and T. Reed. 1985. "Immigrant
    Workers and the American Workplace: The Role of Voc Ed." *ERIC Digest*. Columbus,
    OH: ERIC Clearinghouse on Adult, Career, and Vocational Education. ED 260 304.
McMahon, C., and C. Bruce. 2002. "Information Literacy Needs of Local Staff in Cross-
    Cultural Development Projects." *Journal of International Development* 14, no. 1: 113–137.
Milne, A. Jan. 2007. "Entering the Interactive Age." *Educause Review* 4, no. 1: 13–31.
Misanchuk, E. 1992. *Preparing Instructional Text*. Englewood Cliffs, NJ: Educational
    Technology.
Oblinger, D. 2006. *Learning Spaces*. Boulder, CO: Educause.
Petrina, S., F. Feng, and J. Kim. 2008. "Researching Cognition and Technology: How We
    Learn across the Lifespan." *International Journal of Technology and Design Education* 18:
    375–396.
Rapoport, A. 2008. "The Impact of International Programs on Pedagogical Practices of Their
    Participants." *Teachers and Teaching: Theory and Practice* 14, no. 3: 225–238.
Roblyer, M., and A. Doering. 2009. *Integrating Educational Technology into Teaching*. Boston:
    Allyn & Bacon.
Ryder, M. 2006. *Instructional Design Models*. Denver: University of Colorado. http://carbon
    .ucdenver.edu/~mryder/itc/idmodels.html#comparative.
Sarkodie-Manash, K., ed. 2000. *Reference Services for the Adult Learner*. Binghamton, NY:
    Haworth Press.
Smith, P., and T. Ragan. 2005. *Instructional Design*. 3rd ed. New York: John Wiley and Sons.
Strange, C., and H. Banning. 2001. *Educating by Design: Creating Campus Learning
    Environments That Work*. San Francisco: Jossey-Bass.
Teresi, J., D. Holmes, M. Ramirez, B. Gurland, and R. Lantiqua. 2001. "Performance of
    Cognitive Tests among Different Racial/Ethnic and Education Groups: Findings of
    Differential Item Functioning and Possible Item Bias." *Journal of Mental Health & Aging*
    7, no. 1: 79–89.

Learning with technology, learning about technology

Technology adds another dimension to learning. It exponentially expands access to information as well as ways that knowledge is represented. Learning *with* technology differs from learning *about* technology, just as learning using information literacy differs from learning *about* it. The former focuses on process while the latter emphasizes content matter.

When technology is integrated into instructional design, its manipulation needs to be taken into account as well as the academic concepts to be mastered; a separate, and sometimes related, set of knowledge and skills must be addressed. If learners do not know how to create a PowerPoint presentation, then they will need the opportunity—and the time—to learn and practice that skill. Therefore, you need to figure out how that learning will occur. Do learners have access to the hardware and software at home or elsewhere? Do they have the time inside or outside of class to access and learn the application? Must some class time be dedicated to that learning? These are just a few of the issues that need to be considered.

The impact of technology on learning

Today's technology has substantially changed the face of learning. First, technology significantly expands and speeds up access to the world of information. Telecommunications has collapsed time and space. People potentially have more access, more quickly, to information around the world. Moreover, people can respond to one another and share group information much more easily than in the past. The convergence of communication industries such as telephony and television further expands the dissemination of information.

The nature of the information itself has been affected by digital technology. Besides the obvious combination of text, image, and sound, technology facilitates the repurposing and transformation of information to address different objectives or different audiences. More than ever, the user needs to interpret the format of information as well as its content, and their interdependence.

The interface between the information and the user comprises another element that has not been as crucial previously. That same interface also gives rise to interactive and dynamic information. For instance, hypertextuality enables the reader to go to linked information that might be further linked to other documentation; while footnotes and bibliographies serve this purpose hypothetically, they generally do not provide instant connections to the full texts/content. Furthermore, applications such as Google Docs and wikis enable participants to literally change documents on the fly, thereby chipping away at the idea of a permanent recorded document (Iacono, 2010).

In addition, technology impacts the nature of instruction, highlighting the issue of standardization versus customization (Martinez, 2005). On one hand, technology enables instruction to be mass produced and standardized. Course design and resources can be easily duplicated and disseminated. To a degree, grading can be done automatically once a quiz is set up. An online video conference can be scheduled for one time, with the understanding that learners anywhere in the world can meet simultaneously. On the other hand, with so many more resources available because of telecommunications and digitization, learners are more likely to find information that fits their particular needs, and educators can provide learners with more choices in what resource they use or how they can demonstrate knowledge. Technology-based instruction can be structured so that learners can self-pace their work. You can develop automated needs assessment tools that direct the learner to the most appropriate resources and activities based on their responses. Likewise, you can store digital learning objects that can be accessed for a variety of applications across curricula, which can lead to a one-size-fits-all mentality or can support a learner's specific needs, depending on how they are used.

Technology also can change the relationship between teacher and learner— and the nature of learning processes themselves (Wang, Fong, and Kwan, 2010). Because more resources can be accessed independently, and learners can access and manipulate those resources at any time, learners have the opportunity to be more independent. Because access and communication can be asynchronous but still timely (as opposed to traditional correspondence courses), learners may be expected to accomplish more because they have a more flexible window of opportunity; they are not constrained by class time. Indeed, the wall between class time and daily life becomes more porous; conversations can continue nonstop if one so wishes. Moreover, the interactivity of the Internet, particularly Web 2.0 collaborative tools, enables learners to relate to one another more fully. Group projects become more feasible because students do not have to meet at one place at one time; on the other hand, when trying to assess learning progress, you must take additional measures to decipher how each person is contributing to the end result. Your status is likely to shift from sage on the stage to guide on the side, providing an educational environment in which learners can explore.

In short, the incorporation of digital technology fosters more independent, learner-centered learning. Maier and Warren (2000) list several technology-enhanced instructional design strategies that support such a model:

- Flexible learning through ubiquitous access to resources, including the instructor
- Resource-centered learning provided within a virtual environment, which enables learners to use tools to manipulate resources according to individual needs and interests
- Self-paced learning, unhampered by class time or one-shot lectures
- Collaborative learning using web-based tools to compare learning and to generate knowledge together
- Distance learning because course materials and structure can be accessed remotely

Decision points and incorporating technology

One of the first questions in the instructional design process that needs to be answered is "Should technology be used?" The following lists some deciding factors.

Incorporating technology is appropriate when:
- accessing remote digital resources,
- addressing sensory modes via simulations and other knowledge representations,
- building on or repurposing existing digital resources or instruction,
- encouraging repeated practice (e.g., drills for rote learning),
- supporting anytime/anywhere learning, and/or
- recording and archiving communication and effort.

Incorporating technology is less beneficial when:
- focusing on in-house, nontechnical resources,
- face-to-face personal contact is important,
- providing one-time customized training, and/or
- other resources and means are more effective.

A good rule of thumb is to employ the most stable, low-tech format applicable to the concept being taught. Likewise, teaching a technology tool should be done only when an immediate and compelling use of it is needed. Once the decision to use technology is made, regardless of the type of technology used, you need to acknowledge and take advantage of these media. For instance, a podcast can combine voice and music or sound effects.

It should be noted that the choice and implementation of technology need to be addressed in light of the entire instructional design. Throughout the process, you need to determine which technologies will be used—and to what extent. In fact, technology-infused instructional design often requires the use of several technologies. At the very minimum, determine whether technology will be used as a tool to deliver instruction, as a learning aid, or as the outcome itself. Even the instructional focus, whether to emphasize a technology tool or educational task, requires careful consideration. The decision-making process itself may well involve technology, particularly when gathering data using online surveys, PDA observation templates, web counters—and analyzing it using spreadsheets, databases, or content analysis software. Technology-based choices apply at each step in designing instruction, as shown here (Maloy et al., 2011):

- **Assess needs**: online survey, video capture of behavior, analysis of website "hits"
- **Identify learners**: online solicitations, RSS feed subscriptions, organizational lists
- **Identify outcomes**: technology standards, online content standards, online education syllabi
- **Identify indicators**: technology rubrics, technology products, electronic Delphi method (i.e., getting experts to come to consensus on key points)
- **Identify prerequisite skills**: web-based assessment, performance observation, content analysis of sample work
- **Identify curriculum**: online training documents, electronic journal articles, iUniversity podcasts
- **Identify the instructional format**:
  - resources (Internet, DVDs, e-books)
  - instructor (technician, instruction designer, remote-site expert)
  - methods (web tutorial, hands-on instruction, video presentation)
  - time frame (self-paced, real-time, just-in-time)
  - location (computer lab, classroom, home)
  - grouping (individual, online group, work unit)
  - individualization (programmed instruction, choice of technology, coaching)
  - affective domain (wiki, threaded discussion, virtual chat)

- **Contextualize instruction**: webpage within work website, professional development database, digital images of applications
- **Implement the plan**: project planning software program, webpage development, videoconferencing
- **Assess the plan**: personal digital assistant (PDA) questionnaire, videotape, online survey
- **Manage the learning environment**:
  - Use network supervision software to monitor learner use of computers.
  - Create technology-enhanced learning stations.
  - Produce a class website that includes assignments, exemplars, and resources.
  - Create a wiki for learners to share information.

Even with these suggestions, technology is sometimes added on top of existing instruction, like icing on the cake, rather than transforming instructional design. Some of the changed elements include the locus of control from teacher to learner, just-in-time learning, emphasis on resource-rich inquiry, and heightened interaction.

Learners and technology

Technology has made incredible advances in the past few decades, yet many people have not experienced technology-infused learning. Even youngsters might not have used technology educationally if their schools have little access to it or their teachers are uncomfortable about using it in class. On the other hand, many individuals do enjoy using technology for educational purposes; these people tend to exhibit certain characteristics (Harley and Bendixen, 2001; Wilson, 2000):

- Self-directed and self-regulated
- Persistent
- Autonomous
- Prefer anonymity
- Independent
- Egalitarian
- Believe in flexible ability
- Value convenience
- Self-paced
- Work outside nine-to-five time frame
- Technologically comfortable
- Comfortable with complex and ill-defined knowledge domains
- May have "traditional" language or physical barriers
- Tend to be a different population than face-to-face learners

Other studies have examined the characteristics of successful distance-education learners, who differ somewhat from generic online learners (Simonson et al., 2008):

- Younger
- More educated
- Emotionally stable and trusting
- Conforming
- Introverted
- Emotionally supported

Gender issues in learning with technology

While today's youth have always lived in the digital world, their attitudes toward technology reflect gendered expectation with puberty (Hackbarth, 2001). Girls report less positive attitudes, and both sexes consider technology to be the male's domain. Girls are less critical of Internet content, and are more likely to attribute technological success to the equipment (Cooper and Weaver, 2003). In coed situations, boys tend to outperform girls in terms of using technology, but in low-stakes single-sex settings, girls do equally well or outperform boys; girls tend to underrate their ability, and boys tend to overrate themselves (Hargittai and Shafer, 2006). On the other hand, girls constitute the majority of social networking users, particularly as a way to keep in touch with friends (Lenhart and Madden, 2007). As such, technology-embedded activities that incorporate collaborative learning and allow for reflective responses can play to females' strengths.

To compensate for this social "norming," you should set a positive learning atmosphere that encourages intellectual risk taking. Furthermore, online learning environments could prove to be an effective way to offset coed perceptions, particularly when learners are given timely feedback (Cooper and Weaver, 2003). Nevertheless, the degree and quality of online participation may betray the student's inner feelings of frustration, defensiveness, or condescension toward e-learning. Therefore, you should also facilitate confidential ways for students to seek help through writing or private online conversations, especially since females are more likely to ask for help.

Digital natives

Traditional-aged K–16 students are digital natives, shaped by globalization and technology. For them, the Web is an interpersonal experience more than surfing the Net, and they are likely to multitask with technology tools. Technology also reinforces their desire for choice, customization, and immediate results (Carlson, 2005).

Although strong in digital communication skills, these youth are not necessarily strong technology learners. They often do not understand research processes, and are more likely to use the first entries in a Google search or Wikipedia than to perform a Boolean search on subscription databases. In examining the information processes of undergraduates, Holliday and Li (2004) noted how the ease of federated searching and cut-and-paste word processing results in sidestepping critical thinking and other reflective e-learning practices; students tend to settle for "good enough" information.

Some gender differences also exist for this generation of learners, according to Morley (2007). He reported that females exerted more effort and made more commitments relative to technology, although males spent more time on computers and had more positive attitudes about digital libraries.

Adult learners

Because digital technology is a fairly recent experience for most adults, usually after their initial formal education journey, you may need to explicitly help adults accept technology as a learning tool in order to use it as a means to learn content matter. For example, online learning may be out of the question for some adults because in their minds the technology itself poses a barrier to learning; if they cannot accept the online environment, learners will not be able to have physical and intellectual access to the information itself.

As a review, adult learning or andragogy builds on the experiences and needs of adults. Based on Knowles, Swanson, and Holton's (2011) work on andragogy, the following elements pair well with technology.

- **Use of new materials**: Technology provides access to timely information from around the world.
- **Self-directed and independent learning**: Technology resources can be accessed and used independently and usually at the learner's convenience.
- **Control of learning**: Technology can provide a learning environment with tools and resources that the learner can explore and control.
- **Immediate utility**: Technology-based resources support just-in-time learning.
- **Problem orientation**: Technology tools facilitate problem solving, and many digital resources are comprised of how-to instructions, simulations, and models that aid in finding solutions.
- **Diverse, active learning**: Technology expands access to resources that address needs of diverse populations, and Web 2.0 facilitates interactive and social learning.

The following list explains adult learning factors that librarian instructional designers need to apply to technology-embedded learning situations.

- **Experience:** Help adult learners identify what they already know and then build on that knowledge. Realize that adult learners might have little digital information experience so explicit instruction on technological use is necessary.
- **Timing:** E-learning activities have the benefit of typically being able to adjust to existing schedule demands, offering options for self-pacing.
- **Practicality:** Hands-on, concrete technology-rich learning activities that address needed information work well with adults, especially if adults can apply that information to their lives immediately.
- **Socialization:** Provide opportunities for adult learners to share information about technology and via technology. By offering these outlets, learners are more satisfied with technology and learn more.
- **Motivation:** Whenever possible, technology-based learning activities should be developed in response to adult interests and needs. For instance, adults may want information in order to improve their economic status or to solve personal health problems, so perhaps they would be more likely to try using technology than they otherwise would be.
- **Need to know:** An information need determined by adult learners offers an ideal opportunity for you to leverage the opportunity to design and introduce learning activities that incorporate technology.
- **Readiness:** Adults learn when they see a need to learn in order to cope with their lives or improve them. Incorporate technology-rich methods of dealing with change since that aspect of e-learning may be unexpected and uncomfortable.

Psychologist Daniel Levinson (1978) studied men's interaction between their inner lives and external events, and identified their development as "seasons in a man's life." Building on Erikson's stages, Levinson detailed three eras. Each stage includes seasons of upheaval and change as well as seasons of stability and synthesis. Implications for technology-embedded learning follow in italics.

- **Early adult:** 22–40 years old. *These learners are likely to be tech savvy or willing to explore new options. Emphasize the benefits of skill-building to optimize career options.*
- **Middle adult:** 40–60 years old. *Show adults how technology can provide them with balance in their lives, both by being more productive as well as using technology for personal growth.*
- **Late adult:** 60-plus years old. *Older adults can mentor younger learners using Web 2.0 tools. These adults are likely to have less hand dexterity, but can use assistive technology if needed. Their cognitive processes may be slower, but the*

self-pacing aspects of online learning can actually be more comfortable than strict class-time learning, particularly if the online course incorporates easy-to-use options for socializing.

Adult attitudes about technology

What are the attitudes of adults today toward technology? Today's adults are probably the last generation of electronic immigrants; a generation ago few K–12 schools offered digital technology courses or provided Internet access for students. In 2003 the National Science Foundation conducted an in-depth study of U.S. public attitudes and understanding about science and technology. Here are some of their findings:

- About 90 percent of adults stated that they were interested in new technologies. Those with more science and math education reported higher interest.
- Fewer than 15 percent felt well informed about the use of new technologies, and about one-third thought they were poorly informed. Furthermore, people feel increasingly less informed.
- Most adults learn about the newest technology development via television.
- Adults who have home access to the Internet are more positive about technology and know more about science.
- Adults hold stereotypical images about scientists and technology professionals.

It should be noted that having gadgets does not equate to positive technology attitude or competency. A survey by the Pew Internet & American Life Project (Horrigan, 2007) found that some people use just a few technology tools, but are very productive and pleased with them; likewise, other people have cell phones, PDAs, and other equipment but feel overwhelmed by—and dissatisfied with—technology as a whole. Likewise, even digital natives may use technology just for personal entertainment and not equate it with formal learning.

Several models trace individual acceptance of technology. Rogers' seminal research on the diffusion of innovation (1962) focused on the individual within the organization. The four factors involved in diffusion included innovation (new idea, practice, or object), communication channel, time (both decision-making and adoption processes), and the social system. Individuals bring their personality and social characteristics, as well as their perceived need for the innovation as they learn about the innovation, couched within social system norms. As individuals decide whether to accept or reject the innovation, they perceive the innovation's characteristics, including its:

- relative advantage over other available tools,
- compatibility with social practice,
- complexity or simplicity,
- trialability (ease with which innovation can be experimented) before having to commit to it, and
- the observability of its benefits.

The Center for Research and Development in Teaching at the University of Texas at Austin (Hall and Loucks, 1979) developed a seven-step model that identifies issues that concern learners as they progress from unawareness to full integration of technology. The developers asserted that educators need to modify instruction to align with each person's stage of concern. Ideally, one should conduct a needs assessment to ascertain the stage of their students in order to design activities accordingly. Stages and suggested approaches follow.

- **Awareness**: Learners start from ignorance. Get their attention. Online features need to draw attention to the relevant technology.
- **Information**: Learners receive technology via one-way communication. Give objective information about the relevant technology, perhaps giving a video demonstration. The site http://www.commoncraft.com/ is a good source of user-friendly technology information.
- **Personal**: Learners react to technology from a personal perspective. Know the immediate benefit of using technology, such as peer sharing. Have learners share a photo of themselves, and a brief introduction can serve as a good online icebreaker.
- **Management**: Learners try to fit technology into their overall learning experience and practice. Show how the technology concretely contributes to their educational goal.
- **Consequence**: Learners determine whether the effort to learn the technology is worth the effort. At this point, choosing the most appropriate technology for the learning task is a key competence.
- **Collaboration**: Leaders work with others to leverage the impact of technology. Emphasize collaborative technology tools at this point.
- **Refocus**: Learners become proactive experts. Give them opportunities to teach others about technology.

As you take these issues into consideration when incorporating technology, be sure to differentiate resources and activities to accommodate different levels of technology acceptance. For instance, learners should be able to demonstrate competence in a variety of ways, choosing a familiar technology approach so that they can focus on the content rather than the technology itself.

Developmentally appropriate use of technology in learning

Both in terms of learning approaches as well as technological acceptance and use, learners' developmental stages need to be considered when designing and implementing technology-embedded instruction. Gurian and Henley (2001) surveyed successful teachers about developmentally appropriate educational measures that can facilitate learning. Here are some of those tips:

- **Kindergarten:**
    1. Foster experiential learning through hands-on learning environments (e.g., object-based manipulatives, puzzles, games).
    2. Have children use digital cameras to capture positive behavior and learning.
    3. Let children express their feelings; use emoticons to identify and express moods.

- **Elementary grades:**
    1. Encourage kinesthetic learning, including whole-body movement and engagement.
    2. Provide opportunities for a variety of positive online learning experiences that use competitive, cooperative, and individual effort.
    3. Provide many, varied writing experiences, including storytelling.

- **Middle school:**
    1. Express high expectations both academically and socially.
    2. Provide positive rite-of-passage experiences.
    3. Facilitate one-on-one mentoring using social networking.
    4. Teach social and tension coping skills.

- **High school:**
    1. Help students learn and practice communication and negotiation skills.
    2. Encourage and facilitate intellectual risk-taking and service.
    3. Facilitate online one-on-one mentors, and introduce adult role models reflecting a wide variety of interests and skills (e.g., male nurses, female engineers, single fathers, female skydivers).

- **Adult education:**
    1. Create a professional learning community structure that offers practical contexts and authentic performance assessment.
    2. Provide opportunities for socializing and its role in collective intelligence.
    3. Design the course to facilitate self-pacing and self-monitoring.

Instructional design planning for technology

It should come as no surprise that instructional design started when technology became more prevalent in education. The incorporation of technology requires more planning than traditional instruction because it involves hardware in order to access and manipulate information and because it requires learning how to use a tool along with learning concepts. You need to address these considerations long before the delivery of instruction.

Particularly for online learning, you should front-load the conditions (Ko and Rossen, 2010).

- **Physical access:** Instructional resources should be accessible by low-performance equipment and dial-up connectivity. Save text in formats that can be read by open-source software; rtf and pdf files are usually acceptable formats. Unfortunately, while image-rich and multimedia documents take advantage of multiple learning styles, they also require broader bandwidth and may need plug-ins in order to play correctly. Furthermore, instructional materials should be accessible for individuals with disabilities.
- **Intellectual access:** Provide directions on the use of technology tools such as spreadsheets or authoring programs. In some cases, even simple operations such as attaching files need to be explained. Facilitate self-sufficient learning by showing learners how to get technical assistance through help screens, manuals, web FAQs, and online tutorials. While some learners are motivated to use technology proactively, and will make the extra effort to process information, others have a negative attitude toward technology that will impede information processing. These people need extra support and encouragement.
- **Building community:** One of the main drawbacks of e-learning can be a feeling of isolation. With the advent of Web 2.0, students can interact easily with their online peers to build a community of learners. Set up the conditions for interactive learning by designing opportunities for group discussion and collaborative learning activities. Threaded discussion forums, wikis, blogs, and online conferencing are just a few of the tools available. These community-based structures have to be supported through the online training of these tools.

Even with these general provisions, students might not succeed at e-learning because they have differing preexisting attitudes and experiences with technology, particularly if they are adult learners. By its nature, e-learning can be a very personalized experience, and technology can support such differentiation. At the very least, provide students with a variety of instructional materials and learning activities to choose from. Relating to technology is affected by emotional states, so make sure that students can feel safe in taking intellectual risks in trying technology, and are rewarded for their efforts as well as their final products (Rogers, 1962).

Technology-based instructional strategies

As noted before, instructional strategies should involve both cognitive and social aspects, reflecting effective learning principles. Particularly with the incorporation of technology, address learners' fears so that they can find pleasure in learning with technology. If learners are stymied by the technology, they will not be able to concentrate on the content matter that they are supposed to master. To address this issue, assess learners' current technology knowledge base, and frontload instruction with opportunities for technology-challenged learners to get acquainted with the technology needed to engage in the desired content. To that end, make sure that students have opportunities to:

- operate computer and other technological systems (i.e., open and close an application, save a document, print, use a mouse, use a menu and navigation bar, etc.);
- use productivity tools;
- navigate the Internet (i.e., use browsers and search engines, use e-mail, etc.);
- evaluate information critically; and
- communicate digitally.

In addition, you must find ways to ensure equitable access to these technologies. Specifically during the delivery of learning opportunities that explicitly incorporate technological and information literacies, several activities can be incorporated to foster understanding and practice of these literacies.

- Highlight information literacy and technology standards that are explicitly addressed in learner projects.
- Have learners generate concept maps (either manually or with graphic organizer applications) about these literacies before and after a learning session.
- Starting with learner outcomes, identify associated literacies.
- Trace the instructional design process and incorporate the technologies accordingly.
- Pair learners in two different academic or career disciplines to compare literacies' overlap and transference.

Several delivery structures leverage technology to improve the learning experience. Each of the following approaches fosters deep engagement with curriculum because the format lends itself well to packaging and communicating content.

Each approach also fosters interactivity between learner and content, and facilitates collaboration. It should be recognized that if instructors are less comfortable with technology, the librarian or technology specialist may get the entire responsibility for teaching technical skills without any input from the instructor of record. Nevertheless, the extent of course collaboration is usually less dependent on each party's technological expertise than it is on interpersonal trust.

WebQuest

One of the first examples of interactive web-based instructional structures was the WebQuest. In this model, a meaningful task is presented. The WebQuest creator provides the learner with links to appropriate web-based documents in order to complete the task. Often collaborative roles are incorporated into the WebQuest to promote human interaction as well as interaction with resources. Usually a summative assessment is included to evaluate the end product and the process. WebQuests blend information access, manipulation, and presentation. The WebQuest format is attractive to instructional designers for several reasons:

- It is content neutral.
- It provides a safe closed learning environment because the websites are preselected.
- Its technology is simple enough so that learners can focus on the content.
- It offers open-ended solutions based on the learner's perspective.
- It aligns all the components of instructional design.

The WebQuest template is so simple that even elementary school children can develop their own WebQuests, which fosters generative knowledge. Details about WebQuests can be found at http://webquest.sdsu.edu/.

Web 2.0

Web 2.0 is the term given to express the idea of interactivity that now marks some web-based collaborative tools such as wikis and blogs. Rather than one-way communication, Web 2.0 applications enable learners to participate in two-way (or multi-way) active communication to share and create information. In studying information management systems, JISC and SCONUL (2008) noted the impact of Web 2.0 in concentrating the aggregation of information, and diffusing the dissemination and reuse of content. Especially in today's Web 2.0 world, consider incorporating interactivity and social networking features, such as push technology RRS feeds, comment/messaging options, incorporation of learning community repositories, enterprise mash-ups, and user-customizable folksonomy "shells." A number of Web 2.0 tools were mentioned in Chapter 5.

Wikis exemplify participatory Web 2.0 practice. Wikis (based on the Hawaiian term "wiki wiki," which means "fast") are webpages that can be generated without markup language knowledge. Wikis are probably best known because of Wikipedia, a user-built web-based encyclopedia. While some people may dispute Wikipedia's veracity, the concept of collaboratively edited content holds valid potential. Furthermore, most wikis have a feature that allows participants to see the page's history, so that contributions can be tracked accurately. These two features, collaborative editing and tracking, make wikis a useful learning and assessment tool. The website http://www.wikimatrix.org/ lets users compare almost 100 different wiki applications.

Wikis can be used to address academic and professional skills, knowledge, and dispositions: knowledge synthesis and generation, written and media communication skills, collaboration, technical skills, and organizational skills. Some of the activities that can be done using wikis follow.

- **Knowledge management**: Learner research can be organized under one wiki by incorporating frames and tags.
- **Group projects**: Each learner is responsible for one aspect of a project.
- **Point-of-view study**: Each student assumes the role of a different stakeholder.
- **Planning:** Wikis facilitate collaborative planning for learning activities and instructional units and speed up grantsmanship.
- **Lists/bibliographies**: Course-related resources can be developed on a wiki.
- **Literature circles**: Each student leads a discussion on some aspect of a book.
- **Text commentary**: Students can put in comments about a text or image.
- **Case studies**: Students can share their perspectives or develop studies collaboratively.

Today's technology can facilitate collaborative e-learning because learners can work with one another both in real time and asynchronously, anytime and anywhere. Web 2.0 tools have greatly expanded the ways that collaboration can occur to support e-learning (Senior, 2010).

- **Threaded discussions** archive individual contributions and responses chronologically by subject.
- **Social bookmarking** (public lists of recommended websites) helps build sources of peer-reviewed information.
- **Blogs** (web logs) enable individuals to write about their experiences chronologically, and others can comment on the entries.
- **Wikis** (quick-edit webpages) facilitate joint production of webpages that reflect collaborative knowledge.
- **Multimedia** programs such as VoiceThread enable users to develop and share online group albums.

- **Image-sharing** programs such as Flickr enable users to upload and share photos and other images; these items can be combined into albums that reflect content matter learned.
- **Online chats** enable individuals to discuss issues in real time. Some chat programs include features that allow documents and webpages to be viewed in common.
- **Web-based conferencing** incorporates text, images, and sound to more closely approximate physical interaction.
- **Virtual environments** (object-oriented online environments) enable individuals to interact virtually using avatars. Virtual environments usually have ways for applications to be embedded and documents to be stored.

Videoconferencing

Videoconferencing links video equipment and telecommunications to enable people to converse fully in real time, including interpreting body language. Videoconferencing is especially effective for virtual field trips and other interactions with remote experts.

At its simplest, videoconference can be done with two Internet-connected desktop computers with webcams and microphones. A software program such as Windows Meeting Space enables the two systems to communicate. Higher-end dedicated systems are more costly, but they can support multiple input devices and larger audiences. Nevertheless, more technical preplanning is required for virtual meetings than for face-to-face events: scheduling, coordinating, and supporting available video technology systems. Microphones should be placed around the room to facilitate wide participation; in addition, the videoconference should be held in a shallow room rather than a long, narrow one, particularly if the video camera can pan. Talk is more task oriented, so you need to explicitly build in opportunities for socializing, such as introductions and icebreaker activities. A pecking order may emerge, with each side considering itself more worthy than the other, so you should give each group a unique task to perform, which can display each unique contribution (Anderson, McEwan, and Carletta, 2007).

Webcasts and videoconferencing have more learning impact if done on a regular basis with a consistent set of people. In that way groups can form communities that can advance their practice through mutual support and accountability. You need to reinforce these long-term commitments between online sessions through telecommunications and online archiving and sharing of documents (Weinfan and Davis, 2004).

E-gaming

E-gaming (electronic games) constitutes a new form of instructional strategy that enables learners to explore issues within a prescribed virtual environment, often interacting with other players. In terms of gaining knowledge, e-games can introduce learners to technology through motivating activities. Social gaming can lead to positive identity assets: self-esteem, self-employment, personal sense of purpose, and personal positive future orientation (Helmrich and Neiburger, 2007). Many studies have been conducted using games that address historical content, such as *Civilization, Revolution,* and *Age of Mythology.* These games proved to be intellectually engaging, highly challenging, and complex learning activities (De Kanter, 2005; Gee, 2007; Squire, 2006).

Many e-games meld educational and recreational components, combining cognitive and affective domains; in order to be engaging to learners, games should be both fun and interactive (Amory et al., 1999). Particularly for females and older adults, the e-gaming protocols need to be easy and intuitive so that the focus is on the content rather than on navigation through a virtual space. On the other hand, if learners have little prior experience learning academically through gaming, they might assume that gaming is strictly a leisure activity. Therefore, consider explaining to students how games offer beneficial learning experiences, and stating explicitly how specific e-games were chosen for an identified learning objective. Halverson (2005) identified four learning environments for e-games: learner centered to help users to apply knowledge, assessment centered, knowledge centered to help users learn, and community centered to build social skills. What characteristics of gaming inform instruction?

- Use of fixed, equitable rules
- Clear roles and expectations
- Internally consistent environment where everything is possible
- Clear goals within a rich context that gives goals personal meaning and relevance
- Opportunities to explore identities
- Cognitive and affective engagement
- (Usually) multiple ways to achieve goals through constructivist strategies
- Specific, timely feedback
- Sense of control and personal investment
- Situated learning
- Sense of reward for effort, including trial and error
- Structured interaction between players, and between players and the game
- Blend of cooperation and competition (DeKanter, 2005; Deubel, 2006; Gee, 2007; Squire, 2006)

Mobile learning

Another popular technology tool affecting instructional strategies is mobile learning, or m-learning. Instructions have used personal digital assistants (PDAs) to help collect observation data and facilitate quick in-class quizzes to check for understanding. The ability of PDAs to "beam" data wirelessly enables instructors to disseminate short documents throughout the class, or create learning stations at which learners can download information for just-in-time learning. Stripped-down application programs such as word processing and concept mapping enable learners to brainstorm and journal their learning experiences easily, and then share those ideas with their peers. Today, smartphones offer a portable world of digital communication, which was facilitated by the convergence of digital services and utilities.

Mobile devices such as smartphones, particularly the iPhone, have ratcheted up m-learning and associated instructional strategies because of their many features: two-way communication, text messaging, photo capture, calendaring, calculating, Internet access, application downloading and operating options, geographic information system (GIS) or global positioning system (GPS) functions, and language support. Clough and colleagues(2008) developed a framework for m-learning instructional suggestions, which these examples concretize:

- **Reference**: Ask learners to access reference sources and e-books online.
- **Interaction**: Hundreds of microprograms are available for free or low cost that can reinforce in-class learning; be aware of these programs in order to recommend them to learners.
- **MicroWorlds**: Ask learners to experience models of downloadable microworld domains as seen in the phone screen.
- **Location awareness**: Ask learners to take photos that demonstrate training concepts, and identify their location using the device's GIS/GPS function. That data can also be used to create class "mashups" of maps and photo info.
- **Data collection**: Give learners observation templates to use to collect observational data out in the field.
- **Collaboration**: Collectively build a database of information, or play educational e-games online.

Digital divide or digital inclusion

At this point, the term *digital divide* usually refers to the "haves" and "have-nots" of technology. The typical image includes powerful white males at state-of-the-art computers doing advanced calculations or sophisticated graphics while poor homeless mothers stare at an isolated Windows 98 system. The actual picture is much more complicated, and effective solutions involve much more than plopping a laptop inside every project complex apartment.

This digital divide discrepancy has a new wrinkle: age. Today's millennial youth have grown up in a digital world; at some point, formal or informal education usually provides youth some technological access. They may be called "digital immigrants." In contrast, most adults over the age of 30 tend to be "digital immigrants"; electronic technology may be considered a second language or culture. In digital-rich industries, youth may be advantaged because of their technological skills; particularly if the corporate culture advances expertise over seniority, the gap between young and old may broaden, sometimes to the disadvantage of seniors. Adults who are used to being considered experts may feel uncomfortable learning from youngsters; they may well leave digital technology in the hands of younger generations, which can seriously jeopardize older adults' own independence and lifelong learning as well as their economic circumstances (Istance, Schuetze, and Schuller, 2002).

Probably the most exerted effort has been made in providing equitable opportunities for individuals with disabilities. The Americans with Disabilities Act of 1990 mandated accommodations so that eligible individuals could access information equitably. Closed-captioned television and videos, accessible websites, universal telephone service, and built-in adaptive features in computers exemplify ways that technology can help this population learn. Other assistive technology includes modified input devices, specialized software, and dedicated hardware.

The digital divide can also impact assessment in that variations among learners' level of technological access and skill may invalidate learners' demonstrated competence (Cowan, 2008). In any case, find out your students' technology realities, and try to provide accessible learning activities for all, or at least make accommodations for online students who have technical constraints. For example, save documents in .rtf format, transcribe video clips, and give learners choices of resources to use.

Emerging technology trends

Technology will continue to change, sometimes in unexpected ways. Many of these technologies have the potential to change instructional design and how adults learn. Some of the technologies appearing on the horizon that could impact learning follow. Library instructional design implications are italicized.

- Cloud computing is basically the ability to store and access information on Internet-accessible servers using a wide variety of devices. Learners can access and store learning objects anytime, anywhere, any way (New Media Consortium, 2010). *These days you can access and have hosted many applications and learning systems "in the cloud," which gives you and learners more flexible access.*
- The Semantic Web already exists, but it is becoming more accurate and multilingual. Search engines are beginning to parse natural language grammar and syntax so that contextualized relationships between terms can be identified. Because languages are constructed differently, search engines can

"cross-walk" linguistic features so that language barriers might be lowered (Raposa, 2008). *In developing instruction, you could use a learning object search agent to locate a set of related topical resources. The Semantic Web can also strengthen knowledge management efforts (Goodman, 2009).*

- Visual immersion systems, from head-mounted visual systems to 3-D "caves," enable learners to experience a visual simulated environment. These systems can sense the learners' movement, and adjust the visual components accordingly (Roblyer & Doering, 2009). *Librarians already use Second Life as a means to provide both formal and informal instruction.*

Sample face-to-face lesson incorporating technology

Technology is not just for distance learning; its tools and resources can enrich face-to-face instructional design as well. This lesson demonstrates how technology can be appropriate for kindergartners and first-graders. Online resources expand students' access to the world outside their community, and help them experience concepts that would be impossible otherwise. The choice of resources reflects this ages' need for realistic images and concepts.

Lesson

Lesson title: Seasons: Impact in Nature

Lesson overview: Seasons impact nature. In temperate zones, nature has predictable seasonal characteristics. Some aspects of seasons are the same, regardless of climate, and others differ because of latitude and geography. Information about the seasons can be garnered from visuals.

Time frame: 1–2 hours

Learning objectives: Learners will:
- Explain seasonal weather.
- Identify characteristics of different seasons.
- Explain how seasonal weather affects animals and humans.
- Gain meaning from images that are communicated digitally.

Science standards: (aligned with Common Core)
- Students know changes in weather occur from day to day and across seasons, affecting Earth and its inhabitants.
- Observe common objects by using the five senses.
- Describe the properties of common objects.

Library standards (aligned with Common Core)
- Understand the concept that printed and digital materials provide information by identifying meaning from simple symbols and pictures.
- Identify types of everyday print and digital materials such as storybooks, poems, newspapers, periodicals, signs, and labels.

Resources

- Technology: Internet-connected computer (with sound) with data projector and screen; installed Google Earth (optional)
- Worksheets (masters found at Teacher's section of http://www.national geographic.com/ngyoungexplorer/0904/)
- Writing/drawing instruments
- Supplies for vocabulary chart/wall as appropriate

Planning for diverse learners

- Have students work in pairs (one typical and one with needs, such as language or physical limitations).
- Have students demonstrate knowledge orally, by drawing, by pointing.
- Read the story aloud to students.

Instructional strategies and learning activities

0. Prepare for the lesson by setting up technology. Create vocabulary cards/wall as needed. Preview the websites.
1. Ask students what season they are experiencing now. Ask what are nature characteristics of the season (such as status of plants, clothing, temperature, length of daylight). As they respond, write simple words or images on a writing surface.
2. Ask students what are the other seasons. Ask what are nature characteristics of each season. A grid can be constructed to show the different seasons, for example:

	Fall	**Winter**	**Spring**	**Summer**
Weather	Fog	Snow	Rain	Sun
Plants	Red leaves	No leaves	Flowers	Dry plants
Temperature	Cool	Cold	Cool	Warm

Some children might not know the answers, which is fine because they will learn during this class.
3. Play the season song found at http://www.youtube.com/watch?v= LTXtSGf1VdY (if the computer has sound). Encourage students to respond as appropriate.

4. Ask students how the seasons impact them, such as the clothing they wear, their play habits, or the food they eat (such as seasonal fruit). Ask them how it impacts animals. Then show the National Geographic stories about the forest in different seasons, starting with the present season. Students can take turns clicking on the page-turn icon.

> The Forest in Fall:
> http://www.nationalgeographic.com/ngyoungexplorer/0809/readstory.html (includes a section on maps)

> The Forest in Winter:
> http://www.nationalgeographic.com/ngyoungexplorer/0811/readstory.html (has worksheet on weather by day)

> The Forest in Spring: http://www.nationalgeographic.com/ngyoungexplorer/0904/readstory.html (has worksheet on animal changes by season)

After the first season, ask students how that season affects each kind of animal. Refer to the pictures, and point out the visual information (such as color, length of fur, body language). Divide the class into the four animal groups, and ask them to focus on that animal for the other two seasons. After each season, ask each group to state how their animal is impacted by the weather, backing their answers by the visual information. Note that there is not a story about the forest in summer. Ask students to predict what the forest would be like in summer, and have them explain why. Students might also state how the vegetation differs.

5. Show "wild weather" images at http://kids.nationalgeographic.com/kids/photos/gallery/wild-weather/. Ask students to identify the season for each, giving the reason for their choice. The teacher can extend the lesson by showing the location of each site on a globe, map, or Google Earth. Alternatively, find images of weather or seasons on http://www.askkids.com. Ask students if they agree about the choice of images generated, and the basis for their decision.

6. Ask students if a season is the same around the world. Ask them why it might be different. This is shown in Forests in Fall (maps) and Forests in Winter (photo spread). Using Google Earth or a geographic map, show them latitude differences, explaining that at the equator, it is warmer, and near the poles it is colder. Similarly, it is colder in the mountains, and warmer during the day in many deserts. Explain that some aspects of seasons are the same throughout the world, such as length of day. Time of the year differs by hemisphere.

7. Replay the season song, and ask students to identify the visual cues about weather. Have students complete the animal changes worksheet.

Variations

- Break up the lesson into different parts, as needed.
- Focus on times of the day.
- Focus on types of weather.
- Focus on geography and weather.
- Focus on plants and seasons.
- Weather snapshot by day (see Forest in Fall worksheet).
- Focus on activities at different seasons (http://www.activityvillage .co.uk/seasonal_pages.htm).
- Study the reason for seasons: http://www.youtube.com/watch?v= DuiQvPLWziQ.
- Have students find images for seasons (can be clip art), and then sort them by season (can do counter-examples).
- Use images from print resources.

Student assessment

Learners are assessed by observation, oral expression, or written work. For instance, students can explain orally or draw what the weather might be during different seasons, depending on the location. The National Geographic worksheet on animal changes can be used as an assessment. The criteria for assessment include:

- Identify characteristics of different seasons: accuracy, completeness of answer.
- Explain how seasonal weather affects animals and humans: accuracy, completeness of answer.
- Interpret visual information: accuracy, completeness of answer.

Additional resources

http://ww2010.atmos.uiuc.edu/(Gh)/guides/maps/home.rxml

http://eo.ucar.edu/webweather/

http://kids.nationalgeographic.com/kids/photos/gallery/wild-weather/

http://www.noaa.gov/wx.html

http://www.nws.noaa.gov/

http://www.photolib.noaa.gov/

http://www.nationalgeographic.com/ngyoungexplorer/0609/

References

Amory, A., K. Naicker, J. Vincent, and C. Adams. 1999. "The Use of Computer Games as an Educational Tool: Identification of Appropriate Game Types and Game Elements." *British Journal of Educational Technology* 30, 311–321.

Anderson, A., R. McEwan, and J. Carletta. 2007. "Virtual Team Meetings: An Analysis of Communication and Context." *Computers in Human Behavior* 23: 2558–2580.

Carlson, S. 2005. "The Net Generation Goes to College." *The Chronicle of Higher Education* 52, no. 7: A34–A37.

Clough, G., A. Jones, P. McAndrew, and E. Scanlon. 2008. "Informal Learning with PDAs and Smartphones." *Journal of Computer Assisted Learning* 24: 359–371.

Cooper, J., and K. Weaver. 2003. *Gender and Computers: Understanding the Digital Divide.* Mahwah, NJ: Lawrence Erlbaum.

Cowan, John E. 2008. "Strategies for Planning Technology-Enhanced Learning Experiences." *Clearing House: A Journal of Educational Strategies, Issues and Ideas* 82, no. 2: 55–59.

DeKanter, N. 2005. "Gaming Redefines Interactivity for Learning." *TechTrends* 49, no. 3: 26–31.

Deubel, P. 2006. "Game On." *T.H.E. Journal* 33, no. 6: 30–41.

Gee, J. 2007. *What Video Games Have to Teach Us about Learning and Literacy.* 2nd ed. Palgrave, UK: Macmillan.

Goodman, V. 2009. *Keeping the User in Mind: Instructional Design and the Modern Library.* London: Chandos.

Gurian, M., and P. Henley. 2001. *Boys and Girls Learn Differently! A Guide for Teachers and Parents.* San Francisco: Jossey-Bass.

Hackbarth, S. 2001. "Changes in Primary Students' Computer Literacy as a Function of Classroom Use and Gender." *TechTrends* 45, no. 4: 19–27.

Hall, G., and S. Loucks. 1979. *Implementing Innovations in Schools: A Concerns-Based Approach.* Austin, TX: Research and Development Center for Teacher Education, University of Texas.

Halverson, R. 2005. "What Can K–12 School Leaders Learn from Video Games and Gaming?" *Innovate* 1, no. 6. http://www.innovateonline.info.

Hargittai, E., and S. Shafer. 2006. "Differences in Actual and Perceived Online Skills: The Role of Gender." *Social Science Quarterly* 87, no. 2: 432–448.

Harley, K., and L. Bendixen. 2001. "Educational Research in the Internet Age: Examining the Role of Individual Characteristics." *Educational Researcher* 30, no. 9: 22–25.

Helmrich, E., and E. Neiburger. 2007. "Video Games as a Service: Three Years Later." *Voice of Youth Advocates* 30, no. 2: 113–115.

Holliday, W., and Q. Li. 2004. "Understanding the Millennials: Updating our Knowledge about Students." *Reference Services Review* 32, no. 4: 356–366.

Horrigan, J. 2007. *A Typology of Information and Communication Technology Users.* Washington, DC: Pew Internet and American Life Project.

Iacono, A. 2010. "OPAC, Users, Web. Future Developments for Online Library Catalogues." *Bollettino AIB* 50, no. 1/2: 69–88.

Istance, D., H. Schuetze, and T. Schuller. 2002. *International Perspectives on Lifelong Learning: From Recurrent Education to the Knowledge Society.* New York: Open University Press.

JISC and SCONUL. 2008. *Library Management Systems Study.* Sheffield, UK: Sero Consulting.

Knowles, M., R. Swanson, and E. Holton. 2011. *The Adult Learner*. 7th ed. Burlington, MA: Butterworth-Heinemann.

Ko, S., and S. Rossen. 2010. *Teaching Online: A Practical Guide*. 3rd ed. New York: Routledge.

Lenhart, A., and M. Madden. 2007. *Social Networking Websites and Teens*. Washington, DC: Pew Internet & American Life Project.

Levinson, D. 1978. *The Seasons of a Man's Life*. New York: Knopf.

Maier, P., and A. Warren. 2000. *Integrating Technology in Learning and Teaching*. Sterling, VA: Kogan Page.

Maloy, R., R. Verock-O'Loughlin, S. Edwards, and B. Woolf. 2011. *Transforming Learning with New Technologies*. Boston: Pearson.

Martinez, M. 2005. "Mass Customization: Designing for Successful Learning." *International Journal of Educational Technology* 2, no. 2: ERIC.

Morley, J. 2000. "Gender Differences and Distance Education." *Journal of Education for Library and Information Science* 48, no. 1: 13–20.

National Science Foundation. 2003. *NSF's Program for Gender Equity in Science, Technology, Engineering and Mathematics*. Washington, DC: National Science Foundation.

New Media Consortium. 2010. *2010 Horizon Report*. Austin, TX: New Media Consortium.

Raposa, J. 2008. "4 Tech Trends to Watch in 2009." *EWeek*, October 20: 32–36.

Roblyer, M., and A. Doering. 2009. *Integrating Educational Technology into Teaching*. Boston: Allyn & Bacon.

Rogers, E. 1962. *Diffusion of Innovation*. New York: Free Press.

Senior, R. 2010. "Connectivity: A Framework for Understanding Effective Language Teaching in Face-to-Face and Online Learning Communities." *RELC Journal: A Journal of Language Teaching and Research* 41, no. 2: 137–147.

Simonson, M., S. E. Smaldino, M. Albright, and S. Zvacek. 2008. *Teaching and Learning at a Distance*. 4th ed. Upper Saddle River, NJ: Merrill.

Squire, K. 2006. "From Content to Context: Videogames as Designed Experience." *Educational Researcher* 35, no. 8: 19–29.

Wang, F, J. Fong, and R. Kwan. 2010. *Handbook of Research on Hybrid Learning Models: Advanced Tools, Technologies, and Applications*. Hershey, PA: Information Science Reference.

Weinfan, L., and P. Davis. 2004. *Challenges in Virtual Communication: Videoconferencing, Audioconferencing, and Computer-Mediated Communications*. Santa Monica, CA: RAND Corporation.

Wilson, M. 2000. "Evolution or Entropy: Changing Reference/User Culture and the Future of Reference Librarians." *Reference & User Services Quarterly* 3, no. 4: 387–390.

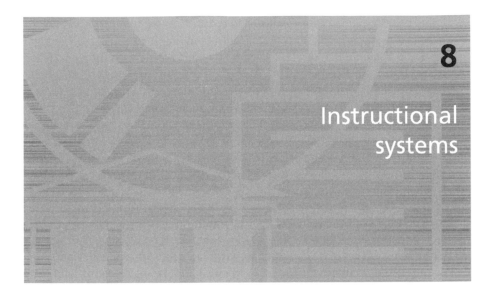

8

Instructional systems

One-shot instructional design can be inefficient. Building an instructional designed scope and sequence offers an articulated learning plan for users. Furthermore, groups of librarians can contribute to an overarching instructional schema to support situational learning. This chapter explains how learning objects and activities can be combined in various ways to address learners' needs. Instruction delivery that combines synchronous and asynchronous modalities can optimize learning. You can also design meaningful instruction collaboratively with communities of learners to provide a sustainable learning environment.

Planning synchronous delivery

The actual delivery of synchronous face-to-face instruction is the result of planning, not only of the curriculum but also the system itself.

Working with the organization

Most instruction is delivered under the auspices of an organization. Some of the details that must be ironed out follow. For each factor, relevant stakeholders and you collaboratively must determine (1) who is responsible; (2) the needed action; (3) the timing; and (4) the cost.

- **Scheduling**: How does the instruction fit sequentially within the curriculum, and how might it impact other curricula? What other instruction is being provided at the desired time? What facilities are available? What technology support is available? What building security is needed and available? It should be noted that learners need a break after two hours of instruction.

- **Publicity**: How will potential learners find out about the instructional delivery session? Who does the publicity: creating and disseminating information? What communication channels will be used? How will the publicity be timed? (More details about these characteristics will be provided in Chapter 9.) Even on the day of the instructional session, directional signs are often needed, particularly if the participants are new to the curriculum or facility.
- **Registration**: Learners need to commit to the learning venue in some manner; registration is usually the means. What kind of registration is needed? Who will handle it? What will be the form of registration? If the form is digital, how will potential participants without technology get access? What cost will be involved (for staffing, materials, facilities, food, overhead, administration, credit)? How will the registration cost be calculated (for instance, to cover costs, to make money, to recruit members)? What will be the timing for registration? How will cancellations be handled? What privacy measures need to be taken (such as credit card information)?
- **Material resources**: What instructional materials and supplies are needed: teaching and learning aids, communication tools (e.g., newsprint, chalkboard, interactive whiteboard, writing utensils), software? Who will provide them? What copyright permissions are needed, and who will procure them?
- **Equipment and connectivity**: What equipment and peripherals (e.g., cables, connectors, webcams, projectors) are needed? Is there sufficient power, and is it handy? Are power strips and extension cords needed? Who will provide them? How can their operability be guaranteed? Who needs to set them up? What software is needed, and who will install it, and make sure it works? What is the backup plan? What technical support is available? What kind of connectivity is needed and available? What log-on procedures and authentication are needed?
- **Facilities**: What are the dimensions of the room(s)? How many people can it accommodate? What features does it have (e.g., windows, doors, poles, heating/air) that might impact delivery (e.g., impossible to get the room dark enough, obstacles to viewing)? To what degree can features be controlled within the room (e.g., turning on the air conditioner)? How convenient is it to the library, restrooms, eating areas, parking? Can food and drink be brought in? Is it ADA accessible? What security is needed, and who will handle it? What insurance or waivers are needed? Who is covered? Who will handle it?
- **Lighting**: What is the nature of the lighting? Can it be differentiated by area? Who can control it? Is ambient light available?

- **Furniture**: Does the furniture fit the activity? What is the seating arrangement; can furniture be moved? What writing surfaces are available? What setup and cleanup details are needed, and who will handle them?
- **Budget**: How will be budget be determined? Who will handle the finances? How will the instruction delivery be underwritten?

Planning details on the day of the instruction delivery

On the day of instruction, be early, prepared, organized, and enthusiastic. All arrangements for opening and setting up the facility should be in order. All personnel should be in place for greeting, parking, registering, hosting, and otherwise supporting the session. The tone for the session needs to be welcoming and productive, so that the cognitive, affective, and social aspects of learning will be optimized.

Even before the formal delivery begins, provide a way to orient learners, such as "early bird" activities like reading content matter, providing food, or helping them get to know one another. Find out about special needs such as hearing or visual impairments, or limited mobility.

At the beginning of the session, make introductions: of the curriculum, the agenda, the participants, the site, and yourself. Clarify expectations and group norms. Explain "housekeeping" details such as restrooms, breaks, parking, and food. Begin learner interaction with the content and peers using a warm-up activity such as the following:

- One-minute peer introductions, including hopes for the session
- Group hands-up census of background, experience, expectations
- Mix-and-mingle activity so learners can gather information from one another (e.g., completing sentences about the curriculum, completing a bingo card about curriculum), which also serves as a diagnostic assessment
- Peer sharing of memories or perceptions about the curriculum
- Drawing or concept map about the content to be covered
- Group walkabout, writing first thoughts or perceptions on newsprint or other writing surface about different aspects of the session's content matter
- Diagnostic assessment in the form of a game (e.g., Jeopardy, trivia)
- Prioritizing content using labeled index cards

The heart of instruction focuses on interaction with the curriculum, as detailed in Chapter 6. Give learners opportunities to practice, reflect upon, and share new knowledge as well as ask for clarification or other assistance. Monitor learning carefully, so that just-in-time modifications can be implemented as needed. Throughout the session, make sure that you are speaking clearly and distinctly in a relaxed and natural way. Deep breathe.

At the closing, provide a sense of closure: review the curriculum, and suggest follow-up activities so learners can transfer and apply knowledge to their own environment. Start cleanup activity before everyone leaves, to take advantage of willing available hands. Assess the session along several dimensions: content, resources, delivery, learning, satisfaction. One good question to ask is "What do you want to learn next, as a result of this session?" The responses can help design follow-up instruction. The delivery should constitute one session in a planned curricular program.

After the session, thank those people involved in its planning and implementation. Wrap up any lingering fiscal and other administrative details.

Course management systems

Increasingly, education is incorporating online course management systems (CMS) or learning management systems (LMS) as part of their curriculum delivery system. This method facilitates distance learning as well as offers increased interaction. However, care must be taken to make good use of its features in designing and implementing courses.

Courseware

Online instructional packaging business has increased dramatically in correlation to the drive for distributed education. Particularly as the Internet becomes ubiquitous, web-based products can facilitate asynchronous learning and address issues of space constraints in education. Particularly with robust programs, learners can consider the courseware as a one-stop learning space that gives them individual control of their learning. CMS also offer nonlinear learning experiences that respond to learners' immediate needs. Its hypermedia features provide another dimension to learning as students self-identify the extent of knowledge needed, and access resources worldwide. Most courseware also provides real-time conversation (chats) as well as asynchronous sharing of reflective learning. On the instructor's part, most courseware includes grading, calendaring, and monitoring features that help one manage the course. Representative CMS products include commercial packages (such as Blackboard, Desire2Learn, eCollege, HotChalk, Informetica, JoomlaLMS, Learn, Meridian, and SharePointLMS) and open-source packages (such as Moodle, Sakai, Haiku, and ATutor). It should be noted that open-source solutions may seem attractive because they tend to be free in the public domain, but they require significant programming skill and technical support, which can be costly. By far, the most used CMS product is Blackboard, partly because they bought out WebCT and Angel. For that reason, the model courseware package detailed in this chapter is Blackboard, with its following features: announcements, course information, staff information, course documents, assignments, communication, links, and resources.

Taxonomies of courseware use

As instructional designers have incorporated courseware such as CMS, patterns of use have emerged. Several models have been developed, which are described here.

Salmon's model of web-based course development (2004) focuses on e-learning, and posits five phases, stepwise leading to increased learning. The model also recognizes the technical and instructional aspects of online course development, and folds those elements into each phase.

1. Student access requires setting up the system, as well as welcoming students.
2. Socialization requires telecommunications setup as well as facilitating interpersonal relationships.
3. Information exchange requires orientation to the software as well as providing feedback.
4. Knowledge construction requires collaborative tools setup as well as facilitating group dynamics.
5. Learning development requires links as well as monitoring.

Broadbent (2002) identified four key attributes to online instruction and learning: learning professionals, learners, content, and technology. She then identified characteristics of each attribute and how each figures in the online learning environment. Thus:

- Learning professionals need to be skillful developers, and should act knowledgably.
- Learners need to be computer proficient coming to the course, and need to act independently to achieve.
- Content must be authoritative, and delivered in the optimum way online.
- Technology needs to be reliable and robust during its use online.

Barnum and Paarmann (2002) adopted a blended learning model that incorporated face-to-face and online interaction, which more closely relates to the use of courseware in hybrid courses. They identified the following pieces: web-based delivery, face-to-face processing, creating deliverables, and collaborative extension of learning.

Northrup (2001) focused on interactivity in framing web-based instruction, identifying five attributes of interaction on the Web:

1. Interaction with content
2. Collaboration
3. Conversation
4. Intrapersonal interaction
5. Performance support

Within this framework, Northrup asserts that the approach to these attributes may be instructor centered or student centered.

In researching the areas of concern related to students' learning time in information literacy skills instruction in a web-based environment, Carey and Gregory (2002) identified three groupings: student characteristics, subject-matter content, and pedagogy characteristics. Using information as one continuum and student engagement as another continuum, they mapped pedagogy along a continuum of objectivist to constructivist.

Gallini (2001) provided the most complex model to describe the relationships between variables while studying technology-mediated learning environments. She posited three domains: background, design, and impact. Background deals with the instructor's and student's beliefs, and instructional goals. Design deals with type of technology, degree of technology integration, degree of online task structure, and online technology tools. Impact is student centered; it includes learning assessments, interaction, student engagement, and collaborative learning.

In reviewing effective instructional strategies in web-based learning, Kanuka (2005) identified seven principles and associated technology-enhanced practices:

1. Engagement with abstracted phenomena: concept mapping, role-play
2. Presentation of multiple perspectives: multiple readings, WebQuests, online debates
3. Relevant content: online remote experts and case studies
4. Diverse ways of knowing: WebQuests, problem-based learning
5. Learner responsibility: group projects, learner presentations
6. Building meaning: threaded discussion, joint course building
7. Expanding worldview: brainstorming, heterogeneous groupings

Focusing on librarians, Sharpless (2010) listed the following criteria for evaluating web-based instruction:

- Instructional design: clear objectives, examples, practice, and feedback
- Subject content: quantity, quality, "chunking"
- Audience consideration: appropriateness, engagement, relevance, student control
- Use of media: enhancement of learning, need for plug-ins, ease of transfer
- Visual design: clarity, consistency, cohesion, aesthetics
- Ease of use: intuitive, quick loading
- Evaluation: feedback features
- Accessibility

In researching teacher-preparation faculty use of the university's online course management system, Farmer (2004) noted the following benefits related to the affective domain:

- Increased frequency and quality of out-of-class, student-to-student dialogue (e.g., collaboration on assignments and projects; peer review of work, etc.) via e-mail, online chat and discussion group facilities
- Increased opportunity for faculty-student communication through individual and group e-mail
- Ability of instructors to evaluate efficiently the quality of student work by means of online quizzes and exams and to monitor student effort and engagement in the subject matter on a more frequent and regular basis through the use of online discussion groups
- Mutual reinforcement of out-of-class and in-class student interaction
- Increased student confidence in their ability to use facilities such as e-mail, chat rooms, and discussion boards

CMS instructional strategies

To concretize these principles, representative instructional strategies using CMS are detailed below.

Resources. Besides the course syllabus and general information, the CMS structure facilitates instruction through its resource manager function. Both you and learners can post readings, lecture notes, and presentation stacks, thereby maximizing access while conserving paper. In addition, hot links to online sources are possible in CMS, which streamlines course content and ensures compliance with copyright law. To increase learning, you can provide learner access to online tutorials, simulations, and WebQuests.

Communication. CMS offer a central telecommunications mechanism that can act in both a one-way and two-way delivery system. Up-front announcements facilitate timely changes. You can e-mail individuals, groups, or the entire class. Most threaded discussions can be sorted according to date, author, or topic for easy analysis. Small-group discussion can remain closed to anyone outside the group—except for the instructor. On the other hand, outside experts can communicate with the class synchronously or asynchronously. Learners can communicate their own interests via their personal online homepage within the course, and they can submit their work to the instructor via a drop-off box feature. It has been found the communication can increase with CMS; learners who might sit passively in the back row now become equal participants, and English learners have the time to think and find the right words to better demonstrate their own knowledge.

Learner engagement. With the variety of communications means, learners can increase their engagement with resources, peers, and their instructor. The act of using CMS helps kinesthetic learners. Learners appreciate the sense of an interactive and open-ended learning environment that is theirs to explore according to their own time and needs parameters. Online activities such as WebQuests and simulations foster interactivity and reflective learning. Discussion forums and virtual classrooms expand communication opportunities, and also enable learners to initiate their own threads; no longer can the learner hide behind someone. Learners learn more about their peers through personal homepages, and they work more easily with the group pages. You can use quizzes and surveys to help learners self-assess their own progress, and learners appreciate the faster feedback of online grading throughout the course period.

Collaboration. The communication and engagement approach certainly fosters collaborative learning activities. As already mentioned, threaded discussion forums, chats, and grouped projects expand traditional means of collaborating. Tele-based experts offer a link between the classroom and the professional world. On a very real level, CMS facilitate knowledge management as shared learning ramps up the class's own expertise. Reinforcing the idea of a learning community, learners can specialize their research and share it with peers, and receive in turn a myriad of research findings.

Equity. With its combination of text, visual, and aural information, a CMS can accommodate a variety of learning preferences, which might be more difficult to attain in a face-to-face environment. Asynchronous online communication helps level the playing field of learning. In the typical classroom, some learners talk more than others for a variety of reasons: knowledge of the topic, verbal ability, higher risk-taking behavior, extroversion versus introversion, cultural/social norms and expectations, language/vocabulary knowledge. English-language learners and women, in particular, benefit from this type of participation because they can self-pace and control their contributions. In addition, learners with physical disabilities can use assistive technology to permit them to communicate with others; the hearing impaired certainly benefit because so much of the information is communicated by text, and the visually impaired can use software to read aloud documents and input their ideas via speech recognition programs. If information remains available throughout the course, learners can preview and review it upon need or as time permits.

Dynamic course building. Unless the entire CMS site is developed ahead of time, and remains static throughout the semester, opportunities exist for learners to request additional materials to be incorporated—and for them to contribute to the CMS themselves. In that way, CMS-enhanced courses can be ongoing, responsive learning "journeys." Some of the means to develop and hone a course during the time period include developing course topics and content based on diagnosis of learner needs and wants, and creating a database of learner work.

Here are more tips for optimizing instructional strategies using CMS:

- Explore the software's features and potential.
- Clarify all instructions, assignments, and feedback.
- Work offline and upload content.
- Test layout and content conversion.
- Train learners in navigating the course work, and have veteran learners coach their peers.
- Check for understanding: never assign a resource without requiring some kind of learner action.
- Warn learners if the site will be dynamic (that is, content will change).
- Distribute instructional responsibility: have learner take lecture notes, create study guides, locate good readings.

Regardless of the specific use of CMS features, learners are by necessity placed in a situation where they have to be more responsible for their learning. Instructional designers tend to consider this situation as positive, believing that the more these students control their learning, the more effective learners they will become. Even those students who are reluctant to use a CMS at first may feel very good about themselves once they "master" the technology. This kind of empowerment can have lasting effects, helping students become self-sufficient lifelong learners.

Delivery use of CMS

You have to decide how to incorporate a CMS in light of the overall curriculum and its structure within the larger organization. Just because the CMS itself is online does not mean that the course itself must be delivered online.

Dimensions of time

The CMS can be used to store and manage resources, which may be consulted in class. In addition, quick quizzes and in-class writing can take advantage of the communications features of the CMS, and provide easy assessment and timely intervention.

Some instructional designers prefer a hybrid course delivery model: typically, one-third to two-thirds of face-to-face class time is eliminated, and virtual contact time increases by the same amount. In this scenario, face-to-face time is usually dedicated to work and interaction that is unfeasible independently, such as role-playing and extended seminar discussion. Those activities that can be done independently at any time, such as critiquing an article or learning declarative knowledge, are good candidates for online or distance learning.

Sometimes a learner may consider taking an online course, only to discover that this medium is not a good instructional "match." As an interesting alternative, some instructors provide class-equivalent activities to accommodate learners who prefer online instruction and those who prefer face-to-face instruction; the same content is provided both ways, but the actual learning activity varies in that online learners work within their local setting and record their learning.

While online courses tend to have more flexibility, you might rue such a feature because students sometimes have a tacit expectation that instructors are always available; clearly communicating expectations about replying to messages (such as 24 hours) and giving feedback to work (such as 4 days) provides predictability and eases workloads. In addition, some courses are entirely self-paced, which may run the danger of learner procrastination as well as negative impact on group discussion; setting deadlines as least monthly ameliorates pacing discrepancies.

Management tool

The CMS can be used strictly as a management tool. The software provides a framework to structure course delivery, which lowers the cognitive load for beginning instructional designers—and sometimes frustrates more experienced designers. Certainly, having a predictable course structure lowers learners' cognitive load. Learners especially like having a one-stop learning environment. The CMS can also facilitate assessment management: submitting learner work and assessing it. A CMS calendar and timely announcements can serve as reminders to learners about due dates as well. The CMS Grading function usually facilitates that administrative work, and enables learners to see their grades more conveniently.

Granularity

It should also be mentioned that the term LMS is actually more accurate than CMS for several reasons:

- Organizations can have separate dedicated sites.
- Learning objects can be used by several courses (of special import to librarians).
- Courses can be linked both within and across programs.
- The unit size can vary such that the curriculum can be structured as a series of modules having different numbers of credits attached to each so that courses can be configured in different ways or a learner can take modules instead of courses (Mairn, 2010).

Technology facilitates such flexibility; the main obstacle now is bureaucratic rather than instructional.

Online structure

Online course organization tends to be more highly structured than that of face-to-face courses because students must be able to navigate the learning environment independently. The lesson in Chapter 3 exemplifies this explicit approach. Most online courses include the following features:

- Course information and syllabus/"green sheet"
- A sequence of units, subdivided into lessons
- Assignments and assessments, which may be accessed separately or embedded in the lesson
- Resources, which may be accessed separately or embedded in the lesson
- Grading function
- Communication functions

Sharing curriculum

As mentioned in previous chapters, the curriculum provides content for learners to understand and use. Curriculum may be developed as a one-time targeted training as well as international multi-university set of programs. While instructional design may be developed largely by one person for a distinct set of content, most instructional design draws upon existing content matter and resources, and so has the potential to be shared beyond its original learning environment and target learners.

The most granular resource is a learning object: a self-contained learning aid such as a lecturette presentation, a simulation, a set of images, or a quiz. These learning objects can be used in different courses for different purposes. For instance, a WebQuest on Paris could be used in a French class or a world geography class. Using learning objects has several advantages:

- They have been learner tested.
- They are usually created by experienced instructors.
- They are often free.
- They can be repurposed and usually customized to address a specific set of learners.
- They serve as good models when creating learning aids from scratch.

In fact, learning objects can be used to provide mass customization of learning plans.

Within a curricular program, you should share your learning objects and other curricular materials with your colleagues, particularly if all the learners in the program have to meet the same standards. With external accreditation, curricular programs tend to develop "signature" assignments that assess how well a learner meets a program standard. Everyone who teaches the course is required to give this same significant assignment, and learner results are used to assess learners, the instructor, the instructional design, the curriculum, and the program as a whole. This practice not only helps provide consistent content matter so learners have equitable experience, but shares the burden of designing instruction. Furthermore, peers can review and improve these learning aids. Increasingly, signature assignments and other curricular learning resources are uploaded to a center site for efficient storage and retrieval. Course and learning management systems may include this feature, and repositories of resources are also being developed for this purpose. At this point, curriculum-specific repositories exist from the local level all the way to international scope. The management of these repositories is detailed in Chapter 9.

Collaborative instructional design most often occurs at the course level. For instance, all the mathematics teachers would get together to design the algebra, geometry, and advanced math courses. Standard course outlines constitute the typical product; they specify the learning outcomes, the content matter, the required resources, and the assessment methods. Instructors still have autonomy to make decisions about the delivery of that content matter. Such subject matter instructional designers often rely on state-legislated content standards and national standards developed by subject specialists such as the National Council of Teachers of Mathematics. In that respect, curriculum development and sharing can occur at even the international level.

As a librarian, you can be a valuable partner in at least three major ways: as an instructional designer developing curriculum, as an instructional designer and consultant recommending resources, and as an information manager organizing instructional design resources.

Developing curriculum programs

A coherent curricular program is the result of deep thinking and thorough broad-based planning with all the stakeholders. The more extensive the curriculum scope and potential audience, the more involvement and resources are needed. Curriculum development and changes can have several ramifications: course content and sequencing, staffing expertise and needed training, textbook adoption, library collection development, hardware and software acquisitions, changes to classroom furniture and utilities, scheduling, program length, student costs. Here are some representative scenarios.

- A public librarian wants to develop in-house curriculum for training adult library volunteers. He has to determine what functions the volunteers should be able to do in light of the rest of the library volunteer and paid staff. He should involve the rest of the library staff in assessing the functional needs of the library as well as curricular needs, and he should make sure that library administration and the library board approve the curriculum. The library is part of local government, so the public librarian needs to find out what roles volunteers are permitted to play within the organization. Thus, a potential curriculum might not equate with a permissible curriculum. Once the parameters of the curriculum are established, the librarian might need to submit that proposed curriculum to that supervisory body and any unions or other representative labor groups.

- Based on her observations of employee use of the library and the reference questions she receives, a corporate librarian develops a curriculum for employees so they can make more effective use of the library. She should first involve the rest of the library staff, if any, and key library users to get their input and buy-in, and would need her supervisor to review and approve that curriculum. It is likely that the corporation would have a human resources department, which would include a staff development function. The librarian should also ensure that those staff members work with her in designing the curriculum, particularly since some skills might be addressed in other training and because the time and resource cost of the curriculum delivery has to be accounted for fiscally. A labor union might also need to be consulted to make sure that the librarians' and other employees' duties are not negatively affected, or that the scope would overstep contract boundaries.

- In light of the American Association of School Librarians' (AASL) *Standards for the 21st-Century Learner,* a school librarian develops a scope-and-sequence curriculum for the high school. He could theoretically design it alone, and present it to the site council of department chairs for their approval. On their part, they might well okay it, thinking that the curriculum is for library aides. As such, that curriculum will probably be ignored by the classroom teachers. Therefore, the school librarian needs to explicitly link the AASL standards with academic content standards, and involve each academic department in that process to optimize across-grade and across-curricula learning. The administration on its part would need to examine the curriculum in terms of budget, resource, and time allocation, and make recommendations accordingly. These processes would require communication and negotiation within and across departments, and the entire faculty and administration would need to approve the ultimate curriculum. The school board would also need to approve the curriculum, so it would make sense for the school librarian to involve parents and a couple of school board members along the way.

- A regional professional library organization is experiencing a leadership vacuum, and wants to develop incoming librarians with leadership potential. The existing organizational leaders brainstorm what skill sets are needed, and consult similar library and other like-minded professional organizations to find out what kind of leadership training they offer—or think is needed. The organization's ad hoc curriculum committee should also identify some likely leaders-to-be, and interview them about their perceived needs and interests. The committee should also consult their regional library/information school to get their recommendations and identify existing courses that might address this issue. The organization's board would need to review and approve the curriculum, and determine what financial, material, and human resources are available to support the curriculum.

- A state accreditation agency is revising its standards for teacher librarian credential programs. In light of the changes, a university's graduate librarianship program needs to review and perhaps revise its curriculum. The program coordinator needs to make sure that the existing curriculum aligns with and meets new state standards. An existing accredited program would meet the old state standards. The coordinator is likely to compare the old and new standards, and identify the changes. Then the coordinator would map the existing curriculum with the changes to identify any curricular gaps. In collaboration with the rest of the program faculty, the coordinator would then determine what curriculum needs to be added, dropped, or changed. She should have an existing advisory group composed of representative library employers, community members, and students to provide a reality check on the curriculum; in that capacity they would also review and make recommendations about the curriculum. Next the program coordinator would need to consult with her department chair and college dean in terms of the curricular change impact on human and material resources, and should contact other related program coordinators in case the curriculum might impact them; for example, an additional course might need to be offered, which would lengthen the program and cost the university and students more money and time. The proposed curriculum would need to be reviewed and approved by the department curriculum review committee, and then the college curriculum review committee, in light of university regulations. If the curriculum requires course changes, which it probably would, then the program changes would also need approval: by the department, the college, and the university. At the university level, fiscal and resource (such as the library) implications would need to be addressed before the curriculum could be approved; at the college level, the curriculum changes might impact other colleges with similar courses. If the program is approved, at the least the university catalog text would need to be changed.

The organizational context of instructional design

You practice learner-centric authentic instruction daily. When you show a person how to use the Online Public Access Catalog (OPAC), and the learner uses it to find a desired book, then chances are the instruction was effective. As you observe information-using behaviors, you can tell if guidance is needed. Nevertheless, such situationally specific practices do not scale well or guarantee significant impact. A more systematic instructional design approach is needed, which requires organizational support.

The instructional design process itself exists within the context of the organizational entity that is sponsoring the learning experience. Therefore, for instructional design to be incorporated effectively, organizational leadership must have a shared vision for its implementation, the means to allocate resources, and policies to support the instructional design and curriculum. In short, the entire enterprise needs to have the motivation and the capacity to incorporate instructional design into its system (Roblyer and Doering, 2009).

For learners to gain optimal benefit from instructional design, the entire organization in which that design occurs has to support and model its use. Leadership has to promote instructional design as a paradigm for meaningful learning, and they need to ensure that resources are in place to support such efforts. In today's digital world, computer systems (including hardware, software, and programs) and Internet connectivity need to be easily accessible to learners and instructors, including opportunities to use social networking features. Ideally, all stakeholders should map the curriculum so that instructional design is introduced and applied across academic domains and instructional levels to provide an interdependent, articulated set of instructional designs that include assessment tools to be used for improving education throughout the school program. Professional development to support incorporation of instructional design needs to be in place. Administrators need to provide incentives and rewards for teaching staff to incorporate instructional design into their practice. In order to optimize the effective use of instructional design, administrators should also facilitate the effective communication and management of instructional design practice. As a librarian, you are a logical leader in such initiatives; you can collect, organize, and develop databases of effective instructional design practices that can be accessed by the entire organization.

Decision making

For each foundational issue, pay attention to the decision maker who makes things happen: legislators, trustees, school boards, superintendents, principals, other administrators, senior staff, and parents. In large educational systems, several spheres of influence may exist, from cross-campus initiative leaders to program coordinators. Do these decision makers have legitimate power or informal power? Did they get their power based on expertise or on whom they knew (referent power)? How willing are they to share their power? What are their attitudes about different instructional design structures and delivery? Further complicating decision making is the reality that decisions at one level impact those at another (usually from the top down); in some cases, those decision makers closest to the learner may be in a better position to identify and solve curriculum problems, but may be hampered by decisions from those higher up. Probably the most reasonable approach is one of transparent governance and open communication so that the input of all stakeholders is heard and considered.

Technology issues

When technology is intended to be incorporated into instructional design, organizational leadership has to understand that integration and provide the means (such as material, facilities, infrastructure, and technical support) to implement such integration. Technology-related policies also need to be put in place, such as acceptable use, skills baselines, professional development and incentives, hardware specifications and refresh cycles, and equity issues. When technology supports learning, job performance is the focus, and the training department controls the process to a large extent; the organization as a whole is not in flux. When technology is an end in itself, the latter views technology as a means.

Getting the buy-in of all the stakeholders for technology efforts, and involving them throughout the planning process, become critical tasks (Legge and Mumford, 1978). Bjørn-Andersen, Eason, and Robey (1986) further asserted that technology acceptance depended on the affective aspects of control and enhancement, whereby a feeling of less personal control increased resistance while a sense of self-improvement and contributing facilitated adoption. This issue of control within an organization was addressed in Gould and Lewis's 1985 principles for user-centered instructional systems design; they asserted that early focus be given to users and actual tasks, and that design should be a participatory set of activities incorporating user testing and feedback. With technology as an end, systems and organizational goals are the central concern, and advanced project management skills are needed; the entire enterprise changes (Mairn, 2010). In short, the entire enterprise needs to have the motivation and the capacity to incorporate technology into its system (Roblyer and Doering, 2009). A good place to start is the 2008 International Society for Technology in Education's (ISTE) technology standards for administrators, which emphasizes their organizational role. Unfortunately, even in 2009, Gaytan found that even though administrators said that they valued distance education, they preferred face-to-face instruction, and did not think that CMS or other online instruction was as educationally sound as in-class instruction. As a result, support for online instruction was lacking. Gaytan contended that administrators needed more data-based evidence of distance education's effectiveness, which a good deal of research does support.

Community support

Education is ultimately a community-based endeavor. Even with national curriculum and standards, how curriculum is played out depends on the community's resources and expectations. This impact may seem short term as societies become more transient, but it may be equally argued that today's online curriculum may influence the future of people around the globe.

As such, the public sector plays several significant roles in support of instructional design (Khoury, 2004).

- **Facilitation**: providing financial and political backing on curriculum initiatives; providing venues for discussing curriculum priorities; advancing information communication infrastructure
- **Regulation**: providing and enforcing information and communication technology (ICT) laws and regulations; accrediting educational institutions; establishing curricular standards and guidelines
- **Use**: bridging educational and economic curriculum applications; identifying and meeting information needs; producing and disseminating information; keeping current in curricular trends; promoting instructional design

As you design instruction, you need to assess the community's material and human resources as a means to enrich students' engagement with the curriculum, both online and as an extension of the physical community. In this respect, service learning provides authentic experiences where learners can apply their knowledge and can contribute to their community in meaningful ways.

You also need to be aware of community cultural values in order to validate current beliefs and bridge to new understandings. If you veer too far from community values and norms, then disconnects occur: between teachers and learners, between learners and their families, between administrators and community leaders. When organizations serve a variety of cultures, which may clash, then decision makers, including you, need to focus on identifying overriding common programmatic values and goals that all relevant community members can agree to. Otherwise, learners may get mixed messages about the curriculum and its application, and instruction may be undermined by family values. Little positive learning will occur. On the other hand, education and community can inform each other on novel views about curricular issues and the evolving world, so that both parties can adjust to an unforeseeable future. Otherwise, either will be stuck in the past, unable to survive or compete successfully.

Further implications for you

Instructional systems exist in multiple formats, from spontaneous learning groups to consortia of professional organizations, from one-time workshops to multinational corporate human resource programs. Operating within several organizations as an information professional, you have several venues in which to design instruction. Therefore, to succeed, you need to be knowledgeable about curriculum, learners, curriculum delivery formats, and the organization itself.

Both the content knowledge and the social context need to be considered so that you can find the best fit within that learning matrix. In that respect, keep observant and stay flexible; however, the payoff for such a mind-set is the opportunity to craft your instructional designer contributions according to personal needs and interests.

Sample professional development videoconference session

This school librarian professional development session showcases the use of videoconferencing, which facilitates real-time remote interaction and sharing of technology tools. In this case, both the content and delivery mechanism incorporate interactive technology. The content itself is a learning system that you can use for your own professional development or as a tool to teach others.

Videoconference

Title: Exploring Web 2.0

Lesson overview: School librarians need to experience Web 2.0 technologies, and consider implementing them into K–12 curriculum. This lesson introduces them to a self-paced set of online tutorials about Web 2.0 tools and their use in classrooms.

Time frame: 60–90 minutes

Learning objectives: Learners will:
- Describe general characteristics of Web 2.0 tools.
- Describe how to use one Web 2.0 tool.
- Explain how to incorporate at least one Web 2.0 tool into the K–12 classroom.

Curriculum standards
- Advocate for twenty-first-century literacy skills to support the learning needs of the school community.
- Employ strategies to integrate multiple literacies with content curriculum.
- Integrate the use of emerging technologies as a means for effective and creative teaching and to support preschool, K–12, and adult students' conceptual understanding, critical thinking, and creative processes.
- Model and promote ethical, equitable access to and use of physical,

digital, and virtual collections of resources to students, teachers, and administrators.

- Demonstrate knowledge of a variety of information sources and services that support the needs of the diverse learning community.

Resources

- Technology: Internet-connected computers; access to videoconferencing software; microphone

Planning for diverse learners

- The videoconference can be recorded and archived for later use (to aid English learners, individuals with different processing preferences).
- Learners at a distance may work in pairs.

Instructional strategies and study activities

0. Before the lesson, librarian sets up videoconferencing connection (such as Elluminate, NetMeeting, Tandem-based application). IP schedules conference time, and notifies participants. If a room-sized videoconferencing system is used, the room itself has to be set up so all participants can be seen by the camera (wide, shallow room) and their voices heard (microphones disseminated throughout the room). The software and equipment also needs to be checked for audio and video quality, and the features to be used should be tested (such as uploading files and using polling). Librarian locates and gathers possible images to use for module #6.

1. Librarian introduces the videoconference, and explains how to participate by explaining the features and the protocols. Librarian asks demographic questions using the input features, which also provides an icebreaker activity.

2. Librarian asks participants to define Web 2.0 via the site features (chat, mike, shared space). Librarian defines Web 2.0 (interactive Internet). Librarian asks participants to name some Web 2.0 tools (blogs, wikis, social bookmarking, Facebook, etc.). Librarian asks participants how Web 2.0 tools can impact learning and library services (examples: engages learners, reflects student personal use of the Internet, facilitates collaboration).

3. Librarian states the agenda: exploring Web 2.0 tools to incorporate into the curriculum, including information literacy. "To this end, one of the major ways that you will learn is through active participation in '23 Things.' This model started as an article by Steven Abrams in Special Library Association's magazine *Information Outlook*. Steven suggested

23 activities that librarians could do to help themselves keep current in technology. The Charlotte-Mecklenburg Public Library transformed his idea into a self-paced professional development program for their librarians. Later the California School Library Association adapted it for their membership. This version is the one that this session will be using."

4. Librarian shares http://schoollibrarylearning2.csla.net/ on the shared space. Librarian explains the website's structure: nine modules, each of which features a unique set of tools, activities, and curricular links.

5. Librarian can have participants choose which module to try (which is a risky approach because the librarian needs to know the entire site well). A good module to show is module 6, which features images. If participants have a video camera, their pictures can be captured and used to make a librarian trading card. Librarian asks participants to brainstorm other ways to incorporate Flickr and other image Web 2.0 tools (examples: make author trading cards, locate images that represent concepts and processes, evaluate cultural connotations of color).

6. Librarian points out week 1's module, which talks about learning processes. Librarian asks participants how they imagine they will set up a learning schedule. Librarian encourages participants to pair up as study buddies.

7. Librarian points out week 2's module, which discusses blogs. Librarian defines blogs (web diary), and states that blogs are good self-reflective tools. Librarian asks participants to name some advantages of blogs and of self-reflection (examples: documents activities, facilitates sharing, uses metacognitive skills). Librarian encourages participants to do week 1 and week 2 modules as soon as possible, and to view and comment on peer participants' blogs. Librarian asks participants to type in their e-mail addresses to facilitate creating a community of learners.

8. Librarian asks participants one thing they learned during the session.

9. After the session, librarian develops a list of the participants, and e-mails the group. Librarian follows up one month later to check on participant's Web 2.0 learning activities.

Variations

- The lesson can be delivered face-to-face, as a webcast, or as real-time chat (such as http://www.Tappedin.org/).
- The lesson can be provided as a self-paced tutorial without any guidance, or with just-in-time coaching.
- The lesson can take the form of a (PowerPoint) presentation.

Student assessment

Learners are assessed in terms of participation (Table 8.1).

|||||||||||||||||||||||||||||||||||||||||||||||||||||||||||||||||||||||||||||||||||||||||||||||||||||||||||||||

Table 8.1. Web 2.0 rubric

Objectives	Low performance	At or below average	At or above average	Exemplary performance
Learner describes how to use and incorporate a Web 2.0 tool.	Learner makes little use of communication features.	Learner uses basic communication features in response to prompts.	Learner responds to all prompts, and comments appropriately.	Learner contributes insightfully to discussion.

Additional resources

http://k12digitalcitizenship.wikispaces.com/

http://oit.montclair.edu/tsc/training/links.html

http://www.collegeathome.com/blog/2008/05/29/
100-free-library-20-webinars-and-tutorials/

|||||||||||||||||||||||||||||||||||||||||||||||||||||||||||||||||||||||||||||||||||||||||||||||||||||||||||||||

References

Barnum, C., and W. Paarmann. 2002. "Bringing Induction to the Teacher." *T.H.E. Journal* 30, no. 2 (September): 57–62.

Bjørn-Andersen, N., K. Eason, and D. Robey. 1986. *Managing Computer Impact*. Norwood, NJ: Ablex.

Broadbent, B. 2002. *ABCs of E-learning*. San Francisco: Jossey-Bass.

Carey, J., and V. Gregory. 2002. "Students' Perceptions of Academic Motivation in Interactive Participation and Selected Pedagogical and Structural Foundations in Web-Based Distance Learning." *Journal of Education for Library and Information Science* 13, no. 1 (Winter): 6–15.

Farmer, L. 2004. "Investigating an Information Process of Change Impacted by Technology." *Assessment Update* 16, no. 3: 4–6.

Gallini, J. 2001. "A Framework for the Design of Research in Technology-Mediated Learning Environments: A Sociocultural Perspective." *Educational Technology* 41, no. 2: 15–21.

Gaytan, Jorge. 2009. "Analyzing Online Education through the Lens of Institutional Theory and Practice: The Need for Research-Based and -Validated Frameworks for Planning, Designing, Delivering, and Assessing Online Instruction." *Delta Pi Epsilon Journal* 51, no. 2: 62–75.

Gould, J., and C. Lewis. 1985. "Designing for Usability: Key Principles and What Designers Think." *Communications of the ACM* 28, no. 3: 300–311.

International Society for Technology in Education. 2008. *National Educational Technology Standards for Teachers*. Eugene, OR: International Society for Technology in Education.

Kanuka, H. 2005. "An Exploration into Facilitating Higher Levels of Learning in a Text-Based Internet Learning Environment Using Diverse Instructional Strategies." *Journal of Computer-Mediated Communication* 10, no. 3: 1–31.

Khoury, R. 2004. "National ICT Priorities." Paper presented at the Arab Technology for Development Conference, Beirut, September 23, 2004. http://www.pca.org.lb/docs/dr.%20raymond%20khoury.ppt.

Legge, K., and E. Mumford, eds. 1978. *Designing Organizations for Satisfaction and Efficiency.* Teakfield, UK: Gower Press.

Mairn, Chad. 2010. "Enhancing Learning While Creating a Library Presence in Course Management Systems." *Journal of Web Librarianship* 4, no. 1: 55–61.

Northrup, P. 2001. "A Framework for Designing Interactivity into Web-Based Instruction." *Educational Technology* 41, no. 2: 31–35.

Roblyer, M., and A. Doering, A. 2009. *Integrating Educational Technology into Teaching.* Boston: Allyn & Bacon.

Salmon, G. 2004. *E-moderating: The Key to Teaching and Learning Online.* 2nd ed. London: Kogan Page.

Sharpless, S. 2010. *Web-Based Instruction: A Guide for Libraries.* 2nd ed. Chicago: American Library Association.

9

Management issues

Regardless of the scope of instructional design, it needs to be managed. Librarians need to document their processes as well as organize their learning resources for easy retrieval, use, and assessment. Instructional design efforts may need support, be it technical or administrative. Part of good instructional design is effective communication: from marketing to instruction to ongoing reinforcement. More fundamentally, you should plan and assess instructional design efforts as part of an overarching cycle of library program improvement. To this end, this final chapter discusses institutional and organizational management issues that impact instructional design.

Documentation

One of the main management functions of instructional design is documentation. Both instructional designers and learners need to document their work to make it more efficient and to facilitate its sharing. Librarians live in a world of documentation: selecting, gathering, organizing, storing, and facilitating its retrieval and use. Your expertise can help other instructional designers as well as leverage your own role as an instructional designer.

Self-managed learning environments

People tend to seek control of their learning. Such self-regulation reflects metacognition (that is, thinking about thinking), which is a valid indicator of a high level of information literacy. With the advent of technology tools, individuals can manage their learning more effectively. One of the recent applications is readers, such as Google Reader, which collect current information. The creator of the reader page identifies electronic news services that he wants to keep current on; he subscribes to the service through Really Simple Syndication (RSS), and creates a link to his reader. On the reader, the learner can also add his own original content. The learner can also customize the reader's appearance to reflect personal style. This kind of aggregated information builds on the learner's interests, and provides an efficient way to manage lifelong learning (Looi et al., 2010).

Learning objects

Learning objects are usually found in federative repositories that index them and facilitate their retrieval for efficient instructional designer use. Usually the directory or repository provides just a link to the source materials, which typically resides at the author's institutional server. The user is expected to comply with copyright law, and has some leeway because of fair use for research and educational purposes. A model representative education repository is the international website MERLOT (http://www.merlot.org/): Multimedia Educational Resource for Learning and Online Teaching. At the other end of the spectrum, collections of learning objects may be held by an individual instructor. The best collection of learning objects is found at Creative Commons: http://wiki.creativecommons .org/Content_Directories. This organization promotes customized intellectual property rights to advance knowledge.

Academic and special librarians are the most likely groups to collect and organize learning objects into institutional repositories. Setting up these databases can be very labor-intensive as the developers have to determine what kind of information (metadata) needs to be provided to optimize retrieval for instructional design: subject, level, format, type of activity. Controlled vocabularies also have to be established, and the repository's structure must be designed. In addition, instructors must be motivated to contribute to the repository, and stipulate acceptable use and copyright.

Knowledge management

As a vehicle for documenting information, knowledge management has gained attention in learning communities as an effective way to gather, organize, and store information in order to optimize its retrieval and use (Richey, Klein, and Tracey, 2010). Knowledge management enables organizations to systematically gather organizational wisdom, organize those ideas, archive them, and provide for their easy retrieval and dissemination. Examples of such expertise include management techniques, effective communication with employees, diagnosis skills, methods for engaging groups, and tips in broadcasting. Knowledge management codifies these insights and facilitates their use by others so the overall organization can benefit. In addition, it provides a mechanism to sustain learning communities because the shared documentation can outlast an individual's presence within the organization.

Traditionally, librarians have served as information managers. In general, they have gathered information from outside an organization in order to inform the organization and support organizational learning and operations, although they might well archive internal documents. Knowledge management tends to focus on the information generated *within* the organization, which can run the gamut from policies and manuals to informal memos and personal guide sheets, from architectural blueprints to party snapshots, from Dictaphone tapes to podcasts, from code books to spreadsheet templates. In addition, knowledge management is likely to use a decentralized model where information can be stored in several physical and virtual spaces. Centralization occurs in the identification, description, and classification of the information; a portal is usually developed as a means to link and relate the various informational sources (McElroy, 2006). Librarians are well positioned to serve as knowledge managers, although some companies label such experts as chief information officers.

Librarian instructional designers are most likely to keep documentation about their own operations and instructional design and training resources. Other instructional designers benefit from working with librarians to standardize their own documentation practices, identify information that could be collected in order to facilitate learning within the organization, and determine appropriate ways to categorize information to better reflect the organization's operations. By having more effective access to an organization's knowledge base, you can design more accurate and encompassing instruction that will benefit all of the organization's members.

Communications

Instructional design has little impact if no one knows about it. You need to articulate your program's mission and vision with stakeholders and beyond. Maintaining effective relationships is another central priority for leaders: creating alliances and working with opponents. Collaborative leadership fosters communication and mutual interdependence. In short, communication is essential for successful instructional design.

Communication should be ongoing and interactive, building on each stakeholder's efforts. Although communication is both a one-way and two-way endeavor, all stakeholders should be sharing information in order to improve the program as a whole and each person in particular: a learning community. In the process, new information can be generated; information is not just transferred between people in a closed loop but is open to new possibilities.

For communication to be effective, the message must be conveyed clearly, accurately, and usually succinctly. The person conveying the communication needs to consider the target audience—clientele, staff, administrator—in order to customize the message to facilitate understanding. The communication channel also has to be chosen carefully to align the content/message with the audience and the intent. For instance, posters serve as quick reminders while reports can offer in-depth analysis.

With the incorporation of technology, possible communication format choices are impressive: desktop publishing, databases, spreadsheets, presentation programs, telecommunications, Internet, digitized images, audio, video, and mixed media. With the advent of Web 2.0 and the concept of interactive technology, another dimension is added as messages are co-constructed and continue to evolve, thanks to technology. As a result, communication is as much a process as a product. Web 2.0 tools in particular can provide you with much-needed tools to inform and collaborate with stakeholders. Technology impacts communication in several ways.

- Communication and actions can be recorded more easily through e-mails, online chat, and videoconferencing.
- Documents can be digitized for easier access, storage, and retrieval.
- Information can be easily modified and repurposed for different audiences and objectives.
- People can communicate anytime, anywhere either instantly or asynchronously, relatively free from the constraints of time and space.

Managing communication tools can be challenging because of their variety of format and application. Each piece of equipment has been associated with a different media, such as a camera for still images. However, that picture is changing as technology devices such as the smartphone can be used for several kinds of communication, converging information. Nevertheless, you should know the possible communication purposes and features for each kind of equipment, as well as know how each operates. Of course, you should maintain communication technologies and make them easily accessible for the user.

Marketing

What is marketing? How does it differ from PR or advertising or strategic planning? The American Marketing Association defines it as "an organizational function and a set of processes for creating, communicating, and delivering value to customers and for managing customer relationships in ways that benefit the organization and its stakeholders" (Wood, 2010: 2). Core principles are values and relationships. Marketing planning is a six-part structured process, which will be explained briefly. The term "marketing mix" refers to the marketing tools of product, placement (channel), pricing, and promotion (some add the tool of people): the 4 or 5 Ps.

Why does instruction (and instructional design) need marketing? At this point in time, learners have so many choices in educational venues that they may be unaware of potentially well-matched options. You should examine their potential clientele market to better target library efforts. In some cases, that examination may impact their instructional design to make it more effective.

To add value for your stakeholders, you should identify what they can offer in terms of products and services: the internal environment. Analyze the external environment to understand the issues that impact stakeholders. The foundation for market and customer analysis is a SWOT analysis (strength, weakness, opportunity, threat). In libraries, S/W may arise from personnel, boards, support groups, facilities, money, collections, services, tech, customer database, open hours, etc. External issues might be local demographics, competition, tech, politics, government and agencies, economic environment, legal environment, etc. Focusing on instruction, a SWOT analysis would identify the following:

- Current library-related instruction that is happening in-house and offered by competitors
- Existing and potential instructors and instructional designers in-house and elsewhere
- Existing and potential resources, including learning aids, in-house and elsewhere
- Existing and potential learners *and* learning needs, in-house and elsewhere

Once you know what you can offer, you can determine which market to target. If you try to reach everyone, that approach is called mass marketing, and tries to find an issue/value that is the common denominator for everyone. Alternatively, you can focus on a few key market segments to provide more specific services/approaches. In general, librarians tend to segment markets (that is, potential learners) by age or type of use. Each market has subgroups or niches: e.g., seniors who want to volunteer in the library, local businesspeople, mystery buffs. Typically, an organization has resources or services that are underused/undervalued that they want to push. Perhaps they see a target user market potential that has ignored them. In general, try to go for the biggest bang for the buck: the best return on your design. For instance, a likely niche is entering users: new students and employees.

The bottom-line benefit of marketing is impact. In addition, to ensure that goals are reached, support must be present: learner support and internal marketing (getting employees on board). The learner focus and support can be confusing: think of wanting happy readers—librarians need to provide them with good service (e.g., readers advisory, good reading material in stock) to attain the goal. That same philosophy applies to instruction: prepared instructors, accessible materials, good technical support.

Products are more than boxes; they can be goods, services, places, ideas, organizations, and people. Wood (2010) noted: "When planning services, marketers must focus on delivering benefits through the appropriate combination of activities, people, facilities, and information" (p. 82). Product development, as instructional design, needs to go through development processes to ensure its success. And what makes a good product/service? Think about performance, features, reliability, durability, aesthetics, and perceived quality.

Branding distinguishes the product and builds connotations that lead to valuing and loyalty. Think about the Library of Congress's American Memory collections, the Folger Library, or Girl Scouts. That's why ALA has the @your-library campaign: to create memorable branding—and help libraries around the world by providing an easily recognizable brand that libraries can adopt—and leverage at the local level. All of the communication has a consistent look and tone that reinforces the instructional design. In general, posters and fliers should have one message and one graphic; supporting documents can have more detail. Infopeople (http://www.infopeople.org/) is a good example of effective instructional design branding.

Pricing strategy may seem irrelevant for libraries, but instructional design does cost, and educational venues usually include a fee. Organizations need to show good return on investment (ROI) to their corporate/institutional body. Certainly, instructional design and delivery cost time and labor. Publicizing the instruction, for instance with printed fliers and postcards, can run up a bill. CMS and digital resource costs can be significant. Depending on the setting of the instruction, computer lab and demonstration equipment can be sizeable. If you spend considerable time designing and publicizing a thesis workshop and pay for a lab in which to run the session, you will have a low ROI if only a handful of students attend.

The third part of the marketing mix is "place": how, when, where to make the instructional design products/services available to the target market. To do that well requires knowing how that target market accesses goods/services, the external environment (including competitors), as well as the product itself and its life cycle. What value accrues along the way from its inception to its delivery? What is the flow—the logistics? This issue is paramount for librarian instructional designers. In school and academic libraries, the tendency is to deliver instruction in the library, but librarians could conduct a web conference to be shown in the classroom. Increasingly, library instruction is done in the form of self-paced online tutorials so that learners can access the information anywhere at their convenience.

Promotion calls upon the advertising "front-line" and public relations tools as well as other techniques. Wood (2010) emphasizes integrated marketing communication built on analyzing the audience (that is, potential learner), clarifying objectives and budget, identifying issues, and doing background research. Note that communication will change over the life cycle of the instructional design. For instance, needs assessment can serve as a promotional opportunity, leveraging surveys and interviews as ways to inform potential users of potential curriculum. On the other hand, at the point of delivery, other formats such as websites and fliers are more appropriate. Kotler, Bowen, and Makens (2009) asserted that public relations is a set of tools: PENCILS (publications, events, news, community involvement activities, identifying media, lobbying, social responsibility activities). Each of these tools taps into a unique aspect of the prospective clientele and community.

The communication arena has really changed lately because of Web 2.0. For instance, viral marketing, which happens as people pass along marketing messages, has become an effective approach because of interactive telecommunications channels. The trend is to co-opt/enlist the help of the target market to identify the desired product as well as to communicate about it. Be aware that you are sharing control of the message and communication channel, so be prepared: Are you happy with what people Twitter about the instructional design? Potentially, electronic word of mouth may be the most effective advertisement of library instructional offerings.

Another aspect of public relations is relationship marketing, which refers to establishing and maintaining long-term relationships: having loyal "customers." This approach aligns well with library instructional design and implementation, and reinforces the concept of lifelong learning. The underlying idea is that the library staff is interested in its clientele, and addresses their needs in a timely and professional manner. Shaik (2009) stated that three levels of relational marketing exist:

1. Level one: price incentive (most libraries offer free instruction)
2. Level two: social bonding (well evident when users say "OUR library")
3. Level three: developing customized programs to meet user needs (good instructional design should provide this option)

The best marketing plan is the one that sells, that gets optimum results. Did the marketing plan work? You should assess your plan's effectiveness all along the way and make adjustments accordingly. Indeed, the type of assessment measures/instruments should be determined from the start. The concept "metrics" is often used; it refers to numerical measures of specific performance-related activities and outcomes, which can be applied to marketing evaluation. The most obvious result is student learning, which can apply to their work, be it academic or in the workplace. For example, instruction on database use might result in a scientist discovering a seminal paper that facilitates the creation of a groundbreaking invention. In public libraries, instruction on the use of business databases can result in richer patrons.

Sample strategic marketing analysis

This marketing analysis worksheet, adapted from the North Carolina State University College of Humanities and Social Sciences (2008), addresses the library organization's goals and the targeted audience's characteristics. It was developed to determine how best to teach librarians to use research to promote literacy and reading. The organization decided to create a short report of research-based guidelines.

Worksheet

Library Organization: International Federation of Library Associations (IFLA) Literacy and Reading Section

Motivation: Why is effective communication necessary in this situation?
1. *What is the need? What is lacking?* Action
2. *What action are you asking the audience to take?* To integrate research methods as they promote reading and literacy
3. *Ultimately, what do you hope to accomplish through the integrated marketing campaign?* **Goal: To convince librarians and professionals in related organizations to integrate research methods as they promote reading and literacy.**

Audience: Who is the audience in this situation?
1. *Define your audience. Is specific information easily available about audience members or is there more loose and generalized information?* IFLA-affiliated librarians (academic, public, school) in English-speaking countries are the core audience.
2. *Identify the generalized features that audience members have in common.* Well-educated librarians and related organizational members who want their clientele to be literate lifelong readers. The core people tend to be middle-/upper-middle-class individuals with MA+ degrees. 85 percent are Caucasian. 75 percent are female. Age range tends to

be 40–60 years old. 50 percent are married, half of which have children. They are librarians; of that group 80 percent are public librarians and 20 percent are school librarians. Buying habits are conservative. The social group is literate, well read, usually well traveled. Activities include reading, writing, travel, photography, music, art, light sports, collecting, entertainment (film), Internet.

3. *Identify the important similarities between you and your audience (try to find less obvious similarities). This is important to guard against making too many assumptions about the target audience.*
   I am a member of the IFLA Literacy and Reading Section, and associate professional with the core audience. I have a master's degree in library science, and teach school librarianship. I have worked in public and school libraries serving youth. I have taught in Tunisia and Hong Kong. I am a Caucasian female in the upper end of the population, have an adult child, and am widowed. I am well read, enjoy cultural activities, and travel regularly.

4. *Identify the important differences between you and your audience.*
   While I have done some reading promotion and have conducted research, I have not done action research in that capacity. I have not worked in a library in 12 years. Nor have I worked in a library outside of the United States, and have somewhat limited knowledge of literacy and reading promotions in other countries.

5. *What's the audience's current level of knowledge, belief, attitude, action regarding your proposed campaign?*

Knowledge: Research methods and resources (both print and digital) at the consumer level, basic reading and literacy promotion strategies, a little knowledge about reading and literacy development, in-depth knowledge about clientele's reading interests.

Belief: Strong belief in the value of literacy and reading, strong belief in the value of reading enjoyment, varying beliefs in their effectiveness to impact clientele's reading and literacy competencies and attitudes, varying beliefs about reading and literacy promotion (in terms of their job description), varying beliefs in the need for and impact of research-based reading/literacy promotion, depending on research background, medium to strong belief in collaboration.

Attitudes: Likes reading, usually considers literacy/reading promotion *and* research time-intensive (and may think there's not enough time to do it), may consider literacy/reading promotion *and* research outside of their scope of work, have personal age preferences/de-preferences, may think that they already know how to do research-based reading/literacy promotion so the added information is not needed (attitude that the issue is time and money, not knowledge—"Don't tell me how to do my job"), varying attitudes about collaboration.

1. *What kind of communication is appropriate in this situation based on your audience analysis?*
   Because the audience comes together only once a year, and is dispersed throughout the world, the instructional communication should be in the form of a set of guidelines to be available in digital and print form (to accommodate those people who have Internet access and those who do not). The guidelines will be presented at the conference through a conference poster session and section business meeting. Information about the guidelines will be disseminated through a flier disseminated at the conference, and through their website.

2. *How is the audience going to use the communication? Specifically, what should/will the audience be able to do after receiving the campaign?*
   Based on reading the communication, the audience should be able to—and be motivated to—make use of existing relevant research, and conduct action and assessment research, in their literacy and reading promotion efforts. A secondary outcome would be to read and participate in other IFLA reading and literacy efforts.

   To measure the outcome, IFLA will leverage their existing communications (e.g., listserv, newsletter, website). They need to add an RSS feed to their website in order to enter the social network area. At the very least, their newsletter and listserv will publicize their communication, and would solicit responses from the readers as to example ways that they have incorporated research into their reading/literacy promotion efforts. IFLA would publicize these efforts, which would then continue to motivate audiences to replicate and expand their own research-based promotion activities. Thus, the number and quality of responses to the prompts would provide evidence of the campaign's effectiveness.

Systems thinking about instructional design assessment

Chapter 4 detailed the use of assessment in instructional design, pointing out the need to identify appropriate instruments at the same time as developing the curricular outcomes. Instructional designers typically look at learner performance relative to their ability and their growth, in comparison to others, and to established criterion (such as standards) (Oosterhof, Conrad, and Ely, 2008). Ongoing

assessment, not just at the preplanning stage, but also during instructional implementation, enables you to make adjustments to the curriculum, resources, and
delivery as well as provide feedback to learners so they can make adjustments to
their own efforts (Richey, Klein, and Tracey, 2010).

While the most obvious use of assessment is to measure learning, the impact
of instructional design needs to be couched in the overall instructional program
and contextualized within the institution as a whole (Killion, 2008). Hence, it
is equally important for you to assess the institutional conditions for enabling
learners to become competent in the field. In determining tasks, you need to
deconstruct the actual design and implementation of learning activities into their
composite elements to determine which actions lead to positive conditions for
gaining competency. Does collaboration between the instructor and industry personnel, for instance, impact adult learning? Does the presence of a rich collection
of current and relevant online resources correlate with content knowledge? In
short, you need to examine the entire enterprise's processes and products in light
of learning throughout the instructional design and implementation process.

An effective approach to assessment is a systems approach where each input
and output factor is identified (Baykal, 2009). The following critical questions
can guide your assessment of your efforts and the learning environment at
benchmark points in the instructional design process: in preplanning, the design
stage, the implementation stage, and the reflective/debriefing stage.

Input

- What *competencies and dispositions* do you bring to the learning environment? Are you credentialed in library information science and other
  domains? Are you new to the field, or do you bring valuable experience from
  other settings—or other fields? Do you have expertise in teaching in online
  environments?
- What *curriculum* are you following? How closely does instructional practice
  align with academic content frameworks or industry standards? Does the
  curriculum reflect the latest trends in the organization and community as
  well as reflect instructional practice? Does the curriculum incorporate technological skills?
- What *resources* are used to deliver the curriculum? Who determines which
  learning systems and program resources to use? Are high-quality electronic
  resources readily available and accessible, including to users with special
  needs? Do you need to develop learning aids; do you have the technical skills
  needed to produce and use them?
- What *instructional strategies* are used? What kinds of learning activities do
  you use to provide learners with opportunities to learn, practice, and demonstrate content competence? How does the learning environment facilitate

content knowledge and application? Do strategies include explicit technical instruction—or resources to help learners use the requisite technology?

- How is *time* allocated: in terms of course and student pacing, relative to learning, and opportunities for help?
- What *governance and enterprise structures* are in place to facilitate instructional design: learning opportunities, databases or repositories to share lessons and best practice, ways to facilitate collaboration, funding for learner participation?
- What background, experiences, skills and dispositions do *learners* bring to the learning environment? You should assess learners' prerequisite skills as they enter the program in order to optimize learning experiences throughout their learning experience. Without addressing these prior skills, both you and learners will be frustrated in their work.
- How do *workplace* and *community members* interface with learners and the rest of the educational enterprise? What resources do they provide? What competing priorities do they reflect?

Output

- Does *learner work* reflect content knowledge and application as well as technological competency? You should routinely examine current student products in order to assess the impact of their instruction.
- How do learners perform on *standardized tests*? Do they "test" consistently, or does their performance depend on content matter or technological circumstances? Whenever possible, you should disaggregate test scores by demographic data, instructor, and technological factors.
- What course *grades* are learners receiving? How consistent is grading between instructors, especially those teaching the same content? Is there a connection between grades and technological incorporation?
- What *courses* are learners taking? What is the basis for course enrollment? What courses do learners drop? How does the online environment impact course choice?
- What happens to learners when they *exit the program*? On what basis do they leave? Surveying learners after they exit (both after a course or program) provides valuable insights into their sense of being prepared for future efforts.
- Other output measures provide indirect data about learning success: time spent learning, computer "down" time, learner turnover rate.

With the incorporation of technology, the assessment process can increase its effectiveness significantly for several reasons (North Central Regional Educational Laboratory, 2005): speed, archiving and retrieval options, timing, level of access, standardization and customization, statistical data analysis facilitation, equity.

In addition, technology increases facilitate metacognitive processes; participants can transcend reactive activity and become more engaged and productive.

Data analysis

It is not enough to collect data. The results need to be analyzed and acted upon. Ultimately, the point person in control of the assessment should also be the person who directs the data analysis. Cook and Farmer (2011) outline several steps that need to be accomplished along the way.

Once the data are collected, you need to organize and present them in a way that can be analyzed. Depending on how online questionnaires are developed, you can export the responses into spreadsheet or statistical programs. Charting the data facilitates understanding. You also need to address missing and bogus data; should an incomplete questionnaire be eliminated or should blatantly dishonest responses be ignored?

Open-ended questions are more problematic. Interviews should be recorded and then transcribed; typically, it takes six to eight hours to transcribe one hour's worth of recording manually; fortunately, online chat automatically provides a transcript. You need to code responses to generate patterns. You should read over the responses to get an overall sense of the data as well as start to pick up reoccurring phrases or themes; jot down notes while examining the responses to help generate useful categories. A second, closer reading can verify and refine the initial categories. At this point, you can generate a grid, cross-referencing the content with demographics; do males search the Internet differently from females, for instance? (They do.) Subsequent readings can pick up nuances. While software programs such as Nudist and Atlas/ti can help in this process if items are already in digital form, remember that these programs work based on word-frequency and word-proximity algorithms, so they may be somewhat arbitrary in their associations; they are best used as a starting point.

Once you organize the data, then statistics may be applied. Often the population is small enough that only descriptive statistics may be used: frequency, range, mean, median, mode, variance. These figures can still give the audience an idea of the scope of the findings, and you can start to see if two sets of findings reflect similar or different populations. Inferential statistics usually make or *infer* generalizations about significantly large populations based on sampling; typically, analysis tries to find correlations between two variables, such as number of books read and reading comprehension ability. The most important statistical consideration is the characteristic of the derived numbers; misaligning a statistical method with number property causes misleading conclusions. The chief "offender" is ascribing mathematical equations to emotions (e.g., one person is 2.5 times as satisfied as another person). Data may also be distinguished as discrete (whole numbers such as the number of students) or continuous (analog such as length). Most numbers in assessment are discrete ordinal or interval kinds (Farmer, 2003).

As much as possible, disaggregate data by demographics such as sex, age, ethnicity, and socioeconomic background in order to help identify at-risk groups; if possible, disaggregate data by preferred learning style or preferred subject matter. For example, males tend to have lower reading scores so interventions should be custom designed to motivate and help that group. Another way to disaggregate data is by quartiles or other score rankings; one cost-effective practice is to focus on those groups who *almost* meet a standard because a specifically targeted intervention may be relatively easy to implement and result in a significant return on investment.

Acting on findings

By analyzing the data derived from assessments, you and the rest of the assessment team can make recommendations to address the emergent issues. For instance, if research bibliographies cite webpages inaccurately, then you can emphasize that source in lessons or guide sheets. If industry standards are seldom mentioned in design briefs, mention them explicitly in instruction or make them more visible on websites; follow-up assessment can determine the basis for low usage. Consider both process-based and product-based interventions. In identifying an effective solution, examine the entire system since any of the entities might impact the outcome.

You should communicate assessment findings, analysis, and recommendations with all stakeholders and those being assessed in order to show that their interest and participation made a difference. These groups can also provide input to refine recommendations. The communiqué should include the background need, the results, and intended recommendations. Technology can facilitate broadcasting and repurposing of information. The ultimate uses of assessment, though, are learner competency and program improvement.

Additional implications for you

Management of instructional design encompasses both internal practices and collaboration with learners and the relevant organization. As a resource and information-processing expert, you are uniquely positioned to document, communicate about, and assess instructional design. Consider each level of instructional design, from a single learning activity to the development and marketing of long-term consortia curriculum. Concurrently, assess each step to ensure that it is done effectively, the bottom line being lifelong learning and organizational improvement.

References

Baykal, A. 2009. "Open Systems Metaphor in Instructional Design." *Procedia – Social and Behavioral Sciences* 1, no. 1: 2027–2031.

Cook, D., and L. Farmer, eds. 2011. *Using Qualitative Methods in Action Research: How Librarians Can Get to the Why of Data*. Chicago: American Library Association.

Farmer, L. 2003. *How to Conduct Action Research: A Guide for Library Media Specialists*. Chicago: American Library Association.

Killion, J. 2008. *Assessing Impact*. 2nd ed. Thousand Oaks, CA: Corwin Press.

Kotler, P., J. Bowen, and J. Makens. 2009. *Marketing for Hospitality and Tourism*. 5th ed. Upper Saddle River, NJ: Pearson Education.

Looi, C., P. Seow, B. Zhang, H. So, W. Chen, and L.Wong. 2010. "Leveraging Mobile Technology for Sustainable Seamless Learning: A Research Agenda." *British Journal of Educational Technology* 41, no. 2: 154–169.

McElroy, M. 2006. *The New Knowledge Management: Complexity, Learning and Sustainable Innovation*. Boston: Elsevier Science.

North Carolina State University. College of Humanities and Social Sciences. 2008. *Marketing Analytics*. Raleigh: North Carolina State University.

North Central Regional Educational Laboratory. 2005. *Critical Issue: Using Technology to Improve Student Achievement*. Naperville, IL: North Central Regional Educational Laboratory. http://www.ncrel.org/sdrs/areas/issues/methods/technlgy/te800.htm.

Oosterhof, A., R. Conrad, and D. Ely. 2008. *Assessing Learners Online*. Upper Saddle River, NJ: Prentice Hall.

Richey, R., J. Klein, and M. Tracey. 2010. *The Instructional Design Knowledge Base*. New York: Routledge.

Shaik, N. 2009. Marketing Strategies Distance Learning Programs: A Theoretical Framework. In *The Challenges for Marketing Distance Education in Online Environments: An Integrated Approach*, edited by U. Demiray and N. Sever, 125–171. Eskisehir, Turkey: Anadolu University.

Wood, M. 2010. *The Marketing Plan Handbook*. 4th ed. Upper Saddle River, NJ: Prentice Hall.

Instructional design resources

Organizations

American Library Association (and its divisions): http://www.ala.org/

Association for Educational Communications and Technology: http://www.aect.org/

Association for Supervision and Curriculum Development: http://www.ascd.org/

Center for Applied Special Technology: http://www.cast.org/

International Society for Technology in Education: http://www.iste.org/

LOEX (Library Orientation Exchange): http://www.emich.edu/public/loex/index.html

LibraryInstruction.com: http://www.libraryinstruction.com/

National Staff Development Council: http://www.nsdc.org/

WestEd: http://rtecexchange.edgateway.net/cs/rtecp/view/rtec_str/2

World Wide Web Consortium: http://www.w3.org/

Instructional design

A to Z Teacher Stuff: http://www.atozteacherstuff.com/

Creative Commons: http://www.creativecommons.org/

Education World: http://www.educationworld.com/

Lesson Plans Page: http://www.lessonplanspage.com/

Teachers Page: http://teachers.net/

Teach-nology: http://www.teach-nology.com/

Information and technology literacy

American Library Association Reference and User Services Association: http://www.ala.org/ala/mgrps/divs/rusa/index.cfm

Educator's Reference Desk: Information Literacy: http://www.eduref.org/cgi-bin/print.cgi/Resources/Subjects/Information_Literacy/ Information_Literacy.html ICT Literacy: http://www.ictliteracy.info

InfoPeople: http://www.infopeople.org/

Information Literacy for K–16 Settings: http://www.csulb.edu/~lfarmer/infolitwebstyle.htm

Information Skills Modules: http://ism-1.lib.vt.edu/

K12 Digital Citizenship: http://k12digitalcitizenship.wikispaces.com/

LE@D (Lifelong Education @ Desktop): http://www.leadonline.info/

Library Research Guides: http://www.lib.berkeley.edu/TeachingLib/Guides

OASIS: Online Advancement of Student Information Skills: http://oasis.sfsu.edu/

PRIMO: Peer-Reviewed Instructional Materials Online Database: http://www.ala.org/apps/primo/public/search.cfm

Tame the Web: http://tametheweb.com/

University of Massachusetts Instruction and Information Literacy: http://www.library.umass.edu/services/instruction/

University of Texas Libraries Instructional Services: http://www.lib.utexas.edu/services/instruction/

WebJunction: http://www.webjunction.org/

Information packaging

21 Classes: http://www.21classes.com/

CAST: http://www.cast.org/

Flickr: http://www.flickr.com/

Good Practices Web Design: http://goodpractices.com/

Google Docs: http://docs.google.com/

Joyce Valenza: http://joycevalenza.edublogs.org/2007/05/26/
from-my-study-how-are-school-library-sites-changing/

Ning: http://www.ning.com/

PB Wiki: http://www.pbwiki.com/

School Library Directory: http://www.sldirectory.com/libsf/resf/wpages.html

Viddler: http://www.viddler.com/

Vimeo: http://www.vimeo.com/

VoiceThread: http://www.voicethread.com/

YouTube: http://www.youtube.com/

Zoho: http://zoho.com/

Index

Page numbers followed by the letter "f" indicate figures; those followed by the letter "t" indicate tables.

About the author

Dr. Lesley S. J. Farmer, Professor at California State University Long Beach, coordinates the Librarianship program. She earned her MS in Library Science at the University of North Carolina Chapel Hill, and received her doctorate in Adult Education from Temple University. Dr. Farmer has worked as a teacher-librarian in K–12 school settings as well as in public, special, and academic libraries, instructing many types of learners. She also taught in formal educational institutions: K–12 to graduate school. Her teaching credentials include K–12 library media specialist, secondary-school English and math, community college, and adult education. She chaired the Education Section of the Special Libraries Association, and is the International Association of School Librarianship Vice-President of Association Relations. A frequent presenter and writer for the profession, Dr. Farmer's research interests include information literacy, assessment, collaboration, and educational technology. Her most recent book is the *Neal-Schuman Technology Management Handbook for School Library Media Centers* (2010), co-authored with Marc McPhee.